The Million Dollar Contest Cook-book

By Jean Sanderson
With A Foreword by Mary Ellen

Mary Ellen Family Books/Doubleday
Garden City, New York

THE MILLION DOLLAR CONTEST COOKBOOK
Copyright © 1983 by Jean Sanderson

Art Director: Heidi Jo Skaret
Editor: David Laraway
Cover Photo: Jim Sanderson

ISBN: 0-385-19145-6

C.I.P. Data applied for
Printed in the United States of America
FIRST EDITION

FOREWORD

Have you ever spent a lot of money for a big, fat cookbook only to find that you use just a fraction of the recipes? Well, you don't have to worry about that with *this* book. Jean has collected prizewinning recipes from the biggest cooking contests in the country, so you *know* they have to be good. You will find the absolute best of the best represented here—from the best hors d'oeuvre recipes to the best desserts. What's more, when I use the recipes I find them remarkably uncomplicated and easy to make. Almost all of them use products and ingredients that you probably have on your cupboard shelves or in your refrigerator right now.

Another feature that makes this cookbook unique is Jean's chapter of hints and information for entering cooking contests yourself. As Jean points out, you don't need to be a gourmet cook to win these contests, but just have "a desire to win and a love of cooking." If you have these, Jean's advice just might give you the edge you need to win.

Any one of these recipes will make you a winner with your family and friends. And who knows, they could inspire you to create a contest-winning recipe of your own.

Here's to good cooking!

Mary Ellen

To my loving family- - -
    who, through years of tasting
    and testing, made this book possible. . .

And with Special Thanks- - -
    to the Food Companies and Food Editors
    without whose support there would
    be no contest cooking.

CONTENTS

PART I

PART II

High Stakes, the Easy Way

It's 7 a.m. as you slowly rise and make your way to the kitchen. Breakfast begins — usually served in shifts to a family on the move.

By 9 a.m. you've completed breakfast. But around noon, just a few hours after the early morning shift ends, you're in the kitchen again. This time it's lunch.

Before you know it, it's 4 p.m., and you're thinking in terms of dinner. You begin to prepare a meal to satisfy a hungry family around 6:30 p.m.

Think about it. You spend a good part of the day in that kitchen. You do it not because you have to so much as you enjoy cooking for people who like to eat. And you've become pretty good at it too.

So for about five hours today you lived in the room that somehow has become the center of family life — the kitchen.

When you were not in the kitchen you may have gone shopping for groceries. Did you read the local specials in the morning paper? Clip coupons perhaps? Stop at the store's reduced shelves hunting for a bargain?

If this is frequently the structure of your day, you probably don't realize how close you are to being in the money. You can turn the job of cooking into a contest-winning art and make your own brand of kitchen ingenuity profitable.

You can participate (expenses paid) in cooking contests of all sorts across the country. That's right. You, with all your daily kitchen experiences and your well-honed shopping sense, have all the ingredients for participating in these cooking contests and winning — winning money, prizes, awards and recognition.

Welcome to the world of contest cooking. This is where common sense and basic cooking skills, both of which you use daily, can lead you down the road to opportunity.

Thousands and thousands of dollars in cash and prizes are awarded to cooks much like you every year. The contests are held to promote the grocery products you buy weekly and probably use daily.

So you aren't a gourmet cook. Don't worry, a Julia Child or James Beard isn't required here. Only a sensible cook who can use his or her already well-tuned knowledge to make a dent in the cooking prize market. And that is very likely a description that fits you.

I know because I have won an array of cooking contests without any extraordinary talent, other than a desire to win and a love of cooking.

There are not just a few cooking contests to be won. There are many. Some are annual and others are announced from month to month. Magazines (*Better Homes and Gardens, Family Circle, Woman's Day, Bon Appetit,* etc.) are some of the best sources of cooking contest news. Publications listing current cooking contests are Shepherd Contest Bulletin, 33 Country Club Rd., Willingboro NJ 08046, Contest News-Letter, P.O.

Box 1059, Fernandina Beach, FL 32034, and ITS — 31 Woodland St., M—3, Hartford, CT 06105. Newspaper food sections are also a good way to keep track of what contests are going on and when.

It's important that you begin collecting recipe ideas for annual contests now, and continue all year round. That way you can experiment with them and perfect them well before the entry deadline.

Search cookbooks in your own collection, in your neighbors' homes and the public library. Excellent sources for recipes are the brochures, leaflets and advertising materials of product manufacturers — many of which can be found on supermarket shelves and advertising displays.

Of course, contest cooking is quickly becoming a national sport of sorts. Its popularity is evident everywhere — the media, bridge club, the family reunion.

And would it be popular unless it was something almost anyone could do and enjoy? No.

You still don't believe you can do it? I assumed you wouldn't. In the following pages you will find all you need to know to win big in any of a number of cooking contests going on in this country. And you'll also find a collection of winning recipes to enjoy now.

A Dash of Creativity Makes a Winner

If you're already in the kitchen several hours a day, why not make it more worth your while? And, more importantly, why not have a little fun?

Creativity — remember that word. It's the key to winning most cooking contests, and to stockpiling three or four recipes for each one you already have.

Everyone has a capacity for being creative. Creativity can be developed by exercise. And in cooking contests circles it can win you a new car, buy you a new kitchen, send you to Hawaii or put cash in your bank account.

It's important to remember from the start that your first recipe entries may not win. But unlike some contests, cooking contests do not require years of experience before you become a true contender. In fact, at this moment success may be only as far as a few changes in a family favorite recipe.

It's also a low-overhead business. Your only investments are 1) your time — which you were already spending in the kitchen, and 2) your groceries — which you were already purchasing. In your family you have the perfect sounding, or tasting board, too.

Chances are they will love your new cooking approach and gladly join in the fun. My children were willing tasters except for an occasional "Oh Mother, not again!" To insure their cooperation, I made a deal with them. I told them if they tasted, they shared in whatever winnings came out of that recipe. When I won $5,000 I gave them each a check.

So what is cooking creativity? It is the process by which you look at a tried and true recipe and imagine something entirely new. It is a new version of a longtime favorite.

For example, one of my first contest winners, and many thereafter, were offspring of an old favorite, Chicken Kiev.

Chicken Kiev is boned chicken breasts filled with chilled butter and seasonings, rolled, dipped in flour, beaten egg and fine bread crumbs, and deep-fried.

My first creative cooking effort, in 1971, was Crescent Chicken Kiev. I used refrigerated quick crescent dinner rolls, filled them with chopped mushrooms, cream cheese and chives, butter, cubed chicken and seasoning. They were dipped in melted butter and crushed seasoned crouton crumbs and baked 20-25 minutes. My creative effort won a trip to the 22nd Pillsbury BAKE-OFF® contest in Hawaii. It was titled Chicken a la Crescents.

There was even more creativity to be found in the likes of old Chicken Kiev though. I competed in the National Chicken Cooking Contest in Birmingham, AL, in 1972, with Mexican Chicken Kiev (deep-fried with a cheese and green chili filling).

That was not the end of it. I won the General Electric Microwave

Cooking Award sponsored by General Electric in the 25th BAKE-OFF® contest (a trip to Phoenix, AZ, $5,000, and a General Electric Microwave Cooking Center) with a recipe for Fiesta Chicken Kiev.

Fiesta Chicken Kiev took two major changes: 1) dipping rolled cheese-filled chicken breasts in butter, then crushed Cheddar cheese crackers mixed with taco seasoning and cooked 10-12 minutes in a GE microwave, and 2) the eight rolled chicken breasts cooked all at once instead of deep frying separately. This quick-cooking method keeps the cheesy butter filling inside the rolled chicken breast producing a crunchy outer coating.

Then, in 1975, still creating the new from the old, I represented Kansas in the National Beef Cook-Off in Denver, CO. My recipe was titled Beef Kiev Ole. I used beef round steak with narrow strips of Cheddar cheese and taco sauce in the center, dipped in butter, rolled in Cheddar cheese cracker crumbs and baked.

Finally, there was the National Catfish Cooking Contest held in Jackson, MS. My recipe was Farm-Raised Catfish Kiev Style — and it was good enough to garner first place.

It contained filleted catfish, filled with butter, cream cheese, chives, lemon pepper seasoning and chopped mushrooms, rolled, secured with food picks, dipped in butter, seasoned crouton crumbs and baked until golden brown.

Bob Finley's "Today's Catch" column in the Chicago Tribune pointed out exactly what made Farm-Raised Catfish Kiev Style a winner:

"Farm-Raised Catfish Kiev Style brings together all the qualities that make a recipe great. It is simple and the ingredients are readily available. It is easily assembled and has a short energy-saving cooking time. The finished recipe has tremendous eye appeal and the mild, pond raised catfish blends perfectly with handy on-the-shelf ingredients to produce a superb flavor combination. It has all the style and interest of a Kiev without the deep frying."

All these Kiev recipes are included in this book. (Reading recipes is a great help in coming up with an idea and cannot be stressed enough.) Kiev is just one example of making a winner out of a dish you already cook — a dish that with a little of your own brand of creativity can go a long way toward winning a cooking contest.

What Winners Are Made Of

Contest cooking is similar, in a way, to the Olympic sport of decathlon. An athlete, such as American's Bruce Jenner, does not win the decathlon due to one single quality. Speed, endurance, accuracy, or strength alone is not enough. It's a combination of all these things in an athlete that enables him to win the decathlon.

Though the qualities are different in cooking competition, the logic is the same. It is not taste or appearance alone that makes a recipe a winner, yet it is these and other qualities together in one recipe that will make your entry stand out from the crowd.

The entrant must keep all these aspects in mind from the time he or she decides to enter a cooking contest. The entrant must always be aware of one thing in particular: Good taste alone does not make a winner.

So what are the most important points upon which a recipe will be judged? That's easy — the same ones you look for in a recipe that you are cooking for your family.

First, you must consider the recipe's appearance. After all, when something doesn't look good, even you will be hesitant to taste it. A winning recipe must be picture perfect.

Color and texture are the two most important aspects of a dish's appearance. Color can be considered when choosing your ingredients. Make sure colors are pleasant and as compatible with each other as possible.

If it lacks color or brightness, a dish can often be improved with a topping or sauce. If the contest rules allow garnish, garnish it with appropriate ingredients. That doesn't mean hide it under big clumps of this or that. Merely dress it up a little.

Texture can be guaranteed, again through proper selection of ingredients, and also by using the correct cooking techniques. Both color and texture are best judged by your family's reaction to the finished dish. If they "ooh" and "aah" about it, then you have no problem. If they back off from it before even tasting it, ask what it is that doesn't appeal to them and make changes accordingly.

When considering a recipe's appearance, also consider the mental images the written recipe will conjure up in the judges' minds. Preliminary judging will take place before anything is cooked so it's imperative to consider what the written recipe looks like.

Every time I hear of a recipe contest I ask myself, "How can I put together a recipe that will create a total picture?" After all, aren't those the recipes you choose when reading a cookbook?

Another important standard your recipe must meet is ease of preparation. The average American, especially when cooking for a family, does not have the time, money or know-how to be a gourmet cook, and a winning recipe is usually one that appeals to that type of person.

Ease of preparation includes the availability of the recipe ingredients, the cost of those ingredients and the time it takes to prepare them.

Be sure that any fruits and vegetables included in the recipe are readily available in most parts of the country. The same goes for seafood. And can those things be obtained for a reasonable price rather than an outrageous "specialty food" price?

The time it takes to cook a recipe will, of course, depend on the complexity of the dish. Cooking procedures should be simple enough that most people feel they can follow them.

Again, only you can be the judge here. How much time is too much time for you to spend cooking a meal?

A contest's rules may well stress time as a factor. Some are judged more heavily than others on ease of preparation. In any case, you should read the rules carefully before entering to make sure you know what factors, including ease of preparation, will be weighed by the judges.

Of course, taste is the most obvious of all qualities of a winning recipe. Though it is a subjective judgment, taste has the advantage of being easily classified by anyone. If something is overly seasoned, bland, too strong, not strong enough, you will know at once. Here again, remember the average American is not a gourmet, nor does he have gourmet taste.

Getting the taste exactly where you want it can only be done through experimentation. This is one reason to work on various creative recipes all year long.

Remember too that taste is perhaps the trickiest of all senses. If something is too sweet, don't just guess you put too much sugar and enter the recipe with a little less. First cook it with less sugar to be sure that was the problem.

Hint: Whether it is specified or not, use of the sponsor's brand name products is important. Use them as frequently as possible. Unless necessary, do not use brand names of any products other than those of the contest's sponsor.

As you can see, a winning recipe is one that has something special, your own personal touch, as well as the other necessary elements described above. Remember, though a decathlon competitor may be able to run faster than the rest of the field, he must be competitive in the high jump, javelin and other aspects to win the contest.

None of this is all that difficult to achieve really. But, in order to win, you must have the know-how to put it all on paper.

Making A Good Entrance

There are several guidelines to follow when you finally begin entering cooking contests. The most important of those is to read and follow contest rules.

You cannot be too careful when following a contest's rules. One slip-up could cause disqualification of a potential winning recipe.

Rules will tell you how many recipes you can enter, how they must be entered and the deadline for entries. Also, they will give you at least some idea, if not specifics, of the judging criteria.

If you can, obtain entry blanks as soon as possible after learning of contests. Since you have been experimenting with recipes all along, you should immediately be able to pull from your files a few to consider entering.

Hint: If you are allowed to enter more than one recipe (and generally you are) enter as many as you can. In this way you can avoid duplications of other entries (which are immediately disqualified) and increase the odds in your favor.

Before you begin completing your entry make sure you have specific measurements for all ingredients. A "dash" simply will not do.

Next experiment with writing it as clearly and in as few words as possible. Nothing is more discouraging to a cook (or a judge) than unclear and rambling directions. Such a mishap will greatly reduce your chances of making it past the contest's preliminary stages.

Titling your recipe is a source of some controversy among cooks. Some feel an elaborate title increases your recipe's chances of standing out. My experience, though, tells me simplicity is the best policy. When a judge reads a recipe title, he should immediately know the recipe's basic idea: It is a chicken recipe, it is a rice recipe, it contains seafood, etc.

Recipes should always be typed or printed neatly. If you do not type, perhaps you can find someone who does. As to form, recipes from good cookbooks are an excellent guide.

Here are the basic rules for typing your contest entry:

1) The title should be centered and all letters in the title should be capitalized.

2) Skip three lines. Type the ingredients, in the order they are to be used, single-spaced, giving specific measurements of each. If packaged or canned ingredients are used, be sure to designate their sizes. Also, capitalize the sponsor's product throughout the recipe.

3) Include any garnishes you use in the list of ingredients.

4) Skip a line after the list of ingredients. Type the directions, again clearly, double-spaced. Give complete directions, pan sizes, baking time and temperature.

5) Skip a line after the directions. Type any serving directions, including use of garnishes, double-spaced.

6) If there is more than one page to the recipe, be sure your name and address are on each page.

7) Use plain white typing paper.

Of course, all of these are subject to the individual contest's rules. Again, follow those rules carefully.

The rules will give specifications as to originality. An original recipe is one created from scratch or via a major change in ingredients or technique of preparation of another recipe. Already published or contest-winning recipes cannot be entered as original recipes and will automatically be disqualified. Know the contest's definition of originality and judge your recipe against it.

Before mailing your entry, check and recheck it. Make sure all ingredients are listed in the directions. Perhaps have someone else read it also. The smallest mistake or typographical error ("tsp." and "tblsp.," for example) can ruin the entire recipe.

Hint: If the contest allows an accompanying statement take advantage of it. Write something that will once again point out the unique appeal of your recipe — ease of preparation, taste, etc.

NATIONAL PINEAPPLE COOKING CLASSIC

PINEAPPLE MERINGUE CAKE

1 cup sifted cake flour
2 teaspoons baking powder
1/8 teaspoon salt
4 large eggs, separated
1 1/2 cups sugar

2 teaspoons vanilla
1/2 cup shortening
5 tablespoons milk
3/4 cup finely chopped pecans
Pineapple Cream Filling

Resift flour with baking powder and salt. Beat egg whites to soft peaks. Gradually beat in 1 cup sugar, continuing to beat until stiff. Fold in 1 teaspoon vanilla. Set aside. Cream shortening with remaining 1/2 cup sugar well. Beat in egg yolks. Blend in flour mixture alternately with milk. Stir in remaining teaspoon vanilla. Divide batter evenly between two well-greased and floured 8 inch layer cake pans. Top each with half the meringue, and sprinkle with pecans. Bake in moderate oven (350 degrees F.) about 35 to 45 minutes, until cake tests done and meringue is a light golden brown. Remove from oven and cool in pans. Loosen edges of cake and meringue with small spatula, and turn out. Place 1 layer, meringue side down, on serving plate and spread with Pineapple Cream Filling. Top with second layer, meringue side up. Refrigerate several hours or overnight before serving. Makes 1 (8 inch) cake, about 12 servings.

Pineapple Cream Filling: Drain a 13 1/2 ounce can crushed pineapple well. Beat 1 cup whipping cream with 1 1/2 teaspoons powdered sugar and 1/4 teaspoon vanilla until stiff. Fold in well-drained crushed pineapple.

Note: Meringue will often spread or be a little crumbly in texture on baking. Press together with hands to shape, if necessary. Cake and filling will mellow on standing.

Won the Grand Prize of $25,000 in the 1977 National Pineapple Cooking Classic, sponsored by the Pineapple Growers Association of Hawaii.
ETHEL KLIEBERT, VACHERIE, LOUISIANA

CAPTAIN'S CHOICE

1 (20 oz.) can pineapple chunks	1/2 cup milk
1 1/2 oz. dark rum	1/2 cup shredded coconut
1 (3 1/2 oz.) package vanilla	1/4 cup sliced macadamia nuts
flavor whipped dessert mix	Maraschino cherries.

Drain pineapple, reserving syrup. Add rum to pineapple and toss gently to thoroughly coat all fruit. Cover; chill in refrigerator several hours or overnight. Put dessert mix in deep bowl. Add cold milk and beat with electric mixer on low speed until well blended, then increase speed to high and beat 1 minute. Drain marinated pineapple chunks. Add enough reserved canned pineapple liquid to marinade to make 1/2 cup. With mixer on low speed, blend this mixture well; increase mixer speed to high and beat for 2 minutes longer. Stir in shredded coconut and drained pineapple chunks. Spoon into dessert dishes. Sprinkle top of each with macadamia nuts, and top with a cherry. Chill in refrigerator for about 1 hour before serving. Makes 6 servings.

Won $10,000 in the 1972 National Pineapple Cooking Classic, sponsored by the Pineapple Growers Association of Hawaii.
MR. NORMAN W. MARTIN, MARBLEHEAD, MASSACHUSETTS

HAWAIIAN POTATO SALAD

4 to 5 medium sized potatoes	3/4 cup thinly sliced celery
3 tablespoons vinegar	2 tablespoons minced onion
2 tablespoons salad oil	4 slices crisp cooked bacon,
1 teaspoon salt	crumbled
1 (5 to 6 oz.) can water chestnuts	3/4 teaspoon powdered ginger
1 (13 1/2 oz.) can pineapple tidbits	1/4 cup mayonnaise

Scrub potatoes. Cook in boiling salted water until tender. Drain and cool. Peel potatoes and dice (makes about 1 quart). Stir together vinegar, oil, salt and pour over potatoes. Mix together lightly. Chill. Drain and slice water chestnuts. Drain pineapple tidbits. Add water chestnuts, pineapple tidbits, celery, onion and bacon to the potato mixture. Stir ginger and mayonnaise together. Combine with potato mixture lightly but thoroughly. Serve chilled. Makes 6 servings.

Won $1,000 in the 1972 National Pineapple Cooking Classic, sponsored by the Pineapple Growers Association of Hawaii.
MRS. KATHLEEN TOVEY, BELLEVUE, WASHINGTON

TRADE WIND MUFFINS

1 (20 oz.) can crushed pineapple
1/2 cup sliced almonds
2 cups sifted all-purpose flour
1 teaspoon soda
1 teaspoon salt
1 (3 oz.) package cream cheese,
    softened

1 cup sugar
2 teaspoons vanilla
1 large egg, beaten
1/2 cup dairy sour cream
Glaze

Drain pineapple, reserving syrup. Heavily grease muffin pans (2 1/2 inches diameter, 1 1/8 inches deep) and sprinkle with almonds. Resift flour with soda and salt. Beat cheese, sugar and vanilla together until smooth. Blend in egg. Add flour mixture alternately with sour cream. Fold in drained pineapple. Spoon into prepared muffin pans. Bake in moderate oven (350 degrees F.) about 35 minutes, until muffins are browned and test done. Remove from oven and let stand in pans 5 to 10 minutes. Turn out onto wire rack and spread Glaze over warm muffins. Makes 16 to 18 muffins.

Glaze: Combine 1 tablespoon soft margarine, 1 cup sifted powdered sugar and 1 tablespoon syrup from pineapple. Blend smooth.

Won $10,000 in the 1977 National Pineapple Cooking Classic, sponsored by the Pineapple Growers Association of Hawaii.
ROBERTA BADGLEY, PHOENIX, ARIZONA

HAWAIIAN PINEAPPLE CAKE

1 (1 lb. 4 oz.) can crushed
    pineapple
2 cups buttermilk baking mix*
1 cup sifted all-purpose flour
1 teaspoon baking soda
1 cup sugar

3/4 cup dairy sour cream
1/2 cup margarine
2 teaspoons vanilla
2 large eggs
2 tablespoons rum**
Glaze

Drain pineapple well, saving syrup for glaze. Stir baking mix, flour and soda together. Beat sugar, sour cream, margarine and vanilla together for 2 minutes. Add eggs, and beat 1 minute. Add flour mixture, and beat 1 minute longer. Mix in drained pineapple and rum. Turn into well-greased 9 inch bundt pan. Bake in moderate oven (350 degrees F.) about 45 minutes, until cake tests done. Remove from oven and spoon about half the glaze over cake. Let stand 10 minutes, then turn out onto serving plate, and spoon on remaining glaze. Cool before cutting. Makes 1 (9 inch) cake.

Glaze: Combine 3/4 cup sugar, 1/4 cup each margarine and syrup from pineapple. Stir over low heat until sugar is dissolved and margarine melted. Remove from heat and stir in 2 tablespoons rum.**

*"Bisquick Buttermilk Baking Mix" used by winner.

**Rum may be omitted, if desired.

Won the Grand Prize of $25,000 in the 1974 National Pineapple Cooking Classic, sponsored by the Pineapple Growers Association of Hawaii.
MARIE SIKKING, VINELAND, NEW JERSEY

HAWAIIAN PINEAPPLE BEEF CHOW

1 pound sirloin steak
2 tablespoons salad oil
1 (2 oz.) can mushrooms
1 (5 oz.) can bamboo shoots,
  drained
1 (5 oz.) can water chestnuts,
  drained
1/2 cup sliced green onion

1/2 cup condensed beef broth
1 tablespoon sugar
1/4 cup soy sauce
2 tablespoons water
2 teaspoons cornstarch
1 (15 1/4 oz.) can pineapple
  chunks, drained
Ginger Rice

Place steak in freezer until surface is frozen. Slice in thin strips. In a heavy skillet, quickly brown steak strips in salad oil. Add mushrooms, bamboo shoots, water chestnuts, onion, broth and sugar. Mix soy sauce, water and cornstarch, and stir into mixture. Cook about 5 minutes. Add drained pineapple chunks, cover and simmer about 5 minutes. Serve over Ginger Rice. Makes 4 to 6 servings.

Ginger Rice: Prepare 2 cups instant rice, adding 1/2 teaspoon ground ginger.

Won $1,000 in the 1973 National Pineapple Cooking Classic, sponsored by the Pineapple Growers Association of Hawaii.
ELIZABETH DYE, SWAINSBORO, GEORGIA

PORTOFINO MOLD

2 (3 oz.) packages raspberry flavor
  gelatin
1 1/4 cups boiling water
1 (1 lb. 4 oz.) can crushed
  pineapple, undrained

1 (1 lb.) can whole cranberry sauce
3/4 cup port wine
1 cup chopped pecans
1 (8 oz.) package cream cheese
1 cup dairy sour cream

Dissolve gelatin in boiling water. Stir in pineapple, cranberry sauce and wine. Chill until mixture thickens slightly. Fold in pecans, and turn into 2 quart serving bowl.* Chill until firm. When gelatin is set, soften cheese, and gradually beat in sour cream until mixture is smooth. Spread over the gelatin. Chill until serving time. Serve from the bowl. Makes 8 or more servings.

*Variation: Or use a 9x9x2 inch pan. Spread with topping when firm. Cut into 9 squares.

Won $10,000 in the 1973 National Pineapple Cooking Classic, sponsored by the Pineapple Growers Association of Hawaii.
JANET BERGSON, SPRINGFIELD, VIRGINIA

PINEAPPLE TEA RING

1 (15 1/4 oz.) can crushed pineapple
1/2 cup brown sugar (packed)
2 tablespoons cornstarch
2 eggs, beaten
1/2 teaspoon cinnamon
1 package active dry yeast
1/2 cup warm water
1 tablespoon granulated sugar
2 1/2 cups buttermilk baking mix*
1 cup natural cereal with raisins and dates
Icing
Maraschino cherries and nuts for decoration (optional)

Drain pineapple, saving syrup for icing. Combine drained pineapple with brown sugar, cornstarch, 1 beaten egg and cinnamon. Cook over low heat, stirring constantly, until thickened. Remove from heat, and cool. Sprinkle yeast over warm water, and let stand 5 minutes. Combine with granulated sugar, baking mix, and remaining egg, beaten. Beat vigorously. Turn out onto board covered with baking mix, and knead smooth, about 20 times. Let rest 5 to 10 minutes. Roll out to a rectangle 16x9 inches. Spread with the cooled pineapple filling, and sprinkle with cereal. Roll up as for jelly roll, starting from long side. Shape into a ring on greased baking sheet, pinching ends together. With kitchen shears, clip about 2/3 of the way through roll at 1 inch intervals. Turn each cut on its side. Cover and let rise in warm place about 1 hour. Bake in moderately hot oven (375 degrees F.) 20 to 25 minutes, until browned. Drizzle with icing while warm. Decorate with cherries and nuts, if desired. Makes 1 ring.

Icing: Stir 1 cup powdered sugar with 1 tablespoon reserved pineapple syrup and 1/2 teaspoon vanilla until smooth.

*"Jiffy" baking mix used by winner.

Won $10,000 in the 1974 National Pineapple Cooking Classic, sponsored by the Pineapple Growers Association of Hawaii.
MARY LOUISE WUNDERLE, KENT, OHIO

PINEAPPLE GOODIE ROLLS

1 package active dry yeast
1 1/4 cups warm water
1 egg, beaten
1 (9 oz.) package white cake mix
1 teaspoon salt
2 1/2 cups sifted all-purpose flour

1 (8 1/4 oz.) can crushed pineapple
1/4 cup margarine, melted
1/4 cup sugar
1/4 cup chopped maraschino
  cherries
1/3 cup chopped pecans
Pineapple Icing

Soften yeast in warm water. Add egg, cake mix, and salt, and mix well. Gradually blend in flour to make a soft dough. Grease top of dough, cover, and let rise in warm place until doubled, about 45 to 60 minutes. Drain pineapple, reserving syrup. On lightly floured board, roll dough to a rectangle about 12x15 inches, and spread with 2 tablespoons margarine. Sprinkle with sugar, pineapple, cherries and pecans. Roll up as for jelly roll, starting from the longer side. Pinch edges together. Cut into 15 (1 inch) slices, and place cut side down in well-greased pan (13x9x2 inches.) Brush tops of rolls with remaining melted margarine. Cover and let rise until doubled, about 45 minutes. Meanwhile, preheat oven to moderately hot (375 degrees F.). Bake rolls about 25 to 30 minutes, until nicely browned. Turn out of pan, and spread with Pineapple Icing. Makes 15 rolls.

Pineapple Icing: Combine 1 cup powdered sugar with 2 tablespoons syrup from pineapple and mix until smooth.

Won $1,000 in the 1973 National Pineapple Cooking Classic, sponsored by the Pineapple Growers Association of Hawaii.
LOIS APPLEDORN, ARTESIA, NEW MEXICO

PINEAPPLE-CHEESE BAKLAVA

1 (1 lb. 4 oz.) can crushed
  pineapple in syrup
1 (8 oz.) package cream cheese,
  softened
1 cup ricotta
1 cup sugar
2 egg yolks

1 teaspoon grated lemon peel
1 teaspoon vanilla
1/2 lb. frozen phyllo pastry leaves,
  thawed (8 leaves)
1/2 cup butter, melted
1 teaspoon lemon juice

Turn pineapple into wire strainer and drain, saving syrup. In mixer bowl, combine cream cheese, ricotta, 1/2 cup sugar, egg yolks, lemon peel and vanilla. Blend together on medium speed. Stir in drained pineapple. Place phyllo leaves between damp towels to keep moist. Place a sheet of pastry in well greased pan (9x13x2 inches). Brush with melted butter.

Repeat with three more leaves. Spoon on the pineapple-cheese mixture, and spread level. Top with remaining phyllo, brushing each sheet with butter as it is layered. Mark pastry into diamonds with point of sharp knife. Bake in moderate oven (350 degrees F.) about 50 ...inutes, or until golden brown. Combine 1/2 cup reserved pineapple syrup, remaining 1/2 cup sugar, and lemon juice, and cook to a thick syrup. When baklava is baked, spoon the hot syrup evenly over top. Cool, then cut into diamonds at markings. Makes 1 large baklava.

Won the Grand Prize of $25,000 in the 1979 National Pineapple Cooking Classic, sponsored by the Pineapple Growers Association of Hawaii.
ANNETTE ERBECK, MASON, OHIO

PINEAPPLE ROYAL REUBEN SALAD

3 small slices rye bread
3 tablespoons soft butter
1 (1 lb. 4 oz.) can pineapple
   chunks
1 (8 oz.) can sauerkraut, chilled
6 cups torn iceberg lettuce

1 (4 oz.) package sliced corned
   beef, cut in strips (1 cup)
4 ounces Swiss cheese, cut in
   strips (1 cup)
1/2 teaspoon caraway seeds
1 cup 1000 Island dressing

Spread bread with butter. Cut into 1/2 inch squares. Bake in slow oven (300 degrees F.) 20 to 25 minutes, until dry and crisp. Turn pineapple into wire strainer and drain well. Rinse, and drain sauerkraut. Place lettuce in large bowl, and top with pineapple, sauerkraut, corned beef, cheese, and croutons. Stir caraway seeds into dressing, pour over salad and toss until well coated. Serve at once. Makes 6 to 8 servings.

Won $2,500 in the 1979 National Pineapple Cooking Classic, sponsored by the Pineapple Growers Association of Hawaii.
MARGARET ZICKERT, DEERFIELD, WISCONSIN

MAGIC PINEAPPLE DRESSING

1 pint mayonnaise
6 hard cooked eggs, finely chopped
1 large sweet green pepper, finely
   chopped
1 (4 oz.) can pimiento peppers,
   finely chopped
1 small onion, finely chopped

1/4 cup chili sauce
1 cup crushed pineapple, drained
   (8 1/4 oz. can)
1 cup finely chopped cooked ham
   (optional)
Lettuce wedges

Stir together mayonnaise, eggs, green pepper, pimiento, onion and chili sauce. Add the well drained pineapple and ham and mix together very well. Chill overnight in the refrigerator before using. Serve on lettuce wedges. Makes about 5 cups.

Won $10,000 in the 1972 National Pineapple Cooking Classic, sponsored by the National Pineapple Growers Association of Hawaii.
MRS. JACK CRUTTENDEN, BARRY, ILLINOIS

PINEAPPLE LEIS

1 cup milk
1 package active dry yeast
1/4 cup warm water
4 1/4 cups unsifted all-purpose
   flour
1/4 cup sugar

1 teaspoon ground ginger
1 teaspoon salt
1 cup (2 sticks) margarine
2 large eggs, beaten
Pineapple Filling
Glaze

Scald milk; cool to lukewarm. Soften yeast in warm water. Combine flour, sugar, ginger and salt. Cut in margarine, until mixture is consistency of coarse meal. Combine yeast, cooled milk and eggs. Stir into dry mixture to make a soft dough. Cover, and chill at least 2 hours. (Dough may be refrigerated as long as 2 days.) Prepare Pineapple Filling. Divide chilled dough in half. Roll one portion at a time to a thin rectangle 18x 12 inches. Spread half the filling over entire width and 2/3 the length of the dough. Fold in thirds, folding unspread third over first. Cut into 12 (one inch wide) strips. Lift ends of each strip and twist lightly in opposite directions. Bring ends together to make leis. Place on greased baking sheets. Repeat with remaining half of dough and filling. Bake in hot oven (400 degrees F.) 15 to 18 minutes, until browned. Cool on wire racks. Frost with Glaze while warm. Makes 24 leis.

Pineapple Filling: Drain a 15 1/4 ounce can of crushed pineapple in juice well. Mix with 1 (8 oz.) package chopped dates, 1 cup chopped walnuts, 1/2 cup brown sugar (packed) and 1 teaspoon ground ginger.

Glaze: Combine 2 tablespoons melted butter, 1 1/2 cups sifted powdered sugar and 1 to 2 tablespoons milk, to make a thin frosting.

Won $2,500 in the 1977 National Pineapple Cooking Classic, sponsored by the Pineapple Growers Association of Hawaii.
PATSY MORGAN, CYPRESS, CALIFORNIA

LUAU HAM SALAD PIE

1 baked 9-inch pie shell*
1 (8 oz.) can crushed pineapple
   in juice
1 (3 oz.) package lemon flavor
   gelatin
1 cup boiling water
1 (3 oz.) package cream cheese,
   softened
1/3 cup mayonnaise

1/4 teaspoon dry mustard
1 tablespoon vinegar
1/2 cup whipping cream
1 1/2 cups diced cooked ham
1/2 cup chopped celery
1/4 cup chopped green pepper
1 teaspoon grated onion
Toasted slivered almond for
   garnish

Bake and cool pie shell. Drain pineapple, saving juice. Dissolve gelatin in boiling water. Gradually beat into cream cheese. Beat in mayonnaise and mustard. Stir in reserved pineapple juice and vinegar. Chill until mixture begins to thicken. Beat cream to soft peaks. Set gelatin into bowl of ice water, and beat until fluffy. Fold in whipped cream, drained pineapple, ham, celery, green pepper, and onion. Turn into pie shell. Chill until firm. Garnish with slivered almonds if desired. Cut into wedges to serve. Makes 6 or more servings.

*Add 2 tablespoons plain wheat germ to your usual pastry, if desired.

Won $2,500 in the 1977 National Pineapple Cooking Classic, sponsored by the Pineapple Growers Association of Hawaii.
JAMES STRIEBER, TUCSON, ARIZONA

GINGERED PINEAPPLE COFFEE CAKE

1 (8 oz.) can crushed pineapple in
   juice
2 tablespoons lemon juice
1 tablespoon crystallized ginger
1/2 cup golden raisins
Streusel
1/3 cup margarine
3/4 cup sugar

1 egg
1 2/3 cups flour
1 1/2 teaspoons baking powder
1 teaspoon cinnamon
1/2 teaspoon soda
1/2 teaspoon salt
1/2 cup chopped pecans

Turn pineapple into wire strainer and drain, saving juice. Combine juice from pineapple, lemon juice and crystallized ginger; heat to boiling. Remove from heat and add pineapple and raisins. Let stand 15 minutes. Meanwhile, prepare Streusel. Cream margarine, sugar and egg until fluffy. Sift flour, baking powder, cinnamon, soda and salt together. Add to creamed mixture alternately with pineapple mixture, mixing well. Fold in 1/4 cup pecans. Spread half the batter in greased 9 inch square baking dish. Sprinkle with half the Streusel. Cover with remaining batter and top with remaining Streusel. Sprinkle with remaining 1/4 cup pecans. Bake in moderate oven (350 degrees F.) 30 to 35 minutes. Serve warm or cold, cut into 9 squares. Makes 9 servings.

Streusel: Mix together 1/2 cup brown sugar (packed), 2 tablespoons flour, 2 tablespoons melted margarine and 1 teaspoon cinnamon. Stir in 1/4 cup chopped pecans.

Won $10,000 in the 1979 National Pineapple Cooking Classic, sponsored by the Pineapple Growers Association of Hawaii.
LOIS RINEHART, INDEPENDENCE, MISSOURI

HAWAIIAN LAMB LOAF

1 (20 oz.) can crushed pineapple
  in juice
1 1/2 pounds ground lamb
1/2 pound ground lean beef chuck
1 large egg, beaten
1 cup fine bread crumbs, soft
  or dry

1/2 cup finely chopped onion
2 teaspoons salt
1 1/2 teaspoons dried mint leaves,
  finely crumbled
1 teaspoon pepper
Pineapple Topping

Measure out 1/2 cup pineapple and set aside for topping. Mix remaining undrained pineapple with lamb, beef, egg, crumbs, onion, salt, mint and pepper. Pack into two loaf pans (8 1/2 x 4 1/2 x 2 1/2 inches). Bake in moderately slow oven (325 degrees F.) 30 minutes. Drain fat from pans. Spread meat with Pineapple Topping. Return to oven and bake 30 minutes longer. Makes 2 small loaves.

Pineapple Topping: Combine reserved 1/2 cup crushed pineapple with 1/4 cup brown sugar (packed), 2 tablespoons mint jelly, and 1 tablespoon dried mint leaves, finely crumbled.

Note: Entire recipe may be baked in one loaf (9 x 5 x 2 3/4 inches) if desired. Increase baking time to 1 hour 20 minutes.

Won $2,500 in the 1977 National Pineapple Cooking Classic, sponsored by the Pineapple Growers Association of Hawaii.
LOIS BOYDSTON, WAUSEON, OHIO

PINEAPPLE SUNSHINE MUFFINS

1 (8 oz.) can crushed pineapple
3/4 cup all-purpose flour
3/4 cup whole wheat flour
2/3 cup toasted wheat germ
1/2 cup sugar
1/2 cup flaked coconut

1/2 cup chopped nuts
1 1/2 teaspoons baking soda
1/2 teaspoon salt
1 cup plain yogurt
2 eggs
1/4 cup oil

Turn pineapple into wire strainer and drain. Combine flours, wheat germ, sugar, coconut, nuts, soda and salt. In a separate bowl combine drained pineapple, yogurt, eggs and oil, mixing well. Add to dry mixture. Stir lightly, just until all of dry mixture is moistened. Spoon into greased muffin pans (2 3/4 inches diameter) or into paper liners set in muffin pans, filling 3/4 full. Bake in hot oven (400 degrees F.) 18 to 20 minutes. Serve warm with butter. Makes 15 to 18 muffins.

Won $2,500 in the 1979 National Pineapple Cooking Classic, sponsored by the Pineapple Growers Association of Hawaii.
DIANE CHITTENDEN, CLEARWATER, FLORIDA

HAWAIIAN STYLE SHORTRIBS

4 lbs. beef short ribs	2 (13 1/4 oz.) cans pineapple tidbits
1 tablespoon salt	1/4 cup liquid smoke
1/4 teaspoon garlic powder	1/4 cup brown sugar (packed)
3 cups bottled barbecue sauce	1 teaspoon lemon pepper

Have ribs cut in serving pieces. Brown on all sides, placing fat side down first, so no additional fat need be used. When ribs are browned, drain off and discard any fat in pan. Sprinkle with salt and garlic powder. Add water just to cover, and heat to boiling. Cover and simmer 1 1/2 hours, just until meat is tender. Drain meat, saving broth. Place ribs in shallow roasting pan. Combine all remaining ingredients, and pour over meat. Bake in moderate oven (350 degrees F.) 1 1/2 hours, basting frequently. If sauce becomes too thick, add some of the reserved beef broth. Makes 6 to 8 servings.

Won $10,000 in the 1974 National Pineapple Cooking Classic, sponsored by the Pineapple Growers Association of Hawaii.
CHARLENE STOCKBURGER, FAYETTEVILLE, ARKANSAS

SWEET & SOUR PORK ROAST WITH GINGERED PINEAPPLE AND SWEET POTATOES

1 rolled pork roast (5 lb.)	1/4 cup dark brown sugar
3 tablespoons flour	1/4 cup soy sauce
2 tablespoons salad oil	1/2 cup sliced celery
2 cups canned pineapple juice	6 sweet potatoes
1 (8 1/4 oz.) can crushed pineapple, undrained	Gingered pineapple slices (recipe follows)
1/2 cup cider vinegar	1/4 cup cornstarch

Preheat oven to 300 degrees F. Coat meat with flour. Heat salad oil and brown meat on all sides. Place in a roasting pan. Mix together the pineapple juice, crushed pineapple, vinegar, brown sugar, soy sauce, and celery. Spoon pineapple mixture over the browned pork roast. Cover and bake about 3 hours, basting frequently with pineapple mixture while roasting. Meanwhile, pare sweet potatoes. Cook potatoes in lightly salted water for 30 minutes, or just until tender. Drain; keep warm. Prepare the Gingered Pineapple Slices. When meat is tender, remove and place on heated platter and keep warm. Mix cornstarch with a little water to make a thin paste. Stir into pan liquid and cook, stirring, until gravy has thickened. Pour over roast. Garnish platter with sweet potatoes alternating with spiced pineapple slices. Serves 6 to 8.

Gingered Pineapple Slices:

1 (1 lb. 13 oz.) can pineapple
  slices
1/2 cup sugar

2 tablespoons white wine vinegar
1/4 cup dry white wine
1 large piece crystallized ginger

Drain pineapple, saving syrup. Mix drained syrup, sugar, vinegar, wine in saucepan. Cut ginger into 3 pieces lengthwise and add to syrup. Bring to boil; reduce heat and simmer for 5 minutes. Add pineapple slices and continue to simmer for 5 minutes longer, basting frequently.

Won the Grand Prize of $25,000 in the 1972 National Pineapple Cooking Classic, sponsored by the Pineapple Growers Association of Hawaii.
MRS. VIRGINIA F. HARRISON, CLATSKANIE, OREGON

HAM CAKES MAUNA LOA

2 cups ground cooked ham
1/2 cup dry bread crumbs
1 large egg, lightly beaten
1/4 cup finely chopped onion
2 tablespoons margarine

1 (8 oz.) can pineapple slices
  in juice
4 frozen patty shells, thawed*
Curry Sauce

Combine ham, bread crumbs, egg and onion; mix well. Shape into 4 patties. Melt margarine in skillet. Add ham cakes and brown on both sides. Set aside to cool. Drain pineapple well, saving juice for sauce. Roll one patty shell at a time to 6 inch square. Place ham cake on center of each square, and top with pineapple slice. Bring corners of pastry together over top, pinching firmly, to form a peak. Set on flat baking pan.

Bake in hot oven (400 to 425 degrees F.) 20 to 25 minutes, until nicely browned. Meanwhile, prepare Curry Sauce. Serve pastries hot, with the sauce. Makes 4 servings.

Curry Sauce: Drain 1 (8 oz.) can pineapple tidbits, saving juice. Heat 1 (10 3/4 oz.) can condensed cream of mushroom soup with 1/2 cup pineapple juice, 1 teaspoon curry powder and 1/4 teaspoon ginger, stirring until well blended. Stir in drained pineapple tidbits.

*Your favorite biscuit dough may be used. Roll out and cut into 4 (6 inch) squares.

Won $10,000 in the 1977 National Pineapple Cooking Classic, sponsored by the Pineapple Growers Association of Hawaii.
HELEN CREDELL, NORWOOD, NEW JERSEY

SUPER PINEAPPLE SPLIT

1 (12 oz.) package vanilla wafers
1 cup softened butter or margarine
1 (20 oz.) can crushed pineapple
1 (8 oz.) package cream cheese
2 cups sifted powdered sugar
1/2 cup semi-sweet real chocolate pieces
1 1/2 cups undiluted evaporated milk

2 large or 3 small bananas
2 tablespoons orange or lemon juice
1 pint frozen non-dairy topping, thawed
1/2 cup coarsely chopped pecans
1 (3 oz.) jar maraschino cherries, drained

Crush vanilla wafers, and mix well with 1/2 cup softened butter. Press over bottom of a 9x13x2 inch baking pan or dish. Drain pineapple well. Combine 1/4 cup butter with cream cheese, and blend well. Mix in 2/3 the pineapple (about 1 cup). Spread over the wafer crust. Combine remaining 1/4 cup butter, powdered sugar, chocolate pieces and evaporated milk in saucepan. Cook, stirring constantly, until thick and smooth. Cool. Slice bananas 1/2 inch thick, drizzle with orange or lemon juice and drain well. Arrange over pineapple-cream cheese layer. Top with cooled chocolate sauce. Spread non-dairy topping over all. Sprinkle with remaining pineapple, pecans and cherries. Chill thoroughly before serving. Makes 12 or more servings.

Won $2,500 in the 1977 National Pineapple Cooking Classic, sponsored by the Pineapple Growers Association of Hawaii.
MABEL HAUGEN, BELOIT, WISCONSIN

QUICHE WIKI-WIKI

1 (8 oz.) can crushed pineapple in juice
1 (9 inch) frozen deep dish pie shell
4 ounces sliced cooked ham*
4 ounces sliced sharp Cheddar cheese*
4 ounces sliced process Swiss cheese*
1/4 cup butter

1/4 cup chopped onion
1/4 cup chopped green pepper
1/2 cup juice from pineapple
4 eggs
1/2 cup light cream
4 teaspoons Dijon mustard
1/4 teaspoon white pepper
1/4 teaspoon prepared horseradish
1/4 teaspoon beef stock base

Turn pineapple into wire strainer and drain well, saving juice. Press pineapple with back of spoon if necessary, to make 1/2 cup juice. Partially bake pie shell in moderately hot oven (375 degrees F.) 10 minutes. Cut ham and cheeses into julienne strips. Melt half the butter in heavy skillet, add onion and green pepper and cook slowly 4 minutes. Add the 1/2 cup pineapple juice, and cook 4 minutes or until liquid is absorbed. Add pineapple and ham strips, and cook about 4 seconds, just long enough to blend. Spread over bottom of pie shell, reserving 4 tablespoons for topping. Add cheeses in separate clumps to vary color. Beat together eggs, cream, mustard, pepper, horseradish and beef stock base. Pour slowly into pie shell. Sprinkle remaining ham mixture on top. Dot with remaining butter. Bake 30 to 40 minutes in moderately hot oven (375 degrees F.) or until set. Serves 4 as entree, or 8 as appetizer.

*Deli-pack

Won $10,000 in the 1979 National Pineapple Cooking Classic, sponsored by the Pineapple Growers Association of Hawaii.
EILEEN CONWELL, OXNARD, CALIFORNIA

PINEAPPLE-HONEY GLAZED LAMB RIBLETS

1 (8 1/4 oz.) can crushed pineapple
1/2 cup honey
1/2 cup soy sauce
1/4 cup sherry
2 teaspoons chopped candied ginger
3/4 teaspoon garlic powder

1/2 teaspoon thyme
1/2 teaspoon salt
1/4 teaspoon crushed rosemary
1/4 teaspoon black pepper
3 lb. lamb riblets, cut into serving pieces

Drain off 2 tablespoons syrup from pineapple, and mix with 1/4 cup honey. Set aside for glaze. Combine remaining pineapple and syrup,

1/4 cup honey, soy sauce, sherry, candied ginger and seasonings; pour over lamb riblets. Marinate in refrigerator for 1 to 3 hours, turning meat several times. Heat oven to moderate (350 degrees F.). Drain lamb, reserving marinade. Arrange riblets on rack in roasting pan, and bake about 1 hour, basting occasionally with the marinade. Just before serving, heat the honey glaze mixture, and brush over riblets. Broil about 3 inches from heat, for 2 to 4 minutes, until glazed, watching carefully to avoid burning. Makes 4 to 6 servings.

Won $10,000 in the 1973 National Pineapple Cooking Classic, sponsored by the Pineapple Growers Association of Hawaii.
GUDREN FARAH, LAKE OSWEGO, OREGON

HAWAIIAN WEDDING CAKE

Pineapple Garnish	1/3 teaspoon baking powder
1 (1 lb. 4 oz.) can crushed pineapple	1 teaspoon salt
	1 cup vegetable oil
2 cups sugar	4 eggs
2 cups instantized flour	1 1/2 cups grated carrot
1 2/3 teaspoons baking soda	Frosting

Prepare Pineapple Garnish. Preheat oven to moderate (350 degrees F.). Drain crushed pineapple. Set aside 1/4 cup for frosting, and use remainder for cake. Combine sugar, flour, soda, baking powder, salt and oil; mix well. Add eggs, one at a time, beating well after each addition. Fold in carrots and pineapple. Divide batter evenly among 3 greased and floured 8 inch layer cake pans. Bake in preheated oven 35 minutes, until cakes test done. Let stand 10 minutes, then invert onto wire racks to cool. Meanwhile, prepare Frosting. When layers are cold, spread top of each with 1/3 the Frosting, and stack together. Decorate top with a lei made from drained Pineapple Garnish. Makes 1 (8 inch) cake.

Pineapple Garnish: Drain 1 (13 1/4 oz.) can pineapple chunks, and combine with 4 maraschino cherries, halved, and 2 tablespoons rum. Let stand while preparing cake. Drain and save rum for Frosting.

Frosting: Soften 1 (3 oz.) package cream cheese; blend with 1/2 cup butter. Beat in 1 pound powdered sugar, adding enough rum drained from Garnish to make a good spreading consistency. Stir in reserved 1/4 cup crushed pineapple.

Won $1,000 in the 1973 National Pineapple Cooking Classic, sponsored by the Pineapple Growers Association of Hawaii.
TED MORELAND, SEATTLE, WASHINGTON

HAWAII FIVE-O TORTE

1 cup sifted all-purpose flour
1/2 cup butter or margarine
1/3 cup finely ground pecans or
  hickory nuts
1/3 cup flaked coconut
1 (1 lb. 4 oz.) can unsweetened
  crushed pineapple

1 envelope unflavored gelatin
1/4 cup cold water
1 (4 3/4 oz.) package lemon pie
  filling
3/4 cup sugar
3 egg yolks
1 cup dairy sour cream
Powdered sugar

Preheat oven to moderate (350 degrees F.). Combine flour, butter, nuts and coconut, and blend to crumb consistency. Press in even layer in bottom of 8 inch square baking pan. Bake in preheated oven 20 minutes, until very lightly browned. Cool. Drain juice from pineapple and add water to measure 2 cups. Soften gelatin in 1/4 cup water. Prepare lemon pie filling with sugar and egg yolks, reducing liquid to the 2 cups pineapple juice and water. Cook until smooth and thick, stirring constantly. Remove from heat, add softened gelatin, and stir until dissolved. Fold in the drained pineapple. Cool 10 minutes, stirring occasionally. Preheat oven to very hot (500 degrees F.). Fold sour cream into pudding mixture, and turn into cooled crust. Cover with Meringue. Place in the very hot oven, turn heat off at once, and allow torte to remain in oven for several hours, until it is completely cold. Remove torte from oven, and sift powdered sugar over top. Chill several hours before serving. Makes 1 (8 inch) torte, 6 to 9 servings.

Meringue: Beat 3 egg whites with 1/4 teaspoon cream of tartar to a fine foam. Gradually beat in 1 1/4 cups sifted powdered sugar, continuing to beat at high speed until very stiff and shiny.

Won the Grand Prize of $25,000 in the 1973 National Pineapple Cooking Contest, sponsored by the Pineapple Growers Association of Hawaii.
BETTY SAKAR, MILWAUKEE, WISCONSIN

PINEAPPLE BEAN BURGERS

1 pound ground beef
1 egg, beaten
1/3 cup cracker crumbs
1 tablespoon prepared mustard
2 teaspoons prepared horseradish
1 teaspoon salt
1/3 cup finely chopped onion
1 (20 oz.) can pineapple chunks

1 (1 lb.) can pork and beans
1/2 cup brown sugar, packed
1/2 cup catsup
1 teaspoon prepared mustard
16 strips of Cheddar cheese
Pimiento strips
Parsley sprigs

Preheat oven to 450 degrees F. Lightly oil a flat baking pan. Combine ground beef, egg, cracker crumbs, mustard, horseradish, salt, and onion. Divide into four balls. On waxed paper, flatten each into a 5 inch circle. Turn up edges on each circle to form a 1 inch rim. Remove meat circles from paper and place them on the oiled baking pan. Bake for 10 minutes. Meanwhile, drain pineapple. Combine pineapple, beans, brown sugar, catsup, and mustard. Using a slotted spoon to avoid excess liquid, spoon the pineapple-bean mixture into the hamburger nests. Place strips of cheese on top of each. Bake 10 minutes longer. Remove from oven. To serve, garnish with pimiento strips and parsley sprigs. Makes 4 servings.

Won $1,000 in the 1972 National Pineapple Cooking Classic, sponsored by the Pineapple Growers Association of Hawaii.
MISS GWEN GRIFFIN, LAKE FOREST, ILLINOIS

HAWAIIAN PINEAPPLE COBBLER

2 (20 oz.) cans pineapple
  chunks
1 tablespoon sugar
2 tablespoons cornstarch
1/4 teaspoon ground ginger
1 tablespoon lemon juice
1 cup sifted all-purpose flour

1/3 cup sugar
1 1/2 teaspoons baking powder
1/2 teaspoon salt
1 1/2 cups grated Cheddar cheese
1/3 cup butter or margarine,
  melted
1/4 cup milk

Preheat oven to 425 degrees F. Drain pineapple chunks; reserve syrup. In a saucepan, mix together 1 tablespoon sugar, cornstarch, and ginger. Stir in reserved syrup and lemon juice. Place over medium heat and cook, stirring, until syrup thickens. Then boil for one minute. Remove from heat; stir in drained pineapple. Spoon into 9 inch square baking pan. Resift flour with 1/3 cup sugar, baking powder, and salt. Stir in cheese. Add melted butter and milk and stir until all ingredients are well blended. Spoon mixture over pineapple. Bake for 25-30 minutes. Serve warm topped with vanilla ice cream. Serves 6 - 8.

Won $1,000 in the 1972 National Pineapple Cooking Classic, sponsored by the Pineapple Growers Association of Hawaii.
MRS. MILLIE SNOW, SOUTHFIELD, MICHIGAN

PINEAPPLE PRALINE COFFEE CAKE

1 (15 1/4 oz.) can crushed pineapple
1 cup sifted all-purpose flour
1/4 cup granulated sugar
1 1/2 teaspoons baking powder
1/2 teaspoon salt
6 tablespoons pineapple syrup

1/3 cup softened butter or margarine
1 egg, beaten
1/2 cup light brown sugar (packed)
1/2 cup coconut
1/2 cup chopped pecans or walnuts
3 tablespoons butter or margarine, melted

Drain pineapple well, saving syrup. Resift flour with granulated sugar, baking powder and salt. Add 6 tablespoons of the reserved pineapple syrup, the softened butter and egg. Beat just until smooth. Spread in a greased 9 inch square baking pan. Spoon well-drained pineapple over batter, then sprinkle with praline topping. Bake in moderately hot oven (375 degrees F.) 25 to 30 minutes until pick inserted in center comes out clean and dry. Serve warm or cold, cut into squares. Makes 9 squares.

Praline Topping: Combine 1/2 cup each light brown sugar (packed), coconut and chopped pecans or walnuts with 3 tablespoons butter or margarine melted.

Won $1,000 in the 1974 National Pineapple Cooking Classic, sponsored by the Pineapple Growers Association of Hawaii.
TERESA TOMASIK, BRIDGEPORT, WEST VIRGINIA

POLYNESIAN SUNDAY SALAD

1 (1 lb. 4 oz.) can pineapple chunks
2 cups diced cooked chicken
2 cups diced cooked ham
2 cups diced celery

1 medium-sized green pepper, diced
3/4 cup blanched almonds (4 oz.)
Polynesian Dressing
Lettuce

Drain pineapple. Combine chunks with chicken, ham, celery, green pepper and almonds. Chill well. Toss with Polynesian Dressing and serve on crisp lettuce. Makes 8 servings.

Polynesian Dressing: Combine 1 1/2 cup mayonnaise, 3 tablespoons lemon juice, 1 teaspoon each powdered ginger and nutmeg, and a dash salt.

Won $1,000 in the 1974 National Pineapple Cooking Classic, sponsored by the Pineapple Growers Association of Hawaii.
CATHERINE SELBY, CHRISTMAS, FLORIDA

HAWAIIAN CELEBRATION TORTE

1 1/3 cups sifted all-purpose flour
1/2 teaspoon soda
1/2 cup margarine
1/2 cup sugar
1 egg
1 tablespoon maraschino cherry
syrup

2 teaspoons lemon extract
2 tablespoons chopped maraschino
cherries
1/2 cup chopped pecans
Pineapple Filling
1/3 cup toasted coconut

Resift flour with soda. Combine margarine, sugar, egg, cherry syrup and lemon extract in mixing bowl. Add flour mixture, and blend well. Stir in cherries and pecans. Spread in greased 9 inch layer cake pan. Bake in moderate oven (350 degrees F.) 20 to 25 minutes, until browned. Cool. Meanwhile prepare Pineapple Filling. Split cooled baked torte into 2 thin layers, and spread Pineapple Filling over tops of both layers. Stack together. Sprinkle coconut over top. Chill 2 or 3 hours before cutting. Makes 8 servings.

Pineapple Filling: Combine 1 (15 1/4 oz.) can crushed pineapple (undrained), 1 (3 1/4 oz.) package coconut cream pudding mix (not instant), and 1/3 cup sugar in a saucepan. Cook stirring constantly, over moderate heat until mixture comes to a full boil. Remove from heat and cool. Beat 1 cup whipping cream with 1 teaspoon lemon extract until stiff. Fold into cooled pudding mixture along with 1 cup miniature marshmallows.

Won $1,000 in the 1974 National Pineapple Cooking Classic, sponsored by the Pineapple Growers Association of Hawaii.
PERNA MAE RAMSEY, SPENCER, OKLAHOMA

FROSTED POLYNESIAN SALAD

1 (10 oz.) package frozen peas
2 medium green peppers
1 medium red onion
2 (5 oz.) cans water chestnuts
3 medium carrots

2 (15 1/4 oz.) cans pineapple
tidbits
2 (4 oz.) cans sliced mushrooms
1 small head iceberg lettuce
Frosting
Topping

Cook peas as package directs, and drain. Remove seeds and finely dice green peppers. Thinly slice onion and water chestnuts. Pare and coarsely grate carrots. Drain pineapple and mushrooms. Line a 9x13x2 inch baking dish with lettuce leaves. Layer vegetables and pineapple in dish.

Spread Frosting evenly over top. Cover dish and chill overnight. About 2 hours before serving, sprinkle with Topping. Refrigerate until ready to serve. Cut into squares. Makes 8 to 10 servings.

Frosting: Mix 1 1/2 cups mayonnaise, 1 1/2 cups dairy sour cream and 5 tablespoons sugar together.

Topping: Grate 3/4 pound Cheddar cheese. Fry 3/4 pound bacon until crisp. Drain well and crumble. Sprinkle bacon and cheese over chilled salad.

Won $10,000 in the 1977 National Pineapple Cooking Classic, sponsored by the Pineapple Growers Association of Hawaii.
LENTSEY CARLSON, LAKEWOOD, NEW YORK

POLYNESIAN LAMB SALAD

1 (13 1/4 oz.) can pineapple
  tidbits
1 (8 oz.) can water chestnuts
1 medium-sized green pepper
2 cups diced cooked lamb

2 cups diced celery
1/2 cup mandarin orange sections
Polynesian Dressing
Lettuce
2 tablespoons chopped pimiento

Drain pineapple and water chestnuts. Slice water chestnuts and green pepper. Combine with pineapple, lamb, celery and orange sections. Toss gently with Polynesian Dressing. Serve on lettuce and garnish with pimiento. Makes 6 or more servings.

Polynesian Dressing: Mix 1 1/4 cups mayonnaise with 3 tablespoons each lemon juice and chopped preserved ginger, 1/2 teaspoon nutmeg and 1/4 teaspoon salt. Cover and chill.

Won $10,000 in the 1974 National Pineapple Cooking Classic, sponsored by the Pineapple Growers Association of Hawaii.
BETTY CORBETT, SAN JOSE, CALIFORNIA

FESTIVE KABOBS

1 (8 oz.) can pineapple chunks
1/4 cup soy sauce
1/4 cup pineapple preserves
2 tablespoons minced onion
2 tablespoons oil
1 tablespoon light molasses
1 teaspoon dry mustard

1 teaspoon ground ginger
1 pound lamb shoulder, cut in
  1-inch cubes
12 large pimiento-stuffed olives
1 large green pepper, cut into 12
  pieces

Turn pineapple into wire strainer and drain well. Combine soy sauce, pineapple preserves, onion, oil, molasses, dry mustard and ginger. Pour over pineapple chunks, lamb, olives and green pepper. Marinate several hours or overnight. Alternate lamb, olives, pineapple and green pepper on 4 skewers. Oven broil or cook on outdoor grill 3 to 4 inches from heat, about 5 to 7 minutes, to desired degree of doneness, brushing frequently with marinade. Makes 4 servings.

Won $2,500 in the 1979 National Pineapple Cooking Classic, sponsored by the Pineapple Growers Association of Hawaii.
SHARI GOLIGHTLY, GRIMES, IOWA

PINEAPPLE MINI PIES

1 (15 1/4 oz.) can sliced pineapple
2 1/2 cups sifted all-purpose flour
1 teaspoon salt
1/2 teaspoon grated lemon peel
1 cup shortening
6 tablespoons reserved pineapple
   syrup
1/4 cup brown sugar
1/4 teaspoon cinnamon
3/4 cup sifted powdered sugar
3 tablespoons lemon juice
Dairy sour cream (optional)

Preheat oven to 400 degrees F. Drain pineapple, reserving syrup. Resift flour with salt; add lemon peel. Cut in shortening as for pastry. Add 6 tablespoons reserved pineapple syrup, one tablespoon at a time, to moisten mixture. Form into a ball. Roll out on lightly floured board to 1/8 inch thickness. Cut into 16 circles, about 1/2 inch larger than a pineapple slice. Cut small holes in center of 8 pastry circles, resembling doughnuts. Place one pineapple slice on each remaining whole pastry circle: sprinkle each with brown sugar and cinnamon. Top each with remaining pastry slices with holes. Seal edges of pastries with fork. Bake about 12 minutes. Remove from oven. Stir together powdered sugar and lemon juice; drizzle over pastries. If desired, serve topped with sour cream. Makes 8 mini-pies.

Won $10,000 in the 1972 National Pineapple Cooking Classic, sponsored by the Pineapple Growers Association of Hawaii.
JAN PETRING, TUCSON, ARIZONA

PINEAPPLE MUFFS

Granulated sugar for pans
1 (8 1/4 oz.) can crushed
  pineapple
3/4 cup milk
1/2 cup butter or margarine
2 eggs, beaten
2 cups sifted all-purpose flour

1/4 cup sugar
3 teaspoons baking powder
1/2 teaspoon salt
12 teaspoons pineapple preserves
1 teaspoon sesame seeds
1/4 cup powdered sugar

Preheat oven to moderately hot (375 degrees F.). Grease muffin pans (2 1/2 inches diameter), and sprinkle with granulated sugar. Drain pineapple, saving syrup. Warm milk in small saucepan. Add butter, and heat until butter melts. Remove from heat, and add eggs. Resift flour with 1/4 cup sugar, baking powder and salt into a mixing bowl. Make a well in center, and add the crushed pineapple. Add milk and butter mixture all at once, and stir just until all of dry ingredients are moistened. Spoon half the batter into the prepared pans, and place a spoonful of pineapple preserves on each. Cover with remaining batter, and sprinkle with sesame seeds. Bake in preheated oven about 25 minutes, until browned and baked through. Let stand 5 minutes. Meanwhile, mix powdered sugar with 1 1/2 teaspoons syrup from pineapple. Turn muffins out, and drizzle lightly with icing. Makes 12 muffins.

Won $10,000 in the 1973 National Pineapple Cooking Classic, sponsored by the Pineapple Growers Association of Hawaii.
SUYEYO LORANCE, WAHIAWA, HAWAII

PINEAPPLE NEWTON

20 fig newton cookies
1/2 cup melted butter
1 1/4 cups sugar
4 eggs
2 (8 oz.) packages cream cheese

1 (13 1/4 oz.) can crushed
  pineapple, drained
1 1/2 teaspoons vanilla
2 cups (1 pint) dairy sour cream
1/3 cup walnuts, chopped

Preheat oven to 350 degrees F. Put cookies in an electric blender and crumble (or, chop fine). Mix with melted butter and press over bottom and sides of one 10 inch pie plate. Chill. Put 1 cup sugar, eggs, and cream cheese in blender; blend for 1 minute on high speed. Stir in drained pineapple. Pour mixture into crust and bake for 20 minutes. Meanwhile, stir remaining 1/4 cup sugar and vanilla into sour cream. Remove cake from oven and spread sour cream mixture over top. Sprinkle with walnuts. Return cake to oven and bake 10 minutes longer. Cool and refrigerate. Makes one 10 inch cheesecake.

Won $1,000 in the 1972 National Pineapple Cooking Classic, sponsored by the Pineapple Growers Association of Hawaii.
LE NAE HAVLICEK, HUNTINGTON BEACH, CALIFORNIA

PORK FANTANGO

4 center-cut pork chops, (1/2 to
  3/4 inch thick)
Salt and pepper to taste
1/2 teaspoon monosodium
  glutamate
1/2 teaspoon grated lemon peel
1/4 cup bottled Italian Dressing

2 tablespoons butter or margarine
1 (8 1/4 oz.) can crushed
  pineapple
1/2 cup apricot preserves
1/4 cup vinegar
1/4 cup dark rum

Trim excess fat from chops. Sprinkle chops with salt, pepper, mono-sodium glutamate and lemon peel. Arrange in shallow baking dish. Pour Italian Dressing over chops; marinate 2 to 4 hours. Drain, saving marinade. Brown chops on both sides in heated butter. Combine undrained pineapple, preserves, vinegar and reserved marinade, and heat. Pour over chops. Bake, uncovered, in preheated moderate oven (350 degrees F.). 30 minutes, or until pork is tender. Pour rum over chops, and bake 5 minutes longer. Makes 4 servings.

Won $1,000 in the 1974 National Pineapple Cooking Classic, sponsored by the Pineapple Growers Association of Hawaii.
ORVILLE SHELDON, CHICAGO, ILLINOIS

ISLANDER LUNCHEON SALAD

1 bunch fresh spinach
1 cup thinly sliced celery
1/4 cup thinly sliced green onion
1 1/2 cups diced cooked chicken
  (or a 5 oz. can)
1 (13 1/4 oz.) can pineapple
  tidbits, drained

1 (4 oz.) can water chestnuts,
  drained
5 slices crisp bacon, crumbled
Dressing
Pineapple slices for garnish

Wash spinach, discard stems, and shred leaves to measure 5 cups. Combine in a large bowl with celery, onion, chicken, pineapple tidbits, water chestnuts and bacon. Pour dressing over salad and toss lightly. Garnish with pineapple slices.

Dressing: Combine 1 cup salad oil, 1/3 cup each catsup and sugar, 1/4 cup vinegar, 2 teaspoons Worcestershire sauce and 1/2 teaspoon curry powder in a jar. Cover and shake well to blend. Shake again just before serving.

Won $1,000 in the 1973 National Pineapple Cooking Classic, sponsored by the Pineapple Growers Association of Hawaii.
FLORIANA RYALL, RENO, NEVADA

PATTI'S PINA COLADA PIE

Coconut Crust
1 (15 1/4 oz.) can crushed
  pineapple in juice
1 envelope unflavored gelatin
3 large eggs, separated
1/3 cup sugar

1 cup milk
1/4 cup light rum
1/2 cup heavy cream
Topping
1/4 cup toasted coconut

Prepare Coconut Crust; set aside. Turn pineapple into wire strainer, and drain well, saving juice. Sprinkle gelatin over 1/4 cup juice from pineapple; let stand 5 minutes to soften. Beat egg yolks with sugar. Stir in milk. Cook over low heat, stirring constantly, until mixture coats a metal spoon. Remove from heat, add gelatin and stir until dissolved. Stir in rum. Chill until mixture begins to thicken. Beat egg whites to soft peaks. Beat cream stiff. Fold egg whites and cream into cooked mixture. Spoon into crust and chill. (May be frozen at this point, to be topped and served another day.) When pie is chilled, prepare Topping. Spoon over pie in mounds. Sprinkle with toasted coconut. Makes 1 (10 inch) pie.

Coconut Crust: Mix together 2 cups flaked coconut, 1/4 cup flour, and 1/3 cup soft butter. Press over bottom and up sides of 10 inch pie pan. Bake in moderately hot oven (375 degrees F.) 5 to 8 minutes, until lightly browned. Chill before filling.

Topping: Beat 1 egg white to soft peaks. Gradually beat in 2 tablespoons sugar and 1 cup well-drained crushed pineapple; beating until mixture is light and fluffy. Beat 1/2 cup heavy cream stiff. Fold into pineapple mixture.

Won $2,500 in the 1979 National Pineapple Cooking Classic, sponsored by the Pineapple Growers Association of Hawaii.
PATTI MALLIA, OWL'S HEAD, MAINE

CHILLED PINEAPPLE PAELLA SALAD

3 cups warm cooked rice, rinsed
1/2 teaspoon curry powder
1 (1 lb. 4 oz.) can pineapple chunks
2 tablespoons syrup from pineapple
1 1/4 cups mayonnaise
1/3 cup minced green onion

1/3 cup finely chopped green pepper
1/4 teaspoon garlic powder
1 (6 oz.) package frozen cooked shrimp, peeled and deveined
1 tablespoon lemon juice
1 1/4 cup frozen peas
1 1/2 cups 3/4 inch cubes cooked ham
Lettuce

Sprinkle rice with curry powder. Spoon off 2 tablespoons syrup from pineapple and add to rice, along with mayonnaise, onion, green pepper, and garlic powder. Mix well, cover and chill at least 1 hour. Thaw shrimp and cut in halves lengthwise. Sprinkle with lemon juice. Add water to peas as package directs, and bring to a boil. Drain at once; set aside 1/4 cup for garnish. Drain pineapple, and set aside a few chunks for garnish. Combine shrimp, remaining peas and pineapple, and ham. Chill. About half an hour before serving, drain any liquid from shrimp-pineapple mixture. Combine rice and shrimp-pineapple mixture. Spoon into serving bowl lined with lettuce. Garnish with reserved peas and pineapple chunks. Refrigerate until serving time. Makes 6 servings (about 8 1/2 cups).

Won $10,000 in the 1979 National Pineapple Cooking Classic, sponsored by the Pineapple Growers Association of Hawaii.
ELIZABETH ROCKWELL, NEWHALL, CALIFORNIA

THE CHRISTIAN BROTHERS® ANNUAL SHERRY CONTEST

SHERRIED WILD RICE SOUP

1/4 cup butter or margarine
1 medium onion, finely chopped
2 1/2 cups sliced mushrooms
 (about 1/2 pound)
1/2 cup each thinly sliced celery
 and flour
6 cups chicken broth
2 cups cooked wild rice

1/2 teaspoon each salt, curry
 powder, dry mustard, paprika
 and dried chervil
1/4 teaspoon white pepper
2 cups half and half
2/3 cup The Christian Brothers
 Dry Sherry
Chopped parsley or chives

In Dutch oven melt butter over medium heat; add onion. Cook and stir about 5 minutes until golden. Add mushrooms and celery; cook and stir 2 minutes. Mix in flour. Gradually add broth, stirring constantly 5 to 8 minutes until slightly thickened. Stir in rice, salt, curry powder, mustard, paprika, chervil and pepper. Reduce heat to low. Stir in half and half and sherry. Bring to simmer, stirring occasionally. Ladle hot soup into individual bowls; garnish with parsley or chives. Makes about 3 quarts.

Won First Prize of $1,000 plus lavish weekend in San Francisco in the 1980 Christian Brothers® Annual Sherry Recipe Contest.
PEGGY LEMMON, ST. PAUL, MINNESOTA

TROPICAL SHERRY SOUP

1 large sweet onion, chopped
1/4 cup butter
1 tablespoon flour
1 tablespoon curry powder
2 tablespoons flaked coconut
2 quarts chicken broth

1 cup smooth peanut butter
1/4 cup The Christian Brothers
 Dry Sherry
1/2 cup sour cream
Chopped peanuts or macadamia
 nuts

In 3 quart saucepan saute onion in butter until limp. Stir in flour, curry powder, coconut, and one cup of the chicken broth. Bring to boil, stirring constantly. Pour mixture into blender container with peanut butter; whirl smooth. Return mixture to saucepan. Add remaining broth and sherry.

Simmer 5 minutes, stirring. Do not boil. Just before serving, whisk in sour cream to blend. Serve dusted with curry and garnished with dollops of additional sour cream and chopped nuts. Makes 6 - 8 servings.

Won First Prize of $500 plus lavish weekend in San Francisco in the 1979 Christian Brothers® Annual Sherry Recipe Contest.
MARILYN HARRIS, HONOLULU, HAWAII

CALIFORNIA GOLDEN SHERRY PORK ROAST

12 to 14 pitted prunes (about
  4 ounces)
3/4 cup The Christian Brothers
  Golden Sherry
3 pounds lean boned pork loin
1/4 cup honey
3 tablespoons soy sauce

1 small onion, grated
1 1/2 tablespoons finely chopped
  crystallized ginger
1/2 teaspoon salt
1/4 teaspoon pepper
Water
1 tablespoon cornstarch

In small bowl combine prunes with enough sherry to cover. Set aside 1 to 2 hours. Make a slit lengthwise about 2 1/2 inches deep in boned side of pork; fill with drained prunes, reserving sherry. Tie pork around in several places to make a firm roll. In stainless steel pan or glass dish large enough to hold pork, combine reserved sherry (there should be about 1/2 cup), honey, soy sauce, onion, ginger, salt and pepper; blend thoroughly. Add pork; marinate, covered, 2 to 4 hours, turning occasionally. Place pork slit-side-down on rack in roasting pan containing 1 cup water; reserve marinade. Roast in 350 degree oven basting frequently with reserved marinade, 1 1/2 to 2 hours until meat thermometer inserted in center of pork registers 160 degrees. (As pork roasts, add water to moisten pan as needed; cover pork lightly with aluminum foil if necessary to prevent overbrowning.) Remove pork to serving platter; cover lightly and keep warm. Remove rack from roasting pan and place pan over low heat. Combine cornstarch with 2 tablespoons water; add to contents of roasting pan with any remaining marinade, stirring, to thicken sauce and loosen brown particles. Stir in enough additional water to make a syrupy sauce. Strain and serve hot with sliced pork. Makes 8 servings.

Won First Prize of $1,000 plus lavish weekend in San Francisco in the 1980 Christian Brothers® Annual Sherry Recipe Contest.
ELISE LALOR, ROCHESTER, NEW YORK

THE BROTHERS' LAMB SHANKS

1 1/2 teaspoon salt
1/2 teaspoon freshly ground pepper
1/2 teaspoon dried rosemary leaves
4 lamb shanks (3/4 - 1 lb. each)
1 tablespoon tomato paste
3/4 cup The Christian Brothers
  Golden Sherry

1 eggplant (3/4 - 1 lb.) cut in
  chunks
2 large green peppers, cored, seeded,
  and cut in chunks
3 medium onions, cut in wedges
3 medium tomatoes, cut in wedges
2 tablespoons chopped parsley
1 teaspoon garlic, minced

Combine salt, pepper and rosemary. Sprinkle lamb shanks with half the seasoning mixture. Place in 13x9 inch baking pan; broil until golden, about 5 minutes on each side. Remove from oven. Combine tomato paste and sherry. Pour over lamb shanks; set aside to marinate, turning occasionally. Meanwhile, in large bowl combine eggplant, peppers, onions, tomatoes, parsley and garlic. Toss with remaining seasoning mixture. Turn into roasting pan, surrounding lamb shanks. Cover tightly with aluminum foil. Bake in 300 degree oven 30 minutes. Remove pan from oven, uncover and turn lamb and vegetables. If mixture seems dry, add additional sherry diluted with water as needed. Cover and continue baking 30 minutes longer or until lamb is fork tender and vegetables thoroughly cooked. Serve with steamed rice and crusty chunks of garlic bread, if desired. Makes 4 servings.

Won the Grand Prize of $1,000 plus lavish one week vacation in San Francisco in the 1979 Christian Brothers® Annual Sherry Recipe Contest. LUCIA MAGGIANI, NEW YORK, NEW YORK

SHERRY EGG NOG PIE

Crust:

4 egg whites
1/2 teaspoon cream of tartar
1/2 teaspoon vanilla

Dash of salt
1 cup sugar

Filling:

1 envelope (1 tablespoon)
  unflavored gelatin
1/4 cup cold water
4 egg yolks

2/3 cup sugar
1/2 cup The Christian Brothers
  Cream Sherry
1/2 cup whipping cream, whipped

Topping:

1 cup whipping cream
2 tablespoons sugar

1/2 teaspoon vanilla

Prepare crust: In large mixing bowl beat egg whites, cream of tartar, vanilla and salt until frothy. Gradually beat in sugar; beat stiff. Spread on bottom and up sides of buttered 9 inch pie plate. Bake in 275 degree oven about 1 hour, until creamy tan. Set aside.

Prepare Filling: Soften gelatin in cold water; warm over low heat to dissolve. In mixing bowl beat yolks until thick and pale, gradually adding sugar. Mix in dissolved gelatin and sherry; fold in whipped cream. Place in cooled crust. Chill 4 hours or overnight. Whip topping ingredients to soften peaks; spread over filling. Top with chocolate curls, if desired. Chill. Makes 1 (9 inch) pie.

Won First Prize of $500 plus lavish weekend in San Francisco in the 1979 Christian Brothers® Annual Sherry Recipe Contest.
MARCELLA BERGUP, HOT SPRINGS, ARKANSAS

SHERRIED DOME DELIGHT

1 pound semi-sweet chocolate
1/3 cup strong coffee
10 egg yolks
1/3 cup The Christian Brothers
  Meloso Cream Sherry
1 pound butter, slightly softened
1 1/4 cups powdered sugar
6 egg whites
Genoise Layer (recipe follows)

2 cups whipping cream
1/4 cup The Christian Brothers
  Meloso Cream Sherry
2 tablespoons granulated sugar
1/2 cup each chopped blanched
  almonds and crushed vanilla
  wafers
1/3 cup grated semi-sweet chocolate
Chocolate curls
Strawberries, halved

In 1-quart saucepan melt chocolate in coffee over low heat. Thoroughly beat egg yolks; whisk yolks into melted chocolate mixture. Remove from heat; whisk in 1/3 cup sherry; cool to room temperature. In large bowl beat butter and powdered sugar just until fluffy. Gradually beat in cooled chocolate mixture just until smooth and thoroughly blended. In another bowl beat egg whites until stiff but not dry; fold into chocolate mixture, one fourth at a time, just until white streaks disappear. Line an 8 inch mixing bowl with plastic wrap. Fill with chocolate mixture; pack down and smooth top. Cover and chill until firm, 4 to 6 hours. Meanwhile, prepare Genoise Layer; cool. Prepare filling: In large bowl whip cream to form soft peaks; gradually beat in 1/4 cup sherry and granulated sugar. Remove half of cream mixture; cover and chill. Into remaining cream mixture fold almonds, vanilla wafers and grated chocolate. Place Genoise Layer on serving plate; top with almond mixture, spread to within 1/2 inch of edge. Carefully remove chocolate dome from bowl; invert on Genoise Layer and peel off plastic wrap. Fit pastry bag with large star tip. Fill with reserved cream mixture. Garnish dessert with piped cream, chocolate curls and strawberries. Chill. To serve, cut in wedges. Makes 14 to 16 servings.

Note: Genoise Layer on following page.

Genoise Layer:

4 eggs
2/3 cup sugar
1/2 teaspoon vanilla
2/3 cup sifted flour

1/4 cup clarified butter, cooled*
1/3 cup The Christian Brothers
Meloso Cream Sherry

In large bowl set over simmering water mix eggs, sugar and vanilla until lukewarm and syrupy. Remove from heat; beat at high speed for 10 to 15 minutes until mixture is pale and tripled in volume. Sprinkle flour over egg mixture, 1/3 cup at a time, folding in gently after each addition. Gradually fold in butter just until thoroughly blended. Turn into buttered and floured 8 x 2 1/2 inch cake pan or springform pan. Bake in 350 degree oven about 30 minutes until cake is golden and begins to shrink from pan. Remove side of pan; cool. Brush side and top of cake with sherry.

*To clarify butter: Place in small deep pan; melt over low heat. (Be careful not to brown.) Skim foam from top and gently pour off clear portion. Discard sediment.

Note: Genoise Layer may be prepared in advance, wrapped and frozen. Brush with sherry after defrosting.

Won First Prize of $1,000 plus lavish weekend in San Francisco in the 1980 Christian Brothers® Annual Sherry Recipe Contest.
ELAINE MICHAEL, PITTSFORD, NEW YORK

AROMATIC SHERRIED CHICKEN

1/3 cup The Christian Brothers
  Golden Sherry
1/3 cup dried apricots
1 medium onion, sliced

2 tablespoons corn oil
2 1/2 - 3 pound chicken, quartered
1/2 teaspoon basil
1/8 teaspoon cinnamon, or 1
  cinnamon stick

Combine sherry and apricots; set aside. In electric frying pan, saute onion in oil until golden; remove and reserve onion. Brown chicken in oil remaining in pan. Add onion, apricots, sherry, basil and cinnamon. Cover pan. Cook at 200 degrees about 50 minutes or until chicken is tender, turning once. Remove cover last 10 minutes. Makes 4 servings.

Won First Prize of $500 plus lavish weekend in San Francisco in the 1979 Christian Brothers® Annual Sherry Recipe Contest.
NANCY EISENMAN, SIMSBURY, CONNECTICUT

SHERRIED CUSTARD, JAPANESE

Broth:

1/2 cup The Christian Brothers
  Dry Sherry
1 cup clam juice
4 peppercorns
2 thin carrot strips

1 thin onion slice
Bouquet garni (1 sprig parsley,
  1 bay leaf, and 1 sprig thyme)
Shells from 4 shrimp

Scallops:

4 scallops
1/2 teaspoon shallots
1 teaspoon butter

1/4 cup The Christian Brothers
  Dry Sherry
Dash of salt

Custard:

4 eggs
1/2 cup half and half
1/2 teaspoon salt
Liquid reserved from broth
  and scallops

Chicken broth, as needed
4 raw shrimp, shelled, deveined
  and halved lengthwise
8 fresh green peas
4 carrot curls

In saucepan combine broth ingredients. Simmer uncovered 10 minutes. Strain and reserve liquid. Heat scallops, shallots and butter in covered saucepan, 3 - 5 minutes, until scallops tighten slightly. Remove scallops. Add sherry to juices in pan. In mixing bowl beat eggs and salt. Combine reserved liquids from broth and scallops with enough chicken broth to make 2 cups; stir into egg mixture. Pour into 4 custard cups, dividing equally. To each cup add 1 shrimp, 1 scallop quartered, 2 peas and 1 carrot curl. Cover with aluminum foil; set in pan containing 1 inch hot water. Bake in 350 degree oven 30 - 35 minutes until custard is set.

Serve hot, garnished with watercress. Makes 4 servings.

Won First Prize of $500 plus lavish weekend in San Francisco in the 1979 Christian Brothers® Annual Sherry Recipe Contest.
TETSUO OKADA, WASHINGTON, D.C.

GINGER PORK BALLS IN SHERRY-ORANGE SAUCE

1 large slice white bread, crumbled (about 1 cup crumbs)
1/4 cup The Christian Brothers Golden Sherry
1 1/2 pounds lean ground pork
1/2 cup minced water chestnuts

2 tablespoons soy sauce
1 egg yolk
2 teaspoons ground ginger
1 large clove garlic, crushed
Sherry-Orange Sauce (recipe follows)

In large bowl combine bread and sherry; set aside 10 minutes. Add remaining ingredients except Sherry-Orange Sauce. Mix to blend thoroughly. Cover and chill at least 30 minutes. Form into 1 inch balls. Place slightly apart on baking sheet. Bake in 400 degree oven about 20 minutes until cooked through and lightly browned. Meanwhile prepare Sherry-Orange Sauce. Add drained pork balls to sauce. Cook over medium heat until hot through, stirring gently. Remove from heat; gently stir in orange segments (reserved in Sherry-Orange Sauce recipe). Serve hot with cocktail picks for spearing. Makes about 5 dozen.

Sherry-Orange Sauce:

2 (11 oz.) cans Mandarin orange segments
Chicken broth or bouillon (about 3/4 cup)

1/3 cup The Christian Brothers Golden Sherry
2 tablespoons each cornstarch and soy sauce

Drain liquid from orange segments into 2 cup measure; reserve segments. Add broth to orange liquid to make 2 cups. Pour into 2 quart saucepan. Mix sherry, cornstarch and soy sauce; add to saucepan. Cook and stir over medium heat until smooth and thickened. Simmer 1 minute.

Won First Prize of $1,000 plus lavish weekend in San Francisco in the 1980 Christian Brothers® Annual Sherry Recipe Contest.
DIANE SHAW, NORTH SCITUATE, MASSACHUSETTS

RED STAR'S 3RD BAKING RECIPE EXCHANGE

MEXICAN PIZZA

2 1/2 cups all-purpose flour
1/2 cup yellow cornmeal
1 package Red Star Instant Blend
  Dry Yeast
1 teaspoon sugar
1 teaspoon salt
1 cup water
2 tablespoons oil

1 1/2 pound lean ground beef
2 (7 1/2 oz.) cans taco sauce
2 (4 oz.) cans green chilies, drained
  and chopped
1/2 pound natural Monterey Jack
  cheese, sliced 1/8 inch thick
Sliced green onions
Shredded lettuce

In large mixer bowl, combine 1 cup flour, cornmeal, yeast, sugar and salt; mix well. In saucepan, heat water and oil until warm (120 - 130 degrees). Add to flour mixture. Blend at low speed until moistened; beat 3 minutes at medium speed. By hand, gradually stir in enough remaining flour to make a soft dough. Knead on floured surface until smooth and elastic, about 5 minutes. Place in greased bowl, turning to grease top. Cover; let rise in warm place until light and doubled, about 45 minutes. Meanwhile, in large skillet, lightly brown meat; stir in taco sauce. Cook, uncovered, 5 to 10 minutes until almost dry. Remove from heat; cool.

Punch down dough. Divide into 2 parts. Form each half into a ball and place on greased cookie sheets. Using palms of hands, pat each ball into a 12 inch circle, making edges slightly thick. Spread meat mixture over dough to edge. Arrange chilies and cheese over meat. Bake at 425 degrees for 15 to 20 minutes. Sprinkle with onions and lettuce. Serve immediately. Makes two 12-inch pizzas.

Won $100 in Red Star's 3rd Baking Recipe Exchange, "Used by permission," Universal Foods Corporation.
PATTY ROSS, TRENTON, OHIO

SAUERKRAUT RYE BREAD

2 1/2 to 3 cups all-purpose flour
2 cups medium rye flour
2 packages Red Star Instant
  Blend Dry Yeast
1/2 cup nonfat dry milk
2 tablespoons sugar
1 tablespoon whole caraway seed

1 1/2 teaspoons salt
1/4 teaspoon ginger
1 1/4 cups water
2 tablespoons oil
8 oz. undrained sauerkraut, at
  room temperature

In large mixer bowl, combine 1 cup all-purpose flour, 1/4 cup rye flour, yeast, dry milk, sugar, caraway seed, salt and ginger; mix well. In saucepan, heat water and oil until warm (120 - 130 degrees). Add to flour mixture. Blend at low speed until moistened; beat 3 minutes at medium speed. By hand, gradually stir in sauerkraut, remaining rye flour and enough remaining all-purpose flour to make a firm dough. (The amount of flour will depend upon how much juice the sauerkraut has.) Knead on floured surface until smooth and elastic, about 5 minutes.

Divide into 2 parts. On lightly-floured surface, roll or pat each half to a 14x7 inch rectangle. Starting with shorter side, roll up tightly, pressing dough into roll with each turn. Pinch edges and ends to seal. Place in greased 8x4 inch loaf pans. Brush dough lightly with oil. Cover; let rise in warm place until light and doubled, about 1 hour. Bake at 375 degrees for 35 to 40 minutes until loaves sound hollow when tapped. If too dark cover with foil last 10 to 15 minutes of baking. Remove from pans; cool. Makes 2 loaves.

Won $100 in Red Star's 3rd Baking Recipe Exchange, "Used by permission," Universal Foods Corporation.
LINDA YOUNG, LAFAYETTE, COLORADO

SWISS CHEESE BREAD

5 cups all-purpose flour
2 packages Red Star Instant Blend
  Dry yeast
3 tablespoons sugar
1 1/2 tablespoons salt

1 cup water
1 cup milk
2 tablespoons butter or margarine
1 egg
1 1/2 cups shredded Swiss cheese

In large mixer bowl, combine 2 1/2 cups flour, yeast, sugar and salt; mix well. In saucepan, heat water, milk and butter until warm (120 - 130 degrees; butter does not need to melt). Add to flour mixture. Add egg. Blend at low speed until moistened; beat 3 minutes at medium speed.

By hand, gradually stir in cheese and enough remaining flour to make a sticky batter. Cover; let rise in warm place until light and doubled, about 1 hour.

Stir batter down; turn into 2 well-greased 1 quart baking dishes. Bake at 375 degrees for 35 to 40 minutes until golden brown and loaves sound hollow when tapped. If too dark, cover with foil last 10 to 15 minutes of baking. Remove from pans; cool. Makes 2 round loaves.

Won $100 in Red Star's 3rd Baking Recipe Exchange, "Used by permission," Universal Foods Corporation.
MRS. NANCY GEER, EAST BERNE, NEW YORK

CORN CHEDDAR BUBBLE LOAF

4 3/4 to 5 1/4 cups all-purpose flour
1 cup cornmeal
2 packages Red Star Instant Blend Dry Yeast
2 tablespoons sugar
2 teaspoons salt

1 3/4 cups milk
1/2 cup water
2 tablespoons butter
1/2 cup Stella shredded sharp Cheddar cheese
1/3 cup butter or margarine, melted

In large mixer bowl, combine 1 1/2 cups flour, cornmeal, yeast, sugar and salt; mix well. In saucepan, heat milk, water and butter until warm (120 - 130 degrees; butter does not need to melt). Add to flour mixture. Blend at low speed until moistened; beat 3 minutes at medium speed. By hand, add cheese and gradually stir in enough remaining flour to make a firm dough. Knead on floured surface until smooth and elastic, about 5 minutes. Place in greased bowl, turning to grease top. Cover; let rise in warm place until light and doubled, about 1 hour.

Punch down dough; divide into 4 parts. Divide each fourth into 10 pieces. Roll each piece into a ball; dip in melted butter. Arrange in greased 10-inch tube pan. Cover; refrigerate 2 to 24 hours before baking. Bake at 375 degrees for 55 to 60 minutes until golden brown. Remove from pan; brush with butter, if desired. Serve warm. Makes one 10-inch tube cake.

Won $100 in Red Star's 3rd Baking Recipe Exchange, "Used by permission," Universal Foods Corporation.
MRS. ROBERT BIRK, RHINELANDER, WISCONSIN

BREAD "STEW-PENDOUS"

4 to 4 1/2 cups all-purpose flour
2 packages Red Star Instant Blend
   Dry Yeast
1/4 cup sugar
1 envelope (about 1 5/8 oz.) beef
   stew seasoning mix

3/4 cup milk
1/2 cup water
1/4 cup butter or margarine
2 eggs

In large mixer bowl, combine 2 cups flour, yeast, sugar and seasoning mix; mix well. In saucepan, heat milk, water and butter until warm (120 - 130 degrees; butter does not need to melt). Add to flour mixture. Add eggs. Blend at low speed until moistened; beat 3 minutes at medium speed. By hand, gradually stir in enough remaining flour to make a firm dough. Knead on floured surface until smooth and elastic, about 5 minutes. Place in greased bowl, turning to grease top. Cover; let rise in warm place until light and doubled, about 2 hours.

Punch down dough. Divide into 2 parts. On lightly-floured surface, roll or pat each part to a 14x7 inch rectangle. Starting with the shorter side, roll up tightly, pressing dough into roll with each turn. Pinch edges and ends to seal. Place in greased 8x4 inch loaf pans. Cover; let rise in warm place until doubled, about 1 1/2 hours. Bake at 375 degrees for 35 minutes. Remove from pan; brush with butter, if desired. Cool. Makes 2 loaves.

Won $100 in the Red Star's 3rd Baking Recipe Exchange, "Used by permission," Universal Foods Corporation.
MRS. DONALD LE CLAIR, NORTH STONINGTON, CONNECTICUT

COFFEECAKE A LA MERINGUE

3 1/2 to 4 cups all-purpose
   flour
2 packages Red Star Instant
   Blend Dry Yeast
1/4 cup sugar
1 teaspoon salt
1/2 cup sour cream
1/2 cup water

1 cup butter or margarine
3 eggs, separated
1/2 teaspoon vanilla
3/4 cup sugar
1/2 cup raisins
1/2 cup chopped nuts
2 tablespoons cinnamon

In large mixer bowl, combine 1 cup flour, yeast, sugar and salt; mix well. In saucepan, heat sour cream, water and butter until warm (120 - 130 degrees; butter does not need to melt). Add to flour mixture. Add yolks and vanilla. Blend at low speed until moistened; beat 3 minutes at medium speed. By hand, gradually stir in enough remaining flour to make a soft dough. Cover; let rise in warm place until light and doubled, about 1 hour.

Punch down dough. On lightly-floured surface, roll or pat to a 15x12 inch rectangle. In small mixer bowl, beat egg whites until stiff adding sugar gradually. Spread dough with meringue. Combine raisins, nuts and cinnamon. Sprinkle over meringue. Starting with the longer side, carefully roll up. Seal edges; cut into 6 equal parts. Place cut side up in greased loose-bottom tube pan. Cover; let rise in warm place, about 45 minutes. Bake at 350 degrees about 1 hour until golden brown. Cool 10 minutes; remove from pan. Makes 1 coffeecake.

Won $100 in Red Star's 3rd Baking Recipe Exchange, "'Used by permission," Universal Foods Corporation.
MRS. MORTIMER BILENKER, ELIZABETH, NEW JERSEY

KNOX UNFLAVORED GELATINE "KNOX BLOX CONTEST"

SALAD BLOX

2 envelopes Knox Unflavored
  Gelatine
1 (3 oz.) package lime flavored
  gelatine

1 1/2 cups boiling water
2 cups (16 oz.) creamed cottage
  cheese
1/2 cup coarsely chopped walnuts
1/2 cup seedless raisins

In large bowl, mix Knox Unflavored Gelatine and flavored gelatine. Add boiling water and stir until gelatine is completely dissolved; cool. Stir in cottage cheese and pour into 8 or 9 inch square pan. Sprinkle with walnuts and raisins and chill until firm. Cut into squares to serve. Makes about 6 dozen (1 inch) squares.

Pineapple Salad Blox: Add 1 (8 1/4 oz.) can crushed pineapple.

Apple Salad Blox: Add 1 medium apple, finely chopped.

Was a prize-winner in the 1975 "Knox Blox Recipe Contest" sponsored by Thomas J. Lipton, Inc.
SARAH MCCORKLE, WINONA, MISSISSIPPI

SALMON "LOX BLOX"

4 envelopes Knox Unflavored
  Gelatine
3/4 cup cold water
1 1/4 cups boiling water
1 cup sour cream

3/4 cup Wish-Bone®Thousand
  Island Dressing
2 teaspoons lemon juice
1 (7 3/4 oz.) can salmon, drained
  and flaked
3 tablespoons finely chopped
  onion

In large bowl, sprinkle Knox Unflavored Gelatine over cold water. Add boiling water and stir until gelatine is completely dissolved. With wire whip or rotary beater, blend in sour cream, Wish-Bone® Dressing, lemon juice, salmon, and onion. Pour into 8 or 9 inch square baking pan, and chill until firm. Cut into squares to serve. Makes about 6 dozen (1 inch) squares.

Was a prize-winner in the 1975 "Knox Blox Recipe Contest" sponsored by Thomas J. Lipton, Inc.
JULIE HAUBER, WINFIELD, KANSAS

CHICKEN 'N CURRY BLOX

5 envelopes Knox Unflavored
  Gelatine
2 (3 oz.) packages lemon
  flavored gelatine
3 envelopes Lipton® Chicken
  Flavor Cup-a Broth

3 cups boiling water
1 1/2 cups mayonnaise
1 1/2 cups cut-up cooked
  chicken
3/4 cup chopped celery
2 tablespoons finely chopped
  onion
1 1/4 teaspoons curry powder

In large bowl, mix Knox Unflavored Gelatine, flavored gelatine, and Lipton Cup-a-Broth. Add boiling water and stir until gelatine is completely dissolved. With wire whip or rotary beater, blend in mayonnaise, chicken, celery, onion and curry. Pour into 9x13 inch shallow baking pan and chill until firm. Cut into squares to serve. Makes about 10 dozen (1 inch) squares.

Was a prize-winner in the 1975 "Knox Blox Recipe Contest" sponsored by Thomas J. Lipton, Inc.
LARENE WILSON, SEATTLE, WASHINGTON

CRAB LOUIS EN BLOX

6 envelopes Knox Unflavored
  Gelatine
1/4 cup sugar
2 1/2 cups boiling water
1 cup mayonnaise
1/2 cup Wish-Bone® Deluxe
  French or Thousand Island
  Dressing

1/2 cup chili sauce
2 cups flaked cooked crabmeat
1/2 cup chopped celery
1 hard-cooked egg, chopped
  (optional)

In large bowl, mix Knox Unflavored Gelatine and sugar. Add boiling water and stir until gelatine is completely dissolved. With wire whip or rotary beater, blend in mayonnaise, Wish-Bone Dressing, chili sauce, crabmeat, celery, and egg. Pour into 9x13 inch shallow baking pan and chill until firm. Cut into squares to serve. Makes about 10 dozen (1 inch) squares.

Won the Grand Prize of $5,000 in the 1975 "Knox Blox Recipe Contest" sponsored by Thomas J. Lipton, Inc.
PEGGY CREED, FLORISSANT, MISSOURI

WESSON "SALAD OF THE YEAR" CONTEST

CRUNCHY CELERY-CRESS SALAD

1 large bunch of celery
2 cups sliced and drained
   watercress

1 medium red onion, separated
   into rings
1/4 cup grated lemon peel
2 cups unsalted pecan halves

Dressing:

1/4 cup wine vinegar
1/3 cup honey
2 teaspoons salt
1/2 cup Wesson Oil
1/2 cup sour cream

1 teaspoon chopped dill weed
2 tablespoons chopped parsley
1 teaspoon Dijon mustard
Fresh ground pepper to taste

Discard leaves and base of celery. Cut stalks into 1/4 inch slices and combine with watercress, lemon peel and onion rings in medium sized mixing bowl.

In small mixing bowl, combine dressing ingredients and blend well, reserving sour cream for last. Beat in sour cream with wire whisk until dressing is smooth.

Pour over celery-watercress mixture and toss gently. Marinate in covered bowl for 2 - 3 hours in the refrigerator, add pecans just before serving.

Make individual servings on bed of spinach leaves or shredded lettuce. When ready to serve, garnish with hard-boiled egg slices, radishes, and tomato slices. Makes 4 servings.

Won Third Prize of $250 - Appetizer Salad Category in the 1977 Wesson "Salad of the Year" Contest.
SUSAN SMITH, CHICAGO, ILLNOIS

WHITE BEAN SALAD APPETIZER

1 cup dried white beans	1 tablespoon red wine vinegar
1 teaspoon red onion, chopped	1/3 cup Wesson Oil
1 teaspoon chives, chopped	1/4 teaspoon salt
1 teaspoon parsely, chopped	1/8 teaspoon pepper

To prepare: Cook beans as directed on package. Drain and while still warm mix with onion, chives, parsley, vinegar, Wesson Oil, salt and pepper. Chill.

To serve: Lightly spread rounds of cocktail rye bread with Dijon mustard. Mash beans slightly, spread on cocktail rounds. Serves 6 - 8.

Won Second Prize of $1,000 - Appetizer Salad Category in the 1977 Wesson "Salad of the Year" Contest.
PHYLLIS WHITE, MARINA DEL ROY, CALIFORNIA

APPETIZER SALAD

3 cantaloupes	3 tablespoons lime juice
2 cups flaked crab meat	1 teaspoon crushed basil
1 cup chopped walnuts	1 teaspoon sugar
1 (7 oz.) jar maraschino cherries	1 teaspoon salt
1 cup Wesson Oil	1/2 teaspoon pepper
1/2 cup cottage cheese	3 cups shredded lettuce
3 tablespoons tarragon vinegar	

Cut cantaloupes in half. Discard seeds and membrane. Cut out 2 cups of small cantaloupe balls. Trim inside of cantaloupes smooth. Put cantaloupe balls, crab meat, and nuts in bowl, drain cherries, remove stems, rinse, and drain again. Put cherries in the bowl. Mix gently. Put oil, cheese, vinegar, lime juice, basil, sugar, salt, and pepper in blender. Blend smooth. Arrange 1/2 cup of lettuce in each cantaloupe shell. Pour on each 1 tablespoon dressing; put 1 cup salad in each shell. Chill before serving. Serve remaining dressing in separate bowl. Serves 6.

Won First Prize of $3,000 - Appetizer Salad Category in the 1977 Wesson "Salad of the Year" Contest.
TABITHA HENKEN, ARCADIA, CALIFORNIA

MUSHROOM APPETIZER

1 pound fresh mushrooms
1/2 cup Wesson Oil
2 1/2 tablespoons wine vinegar
1 clove garlic, chopped fine
1 large onion, chopped fine
1/2 teaspoon salt
1/2 teaspoon pepper
1/2 teaspoon sugar

2 sprigs parsley chopped
1/8 teaspoon oregano
1/8 teaspoon allspice
1/8 teaspoon cloves
Few dashes of Louisiana Hot Sauce
  or red pepper to taste
1 (12 oz.) can tomato juice
1 tablespoon flour

Slice mushrooms and set aside.

Combine the rest of the ingredients in a saucepan and simmer for 5 minutes to blend the flavor. Add mushrooms making sure they are covered with the liquid. Simmer for 15 minutes.

Mix one tablespoon of flour with a little water to make a thin paste. With mushroom mixture on a low flame, add a little of the flour mixture at a time until the juice is the thickness of gravy.

Cool thoroughly. Serve on lettuce leaves.

Will serve from 4 to 8 persons depending on size of serving.

Won Second Prize of $1,000 - Appetizer Salad Category in the 1977 Wesson "Salad of the Year" Contest.
LAURA E. HEARN, LONG ISLAND CITY, NEW YORK

PEAS IN SNOW SALAD

4 cups cooked baby peas
1 medium onion
3 tablespoons fresh mint
3 tablespoons Wesson Oil

2 tablespoons honey
2 teaspoons salt
1/2 cup sour cream
1 1/2 tablespoons white wine
  vinegar

Cook peas 5 minutes. Cool. Mix with thinly sliced onion and mint. Combine well. Leave overnight in a mixture of oil, honey and salt. Thirty minutes before serving add 1/2 cup sour cream and white wine vinegar. Serve in a bowl or on lettuce cups. Garnish with mint sprigs. Serves 6.

Won First Prize of $3,000 - Side Dish Salad Category in the 1977 Wesson "Salad of the Year" Contest.
LINDA SAUKKONEN, LONGVIEW, WASHINGTON

ORANGE GINGER

1 1/2 tablespoons orange
    marmalade
2 tablespoons crystallized
    ginger, minced
1 tablespoon lemon juice
1/4 teaspoon salt

3 tablespoons Wesson Oil
3 oranges, peeled and thinly
    sliced
8 large stewed prunes
1 (3 oz.) package cream cheese,
    softened

Combine marmalade and ginger together. Add lemon juice and salt. Slowly stir in Wesson Oil. Mix well and pour over oranges and prunes. Marinate at least one hour.

Arrange orange slices on serving plate. Place prunes in center. Beat marinade into softened cheese until creamy. Spoon over oranges. Sprinkle with grated orange rind. Makes 8 servings.

Won Second Prize of $1,000 - Side Dish Salad Category in the 1977 Wesson "Salad of the Year" Contest.
MRS. KATHERINE ROBINSON, WAIMANALO, HAWAII

GREEN BEANS ITALIANO

3/4 cup Wesson Oil
1/3 cup red wine vinegar
1 envelope spaghetti sauce mix
2 tablespoons dry wine, if
    desired
2 (1 lb.) cans Italian green
    beans, drained
1/2 cup sliced ripe olives

1 (3 oz.) can sliced mushrooms,
    drained
1/4 cup chopped onion
2 tablespoons chopped pimiento
3 cups shredded lettuce
2 tablespoons grated Parmesan
    cheese
Whole olives for garnish
1/4 cup diced salami or
    pepperoni, optional

Combine Wesson Oil, vinegar and spaghetti sauce mix. Add wine, if desired. Place beans, olives, mushrooms, onion and pimiento in glass or plastic bowl. Pour dressing mixture over; toss. Cover; refrigerate at least 2 hours. Serve atop shredded lettuce. Sprinkle with Parmesan cheese; toss. Garnish with whole olives and diced salami, if desired. Makes 8 servings.

Won Third Prize of $250 - Side Dish Salad Category in the 1977 Wesson "Salad of the Year" Contest.
JAMES L. STRIEBER, TUCSON, ARIZONA

ORIENTAL CABBAGE SLAW

1 small head white or Chinese
   cabbage, shredded
2 cups snow peas (optional) cut
   diagonally

1 bunch radishes, sliced thin
1/2 cup thinly sliced (long ways)
   green onion
2/3 cup slivered almonds

Mix cabbage, snow peas, radishes and onion together. Toast almonds at 350 degrees for 8 minutes. Set aside.

Sweet Soy Dressing:

1/2 cup Wesson salad oil
1/3 cup white vinegar
3 tablespoons sugar
2 tablespoons soy sauce

3/4 teaspoon ground ginger
1/8 teaspoon cayenne pepper
1/4 teaspoon sesame oil

Combine dressing ingredients.

To serve: Add almonds and dressing to slaw mixture. Toss together lightly.

Won Second Prize of $1,000 - Side Dish Salad Category in the 1977 Wesson "Salad of the Year" Contest.
KATHY PALMER, SANTA CRUZ, CALIFORNIA

CURRY/CREAM CHEESE SALAD

2 cups canned chick peas, drained
1/2 cup Wesson Oil
1/4 cup lemon juice
2 teaspoons salt
1/4 teaspoon white pepper

1 teaspoon curry powder
1 onion, very thinly sliced
1 pound firm cream cheese
1/2 head crisp iceberg lettuce,
   finely shredded

Chill chick peas several hours. Blend Wesson Oil, lemon juice, salt, pepper and curry powder in blender and pour over chick peas. Toss gently with sliced onion. Chill, covered, while you slice firm block of cream cheese into small cubes. Toss cream cheese cubes with chick pea mixture and chill two hours or more. Just before serving, toss mixture with shredded lettuce. Serves 8.

Won Third Prize of $250 - Side Dish Salad Category in the 1977 Wesson "Salad of the Year" Contest.
MRS. JEFFREY H. NEWBY, CORAL GABLES, FLORIDA

APRICROWN JEWEL SPINACH SALAD

Topping:

1/4 cup Wesson Pure Vegetable
  Oil
2 teaspoons Worcestershire
  sauce

1/2 teaspoon garlic salt
4 slices bread, cubed
1/2 cup golden raisins

In large skillet, combine oil with Worcestershire sauce and garlic salt. Heat and add bread cubes, mixing to coat. Add raisins and heat over low heat until bread is toasted, stirring often.

Dressing:

1/2 cup Wesson Pure Vegetable
  Oil
1/3 cup apricot preserves

1 cup sour cream
1 teaspoon rum extract

In small bowl combine Wesson Oil, apricot preserves, 1/2 cup sour cream (reserve remainder), and rum extract. Blend thoroughly and refrigerate.

Salad:

12 ounces spinach
1/2 cup chopped celery
8 small green onions, thinly
  sliced

4 hard cooked eggs, coarsely
  chopped
2 cups cooked ham, cubed
12 apricot halves, drained

Wash spinach and remove stems; break leaves into bite sized pieces in a large salad bowl. Toss lightly with celery, onions, eggs and ham. Refrigerate covered until serving time.

To serve: Toss salad with dressing. Place in four large serving bowls. Sprinkle with topping. Garnish each bowl with three apricot halves and dollops of reserved sour cream. Yields 4 servings.

Won First Prize of $3,000 - Main Dish Salad Category in the 1977 Wesson "Salad of the Year" Contest.
MRS. CLAYTON CURTIS, WINSLOW, INDIANA

PRIZE CATCH SALAD

1/2 cup Wesson Oil
1/2 cup cider vinegar
1 teaspoon salt

1/2 teaspoon pepper
3/4 cup sugar
1 pound shrimp, cooked and
   cleaned

Combine first 5 ingredients, mix to blend well. Marinate shrimp in the Wesson Oil dressing overnight in refrigerator.

The following salad ring accompaniment may be prepared the evening before or on the day it is to be served, allowing time to set.

1 tablespoon plus 2 teaspoons
   plain gelatin
1/4 cup cold water
1 cup boiling water
1 tablespoon cider vinegar
1 cup sugar
3/4 cup chili sauce

2 cups finely chopped, drained
   sauerkraut
1/2 cup chopped green pepper
1/2 cup diced celery
1/2 cup chopped green onion
1 (4 oz.) jar pimientos, drained
   and chopped

Mix gelatin with cold water. Let stand 5 - 10 minutes to soften. Add 1 cup boiling water and stir to dissolve completely. Cool. Add rest of ingredients and mix well. Pour into a Wesson-oiled 1-quart ring mold and set in refrigerator to jell. Unmold on platter, arrange marinated shrimp in center and garnish with endive.

Won Second Prize of $1,000 - Main Dish Salad Category in the 1977 Wesson "Salad of the Year" Contest.
MRS. MARJORIE C. CURTIS, RICHLAND, WASHINGTON

HONEY CREME WALDORF SALAD

Salad Dressing:

1/2 cup sour cream
1/2 cup Wesson Oil
1/2 cup honey

1/2 cup orange juice
1 (3 3/4 oz.) package vanilla
   instant pudding

Beat first 4 ingredients together with a mixer until smooth, then stir in the instant pudding.

Toss together:

4 cups apples, chopped
(unpeeled)
1 cup chopped celery

1/2 cup chopped nuts
1 cup raisins

Mix with Honey Creme Dressing. Serve with slices of Cheddar cheese if desired. Serves 8 - 10.

Won Third Prize of $250 - Dessert Salad Category in the 1977 Wesson "Salad of the Year" Contest.
MRS. MARY TONEY JARVIS, LAPEL, INDIANA

COFFEE FRUIT FONDUE

1 1/2 teaspoons instant coffee
powder
1/2 teaspoon vanilla extract
1/2 teaspoon salt
1/4 cup Wesson Oil
2/3 cup sweetened condensed
milk
1/4 cup lemon juice
1/3 cup canned pineapple juice
1 egg yolk
1 cup heavy whipping cream, stiffly
beaten

2 large bananas, peeled, fluted,
cut into chunks and dipped in
lemon juice
1 1/2 cups watermelon balls
1 cup cherries, pitted stuffed with
pecan halves
1 1/2 cups fresh pineapple cubes
1 1/2 cups fresh strawberries
1 cup seedless grapes
Watercress

Blend together coffee, vanilla and salt; stir in oil. Combine milk, juices and egg yolk; stir in oil mixture. Beat until thickened. Chill. Fold in whipped cream. In center of shallow dish, set small glass bowl with dressing. Around it, arrange fruits in groups. Tuck in watercress between each type of fruit. Serves 8 desserts.

Won Second Prize of $1,000 - Dessert Salad Category in the 1977 Wesson "Salad of the Year" Contest.
MRS. OLIVER CREED, FLORISSANT, MISSOURI

LIDDLE BO BEEP SALAD

Garlic Mint Dressing:

2 teaspoons dried mint leaves,
  finely crushed
1 teaspoon curry powder
1 envelope garlic dressing mix
1 teaspoon paprika

1/3 cup honey
1/3 cup vinegar
1 tablespoon lemon juice
1 teaspoon grated onion
3/4 cup Wesson Oil

Combine mint leaves, curry powder, garlic dressing mix, paprika. Stir in honey, vinegar, lemon juice and onion. Very slowly pour Wesson Oil into mixture, beating constantly with electric beater. Pour into jar with tight lid and refrigerate.

Salad Ingredients:

4 cups diced cooked lamb
1/2 pound young fresh spinach
  washed and torn into bite-sized
  pieces
1 (1 lb.) can sliced carrots, well
  drained
1 cup celery slices, cut diagonal

1/2 cup sliced mushrooms
1/2 cup sliced pitted ripe olives
1/4 cup finely cut dried apricots
1 medium sized green pepper, cut
  in strips
2 tablespoons chopped pimiento
1/2 cup cold cooked rice

In salad bowl combine all salad ingredients. Shake prepared dressing in jar then drizzle over salad ingredients. Toss lightly.

Garnish Accompaniments:

1/2 cup toasted almonds
1/2 cup flaked coconut
1/2 cup watermelon pickles
1/2 cup pineapple chunks, well
  drained

2 large ripe tomatoes, cut in
  wedges
1 can onion rings, heated in oven,
  place in pie tin
4 slices bacon, fried crisp and
  crumbled

Serve these garnishes in small bowls arranged on a tray to pass, or flanking the salad bowl if it's a buffet. Use a colorful India print bedspread as a tablecloth and pick up one of its colors for napkins. Use a brass or copper centerpiece.

Won the Grand Prize of $10,000 in the 1977 Wesson "Salad of the Year" Contest.
GLORIA WARD, MANKATO, MINNESOTA

BASKIN-ROBBINS ICE CREAM SHOW-OFF CONTEST

PEANUTTY BANANA SQUARES

1 1/2 tablespoons sugar
2 tablespoons banana liqueur, optional
1/2 cup heavy or whipping cream, whipped
1/3 cup chunky peanut butter

1/4 cup Baskin-Robbins Hot Fudge Sauce
1 pint Baskin-Robbins Fresh Banana Ice Cream *
1 1/2 cups Baskin-Robbins Chocolate Chip Ice Cream
1 cup crushed peanut brittle

Fold sugar (and liqueur, if used) into whipped cream. Refrigerate. Blend peanut butter and Hot Fudge.

Working quickly, spread Fresh Banana Ice Cream evenly in an 8 inch square pan. With knife, mark off 9 squares, 3 across and 3 down. With back of spoon, make an indentation in center of each square. Spoon 1 tablespoon of peanut butter-fudge mixture into each indentation. Sprinkle 1/2 cup crushed peanut brittle around indentations. Spread Chocolate Chip Ice Cream over all; gently press down to level top. Swirl whipped cream mixture over top; sprinkle with remaining crushed peanut brittle. (Peanut butter-fudge filling will be centered in each square.) Freeze until firm, about 3 hours. To serve, cut into 9 squares. Makes 9 servings.

*(or, use other Baskin-Robbins Banana flavored Ice Cream.)

Was a prize-winner in the 1975 Baskin-Robbins Ice Cream Show-Off Recipe Contest.
DOROTHY BURRIDGE, TUSTIN, CALIFORNIA

HEAVENLY ICE CREAM TRIFLE

8 ladyfingers, split
1/3 cup raspberry or strawberry
   jam
1/3 cup orange juice
3 tablespoons cherry wine
8 almond or coconut macaroons,
   crushed

1 quart Baskin-Robbins Burgundy
   Cherry Ice Cream
3/4 cup heavy or whipping cream
3 tablespoons powdered sugar
1/2 teaspoon vanilla
1/2 cup sliced or slivered almonds,
   toasted

Spread split ladyfingers with jam. Arrange in a single layer, jam side up, in the bottom of an 8 inch square pan. Mix orange juice and cherry wine; pour over ladyfingers. Sprinkle with crushed macaroons and cover with 3/4 of the Ice Cream. Freeze at least 3 hours. (For individual servings, place ladyfingers in bottom of 8 freezer-proof glass dessert or sherbet dishes. Divide ingredients and layers as described above. Freeze.) Just before serving, whip cream, powdered sugar and vanilla. Swirl over Ice Cream. Sprinkle with toasted almonds. Makes 8 to 9 servings.

Was a prize-winner in the 1975 Baskin-Robbins Ice Cream Show-Off Recipe Contest.
LINDA E. NAGY, CLEVELAND, OHIO

HOT JAMOCA® NOG

1/4 cup instant coffee
1/4 cup sugar
1 tablespoon cinnamon
1 tablespoon nutmeg
6 cups boiling water

1 quart Baskin-Robbins Jamoca®
   Ice Cream
Whipped cream or topping
Cinnamon

Mix together the instant coffee, sugar, cinnamon, and nutmeg. Store in tightly covered container.

To serve, place 1 tablespoon of the coffee-sugar mixture into each large coffee mug. Pour boiling water into mugs, filling two-thirds full. Add 1 scoop Ice Cream to each mug; top each with whipped cream and a sprinkle of cinnamon. Serve immediately. Makes 8 to 10 servings.

Was a prize-winner in the 1975 Baskin-Robbins Ice Cream Show-Off Recipe Contest.
MR. AND MRS. RANDY J. POWELL, PRESCOTT, ARIZONA

HAWAIIAN MACADAMIAN SUNDAE

4 tablespoons butter
1 cup salted macadamia nuts,
  coarsely chopped
1 cup whipping or heavy cream

1 cup firmly packed brown sugar
1 quart Baskin-Robbins Nutty
  Coconut* or Fresh Coconut*
  Ice Cream

Melt butter in saucepan, mix in nuts; heat, stirring occasionally, until lightly toasted. Stir in brown sugar and cream. Bring just to a boil and simmer until blended, stirring constantly. Let cool slightly. Spoon warm sauce over individual scoops of Ice Cream. (Sauce can be made ahead, refrigerated and warmed just before serving.) Makes 8 servings.

*(or, use other Baskin-Robbins Coconut flavored Ice Cream.)

Was a prize-winner in the 1975 Baskin-Robbins Ice Cream Show-Off Recipe Contest.
MIRIAM HARTIGAN, WHEATON, ILLINOIS

MARDI GRAS ICE CREAM PIE WITH PRALINE SAUCE

2 tablespoons soft butter
1 (3 1/2 oz.) can flaked coconut
1 quart Baskin-Robbins Butter
  Pecan Ice Cream
1 quart Baskin-Robbins Nutty
  Coconut* Ice Cream
  (or, Fresh Coconut* Ice Cream)
2 cups sugar

1 cup buttermilk
2 tablespoons molasses
1/2 cup butter
3 tablespoons white corn syrup
1 teaspoon baking soda
1 teaspoon vanilla
1/2 cup coarsely chopped pecans,
  or more

Spread the 2 tablespoons of butter in a 9 inch pie pan; press the coconut into the butter. Bake in a 300 degree oven until a light brown, about 20 minutes. (If edges brown too quickly, cover with foil and continue baking until done.) Cool shell. Soften the Butter Pecan Ice Cream and press into bottom of shell. Freeze for 1 hour. Scoop the Coconut Ice Cream over the Butter Pecan Ice Cream. Freeze at least 3 hours. Meanwhile, combine the remaining ingredients, except the vanilla and pecans, in a heavy saucepan. Bring to a gentle boil, simmer for 10 minutes, stirring occasionally; remove from heat. Stir in vanilla and pecans. (Sauce thickens as it cools.) To serve, cut pie into wedges, pass the Praline Sauce. Makes 8 servings.

*(or, use other Baskin-Robbins Coconut flavored Ice Cream, or Chocolate Chip Ice Cream.)

Was a prize-winner in the 1975 Baskin-Robbins Ice Cream Show-Off Recipe Contest.
MRS. LEE R. CONNELL, JR., NEW ORLEANS, LOUISIANA

LEMON CUSTARD ICE CREAM PIE

6 tablespoons butter, softened
1 cup flour
1/4 cup powdered sugar
2 eggs, beaten
3/4 cup sugar
2 tablespoons flour
3 tablespoons lemon juice

1 teaspoon grated lemon peel
1 quart Baskin-Robbins Lemon
  Custard Ice Cream *
1 cup whipping or heavy cream
8 thin slices of lemon

Make a shortbread crust by blending the butter, 1 cup flour and powdered sugar. Press mixture into the bottom and sides of a 9 inch greased pie pan. Bake in a 350 degree oven for 15 minutes (325 degrees for a glass pan). Mix eggs, sugar, 2 tablespoons flour, lemon juice and peel. Pour over hot crust; bake 20 minutes longer. Remove from oven; let cool completely. Fill cooled crust with slightly softened Ice Cream. Freeze. Beat cream, with 2 tablespoons of sugar and 1 teaspoon vanilla, until stiff peaks form. Swirl whipped cream over top of pie. Garnish with twisted lemon slices. Freeze at least 3 hours. Remove from freezer about 10 minutes before serving to mellow. Makes 8 servings.

*(or use other Baskin-Robbins Lemon flavored Ice Cream.)

Won the Grand Prize of a two week trip for two on the Islands, Oahu, Maui and Kauai, in the 1975 Baskin-Robbins Ice Cream Show-Off Recipe Contest.
JEANNE RANDALL, CORNING, NEW YORK

PRESIDENTIAL ICE CREAM PIE

1 (15 oz.) roll refrigerated
  peanut butter cookies
1 cup dates, chopped
2/3 cup water
1/4 cup sugar
3 tablespoons peanut butter

1 1/2 quarts Baskin-Robbins
  Pralines 'n Cream Ice Cream
1 cup whipping cream
1 tablespoon sugar
1 teaspoon vanilla
3 tablespoons chopped peanuts

(Cut cookie roll in half crosswise. Cut half roll into about 30 - 1/8 inch slices; refrigerate remaining half roll.) Lightly butter bottom and sides of 9 inch pie pan. Line bottom of pan with cookie slices, pressing to form a solid crust. Overlap remaining slices on side (not edge) of pan to complete crust. Bake in a 350 degree oven for 10 minutes; cool, chill. In small saucepan cook dates, water and sugar until thick, about 7 minutes, stirring constantly. Remove from heat, stir in peanut butter; cool. Fill pie shell with slightly softened Ice Cream, mounding in center. Spoon date mixture over Ice Cream. Freeze at least 3 hours. To serve: beat whipping cream with sugar and vanilla until it holds its shape. Swirl over pie, sprinkle with peanuts. Makes 8 to 10 servings.

Won the Grand Prize of a two week trip for two in the British Isles in the 1977 Baskin-Robbins Ice Cream Show-Off Recipe Contest.
MARGUERITE BALBACH, LA CRESCENTA, CALIFORNIA

DANDY BRANDY APRICOT-NUT SUNDAE

1 (6 oz.) package dried apricots
  (about 1 cup)
1 cup water
1/2 cup firmly packed brown
  sugar
1/2 cup dark corn syrup

1/4 cup brandy
1/4 cup chopped pecans
1 pint Baskin-Robbins Jamoca®
  Ice Cream
1 pint Baskin-Robbins Butter
  Pecan Ice Cream

Snip apricots fine with scissors. Cook apricots and water in saucepan, covered, until softened. Stir in brown sugar and corn syrup, simmer for 15 to 20 minutes, or until thickened. Cool. Stir in brandy and pecans. Place a scoop each of Jamoca® and Butter Pecan Ice Cream into each of 6 sundae dishes. Spoon on warm sauce. Makes 6 servings.

Was a prize-winner in the 1977 Baskin-Robbins Ice Cream Show-Off Recipe Contest.
MARIE SIEVERWRIGHT, BLOOMFIELD HILLS, MICHIGAN

ROYAL APRICOT BANANA SQUARES

1 1/2 cups dried apricots
3/4 cup sugar
1 cup water
3/4 cup butter
1 cup packed brown sugar
1 1/2 cups all-purpose flour
1 teaspoon baking powder

1 1/2 cups quick oats
2 quarts Baskin-Robbins Banana
   Ice Cream
12 canned apricot halves, (or
   apricot preserves)
Whipped cream, optional

Snip apricots in small pieces; combine with sugar and water in a saucepan. Simmer about 15 minutes, or until thickened, stirring occasionally. Cool slightly. Cream butter and brown sugar. Add flour, baking powder and oats. Mix well. Reserve 2 cups crumb mixture for topping. Press remaining crumb mixture into an 11x7x2 inch pan. Spread apricot filling over first layer. Crumble reserved crumbs over top. Bake in a 375 degree oven for 25 minutes or until lightly browned. Cool; cut into 12 squares. To serve, top each square with a scoop of Ice Cream, an apricot half or a teaspoon of preserves, and whipped cream. Makes 12 servings.

Was a prize-winner in the 1977 Baskin-Robbins Ice Cream Show-Off Recipe Contest.
DOROTHY M. WILLIAMS, SAN CLEMENTE, CALIFORNIA

HOT PEANUT FUDGE SUNDAE

1 (6 oz.) package semi-sweet
   chocolate bits
3/4 cup light cream
1/2 cup chunky peanut butter

1/2 cup marshmallow creme
1 quart Baskin-Robbins Chocolate
   Fudge or Jamoca® Ice Cream
Chopped peanuts

Melt chocolate in a double boiler, or over very low heat. Add cream beat with mixer, or by hand, until well blended. Add peanut butter and marshmallow creme, beat until thoroughly combined. Scoop Ice Cream into 6 sundae dishes. Ladle on warm sauce; garnish with peanuts. Makes 6 servings.

Was a prize-winner in the 1977 Baskin-Robbins Ice Cream Show-Off Recipe Contest.
WANDA PATTON, CLEVELAND, OHIO

TURTLES ON SUNDAE

1 quart Baskin-Robbins Butter
Pecan Ice Cream
1 (9 3/4 oz.) jar Baskin-Robbins
Butterscotch Topping

1 (9 oz.) jar Baskin-Robbins
Hot Fudge, warmed
36 pecan halves

Place a large scoop of Ice Cream in each of 6 shallow dessert dishes. Smooth each with a spoon into an oval mound (to form the turtle's body). On each mound arrange a pecan half to form a head, and 4 halves for feet, and a broken piece for a tail. Top each mound with Butterscotch Topping, then with Hot Fudge. Serve immediately. Makes 6 servings.

Was a prize-winner in the 1975 Baskin-Robbins Ice Cream Show-Off Recipe Contest.
MONICA L. COLE, IOWA CITY, IOWA

KRISPIE KRUNCH TORTE

1/4 cup butter or margarine
35 large marshmallows
5 cups Rice Krispies
2 quarts Baskin-Robbins Pralines
'n Cream or Butter Pecan Ice
Cream

1/2 pint whipping cream
3 tablespoons powdered sugar
1 teaspoon vanilla
8 maraschino cherries, halved
1 (9 oz.) jar Baskin-Robbins
Butterscotch Sauce

Melt butter in a large, heavy saucepan. Add marshmallows, stir constantly until melted. Add cereal, stir until well coated with marshmallow sauce. Divide the mixture between 3 buttered, 9 inch round cake pans. Press mixture lightly and evenly into each pan. When cool, remove cereal layers from pans; wrap, chill, freeze. Prepare 2 plastic-wrap lined 9 inch round cake pans. Slightly soften Ice Cream. Spoon a quart into each prepared 9 inch pan. Press gently to make even layers, freeze at least 2 hours. Assemble torte by placing alternate layers of marshmallow-cereal rounds and Ice Cream on a chilled serving plate, beginning and ending with marshmallow-cereal rounds. Freeze until ready to use. Allow torte to mellow 10 minutes in refrigerator before serving. Meanwhile, beat cream until it begins to thicken, gradually add sugar and vanilla. Beat cream until it holds its shape. Garnish top of torte with dollops of whipped cream and cherry halves. Serve with warm Butterscotch Sauce. Makes 16 servings.

Was a Grand Prize-Winner - Young Adult Competition in the 1977 Baskin-Robbins Ice Cream Show-Off Recipe Contest.
STEPHEN FULLING, PALESTINE, ILLINOIS

TEDDY BEAR PIE

1 peanut butter-graham cracker
   pie crust, recipe follows

1 quart Baskin-Robbins Chocolate
   Almond or Rocky Road Ice
   Cream
2 cups miniature marshmallows

Prepare pie crust according to directions that follow, chill, freeze. When crust is frozen, slightly soften Ice Cream and spoon into frozen crust, press gently into crust, mounding in center. Quickly arrange marshmallows, evenly, on top of pie. Freeze for at least 2 hours. Just before serving preheat broiler for 5 minutes. Place pie 4 inches from heat; and watching carefully, leave just until marshmallows puff and brown lightly. Cut in wedges, serve immediately. Makes 8 servings.

Peanut Butter-Graham Cracker Pie Crust: Prepare 1 1/2 cups of finely crushed graham cracker crumbs (about 10 double crackers). Mix with 3 tablespoons of sugar, blend in 1/4 cup peanut butter, add 1 1/2 tablespoons water, knead gently. Press into bottom and sides of a buttered 9 inch pie pan. Chill, freeze.

Was a prize-winner in the 1977 Baskin-Robbins Ice Cream Show-Off Recipe Contest.
JANET SCHWARTZ, OMAHA, NEBRASKA

NEW ORLEANS FRENCH PARFAIT

3 tablespoons butter
1 1/4 cups chopped pecans
1/2 cup Baskin-Robbins
   Butterscotch Topping
1 tablespoon vanilla

1 quart Baskin-Robbins Butter
   Pecan or French Vanilla Ice
   Cream
Whipped topping, optional

Melt butter in small skillet; stir in 1 cup of the pecans, cook over low heat for 5 minutes. Add Butterscotch Topping and vanilla, cook, stirring, until heated through. Cool. Layer Ice Cream and pecan mixture into each of four parfait glasses. Top, if desired, with whipped topping and remaining chopped pecans. Makes 4 servings.

Was a prize-winner in the 1973 Baskin-Robbins Ice Cream Show-Off Recipe Contest.
ELIN A. HAWKINS, GLENDALE, ARIZONA

HEAVENLY ICE CREAM PUFF FONDUE

36 miniature cream puffs, bakery or homemade (recipe follows)

1 pint Baskin-Robbins Burgundy Cherry Ice Cream*

1 pint Baskin-Robbins Chocolate Mint Ice Cream*

1 pint Baskin-Robbins Jamoca® Ice Cream*

2 cups Chocolate Fondue Sauce (recipe follows)

*(or, any 3 or more of your favorite Baskin-Robbins Flavors.)

Cut top off puffs; pull out any filaments of dough to form hollow shells. Fill and mound six puffs, (using a melon-ball cutter or teaspoon) with one flavor of Ice Cream. Press tops into Ice Cream, place in freezer. Fill six more puffs with first flavor. Freeze. Repeat with second and third flavors. Continue until desired number of puffs are filled, allowing 6 to a serving. When all are frozen, place in a plastic bag, freeze until served. To serve: Gently heat Chocolate Fondue Sauce in a fondue pot or decorative skillet; arrange frozen filled puffs on plates. Each guest spears a puff with fondue fork, dips into the Sauce and swirls to coat. If desired, small bowls of flaked coconut, chopped pecans and sprinkles can be arranged around Sauce in which to dip the chocolate-coated puffs. Makes 6 servings.

Chocolate Fondue Sauce:

1 (14 oz.) can sweetened condensed milk

1 (12 oz.) package semi-sweet chocolate bits

1/2 cup milk

1 (7 oz.) jar marshmallow creme or 1 (6 1/4 oz.) package miniature marshmallows (3 3/4 cups)

1 teaspoon vanilla

Combine all ingredients in saucepan. Heat over medium heat, stirring, just until mixture is smooth and warmed through. Sauce can be made ahead, refrigerated, and reheated. (It will keep indefinitely in the refrigerator.) Add a little milk if sauce becomes too thick. Makes 4 cups.

Miniature Cream Puffs:

(Miniature cream puffs can be ordered, in advance from many bakeries.) Preheat oven to 375 degrees. In small saucepan slowly bring 1/2 cup water, 1/4 cup butter or margarine and 1/4 teaspoon salt to a boil. Turn heat low, stir in 1/2 cup all-purpose flour all at once. Beat, with a wooden spoon, until mixture leaves sides of pan and forms into a small, compact ball. Remove from heat, then add 2 eggs, beating until smooth. Drop dough, by half teaspoonfuls, the size of a nickel, 2 inches apart, onto an ungreased baking sheet. Bake 25 to 30 minutes or until puffed and golden. Cool away from draft. Makes about 36 Miniature Cream Puffs, 1 1/2 inches in diameter.

Won the Grand Prize of a Chevy Vega Hatchback Coupe in the 1973 Baskin-Robbins Ice Cream Show-Off Recipe Contest.
LAURIE H. FREEDMAN, BROOKLYN, NEW YORK

ICE CREAM GRASSHOPPER TARTS

2 cups fine chocolate wafer crumbs
1/2 cup butter, melted
4 tablespoons confectioners' sugar
1/2 cup whipping cream
1 1/2 tablespoons sugar
1 tablespoon white creme de cacao
1 tablespoon white creme de menthe
1 pint Baskin-Robbins Pistachio Almond Fudge Ice Cream*
3 tablespoons sliced almonds
3 tablespoons chopped maraschino cherries

Blend wafer crumbs with butter and confectioners' sugar. Press into bottoms and sides of five 4 inch tart pans. Bake in a 300 degree oven for 15 minutes. Cool. Freeze. Whip cream, fold in sugar, creme de cacao and creme de menthe, blending well. Chill. Put one scoop of Ice Cream in each shell, gently leveling Ice Cream. Carefully remove shells from pans, place on tray. Top and cover each scoop with a generous swirl of the whipped cream mixture; sprinkle with almonds and cherries. Serve immediately or freeze until needed. Makes 5 servings.

*(or, use other Baskin-Robbins pistachio flavored Ice Cream)

Was a prize-winner in the 1973 Baskin-Robbins Ice Cream Show-Off Recipe Contest.
DOROTHY BURRIDGE, TUSTIN, CALIFORNIA

JAMOCA® ALMOND FUDGE TORTE

3 cups unsifted flour
1 1/2 cups sugar
6 tablespoons cocoa
2 1/2 teaspoons baking powder
1 1/2 teaspoons baking soda
1 1/2 cups mayonnaise
1 1/2 cups water

1 1/2 teaspoons vanilla
2 quarts Jamoca® Almond Fudge
  Ice Cream
Mocha Fudge Sauce, recipe follows
Coffee Whipped Cream, recipe
  follows
Toasted, sliced almonds

Prepare 3 (9 inch) round cake pans for baking. Preheat oven to 350 degrees. Sift together dry ingredients into large bowl. Stir in mayonnaise; gradually stir in water and vanilla until well blended. Pour into baking pans; bake for 20 - 25 minutes; cool. Remove from pan and cool completely. Meanwhile, freeze ice cream in 2 (9 inch) layer cake pans.

Cover one cake layer with one frozen ice cream layer, then spread with 1/2 the fudge sauce; repeat. Top with third cake layer. Decorate top of cake with coffee whipped cream, top and bottom edges with whipped cream rosettes, and sprinkle with almonds. Servings: 10 - 12.

Mocha Fudge Sauce: In double boiler, heat 1 (14 oz.) can sweetened condensed milk, 1 ounce square of unsweetened chocolate, 2 tablespoons water, and 1 teaspoon instant coffee powder stirring constantly about 20 minutes or until mixture thickens. Remove from heat; stir in 3 tablespoons almond liquer; cool.

Coffee Whipped Cream: Whip 1 pint heavy cream to soft peaks, then beat in 1/4 cup confectioners sugar until cream is thick. Fold in 1 tablespoon instant coffee powder dissolved in 1 tablespoon water.

Was a prize-winner in the 1977 Baskin-Robbins Ice Cream Show-Off Recipe Contest.
SUE CACCAMO, WAPPINGERS FALLS, NEW YORK

BAKED HAWAII

1 large ripe pineapple
1/4 cup sugar
1 teaspoon rum flavoring
1 pint Baskin-Robbins Fresh
  Coconut Ice Cream*

1 pint Baskin-Robbins Burgundy
  Cherry Ice Cream
Meringue (recipe below)

Lay pineapple on its side. With a sharp heavy knife cut off a 1/2 inch slice lengthwise. Leave green-leafed crown intact. With a thin sharp knife, cut out fruit, leaving a shell. Cut out core from fruit, discard core. Cut 2 cups of fruit into bite-sized pieces, mix with sugar and rum flavoring. Let stand 30 minutes. (Remainder of fruit can be used for salad, compotes, etc.) Wrap leaves of pineapple with foil, freeze for 30 minutes. Drain sweetened fruit. Remove shell from freezer; half fill with slightly softened Fresh Coconut Ice Cream; spoon drained rum-pineapple pieces evenly over Ice Cream. Fill remainder of shell with slightly softened Burgundy Cherry Ice Cream. Freeze for at least two hours.

To make Meringue: Beat 2 eggs with 1/2 teaspoon lemon juice and 1/2 teaspoon rum flavoring until frothy. Gradually beat in 4 tablespoons sugar, a little at a time. Continue beating until stiff. Remove filled pineapple from freezer, lay on small cutting board or baking sheet. Completely cover and seal Ice Cream and edge of shell with meringue. (If desired, freeze up to 24 hours.) Bake in a preheated 500 degree oven, on lowest rack, about 2 minutes or until meringue is delicately browned. Remove foil from leaves. Slice, with heavy sharp knife, or electric knife, through meringue, Ice Cream and shell into one-inch slices. Makes 6 to 8 servings.

*(or, use any other Baskin-Robbins coconut flavored Ice Cream.)

Was a prize-winner in the 1973 Baskin-Robbins Ice Cream Show-Off Recipe Contest.
ANN DICKINSON, INDIANAPOLIS, INDIANA

ENGLISH TOFFEE SUNDAE SQUARES

1 cup sifted flour
1/4 cup crunchy granola
1/4 cup packed brown sugar
1/2 cup butter
1/2 cup chopped walnuts
1 (9 3/4 oz.) jar Baskin-Robbins
  Butterscotch Topping

1 quart Baskin-Robbins English
  Toffee Ice Cream
Whipped cream or topping,
  optional
Maraschino cherries, optional

In bowl, combine flour, granola and brown sugar. Cut butter into mixture until it looks like coarse crumbs; stir in nuts. Pat mixture into a 9x13x2 inch baking pan. Bake for 15 minutes in a preheated 400 degree oven. While still warm, stir to crumble mixture. Cool. Spread half of crumb mixture in a 9x9x2 inch pan. Drizzle half of the Butterscotch topping over crumbs. Slightly soften Ice Cream; carefully spread over crumbs. Drizzle with remaining topping; sprinkle with remaining crumbs. Freeze at least 2 hours. To serve: Remove from freezer about 5 minutes before cutting into squares or bars. If desired, top each serving with whipped cream and a cherry. Makes 9 to 12 servings.

Was a prize-winner in the 1973 Baskin-Robbins Ice Cream Show-Off Recipe Contest.
FRANCIS RAAB, CHELMSFORD, MASSACHUSETTS

PUMPKIN PECAN PARTY PIE

1 1/2 quarts Baskin-Robbins Butter Pecan Ice Cream
1 cup sugar
1 cup canned pumpkin
1 teaspoon cinnamon
1/4 teaspoon each ginger, nutmeg, salt
1 cup whipping cream, whipped
1/4 cup packed light brown sugar
2 tablespoons butter
1 tablespoon water
1/2 cup chopped pecans

(Thirty minutes before preparing Ice Cream crust, put a deep 9 inch pie pan in freezer.) To make crust: Working quickly, line bottom and sides of frozen pan with Ice Cream. Do not put Ice Cream on edge of pan. Build up crust 1/2 inch above edge of pan by overlapping tablespoonfuls of Ice Cream. Freeze at least 2 hours. Combine sugar, pumpkin, spices and salt in a saucepan; cook over low heat for 3 minutes. Cool. Reserve 1/4 cup whipped cream for garnish. Fold remaining whipped cream into pumpkin mixture. Spoon into frozen Ice Cream crust, swirling top. Freeze at least 2 hours. In small saucepan over medium heat, combine brown sugar, butter and water. Bring just to a boil, cook 1 1/2 minutes, remove from heat, stir in pecans. Cool. Spoon mixture around edge between filling and crust. Mound the 1/4 cup of reserved whipped cream in center. Freeze. Let mellow for 10 minutes in refrigerator; cut in wedges. Makes 8 to 10 servings.

Was a prize-winner in the 1973 Baskin-Robbins Ice Cream Show-Off Recipe Contest.
SUSAN T. BURTCH, RICHMOND, VIRGINIA

BANANAS MARTINIQUE

1 quart Baskin-Robbins French
  Vanilla Ice Cream
3 tablespoons butter
1/4 cup sugar
3/4 cup orange juice

1/2 cup apricot jam
1 cup rum
6 ripe bananas
1/4 cup toasted, sliced almonds

Make 6 large scoops of Ice Cream. Place in freezer until serving time. In a large chafing dish, or skillet, melt butter over medium heat, stir in sugar. Cook, stirring, until sugar caramelizes. Mix in orange juice and apricot jam; heat, stirring constantly, until caramelized sugar is dissolved; stir in rum. Peel bananas, slice lengthwise, lay in the hot sauce. Bring just to the simmering point, cook 1 or 2 minutes, turning bananas once. Do not overcook. (If desired, flame with rum.) Place two banana halves on each dessert plate. Top with a scoop of Ice Cream, a generous spoonful of sauce, and a sprinkle of toasted almonds. Makes 6 servings.

Was a prize-winner in the 1973 Baskin-Robbins Ice Cream Show-Off Recipe Contest.
IRENE FRIDAY, OSPREY, FLORIDA

ICE CREAM CONE PIE

1 dozen Baskin-Robbins Ice
  Cream Sugar Cones, crushed
3 tablespoons toasted, slivered
  almonds
2 tablespoons butter

1/2 package (6 oz.) semi-sweet
  chocolate bits
1 quart Baskin-Robbins Chocolate
  Mint Ice Cream

(Reserve 1/4 cup crushed cones for garnish') Combine remaining crushed cones and almonds in a mixing bowl. Gently melt butter and 3 ounces of chocolate bits, pour over crushed cone mixture. Mix thoroughly to coat crushed cones. Press into bottom and sides of a 9 inch pie pan. Chill until firm. Fill pie shell with slightly softened Ice Cream; garnish with the reserved crushed cones. Freeze. Makes 6 to 8 servings.

Was a prize-winner in the 1973 Baskin-Robbins Ice Cream Show-Off Recipe Contest.
J. W. BATTAGLIA, EL PASO, TEXAS

APPLE BUTTER PECAN TARTS

1 pint Baskin-Robbins Butter
 Pecan Ice Cream
1 (16 oz.) can applesauce
1/2 cup light brown sugar
1/2 teaspoon each nutmeg,
 and cinnamon
1/4 teaspoon allspice

5 baked pie-crust tart shells
 (4 inch diameter)
3 egg whites
1/4 teaspoon cream of tartar
1/3 cup packed dark brown
 sugar
1/2 teaspoon vanilla

Make 5 scoops of Ice Cream; put on tray, freeze until firm. Combine applesauce, sugar and spices in a small saucepan. Cook, over low heat, stirring occasionally until mixture is medium thick. Cool, chill. Spoon applesauce mixture into tart shells. Center a scoop of Ice Cream in each shell. Place in freezer. Beat egg whites and cream of tartar until soft peaks form. Gradually add brown sugar and vanilla beating until stiff peaks form and mixture is glossy. Remove tarts from freezer; completely cover Ice Cream with meringue, spreading it to cover edge of shells. (Freeze, at this point, for no longer than 24 hours.) Bake in a preheated 450 degree oven for 2 or 3 minutes, or until meringue is a light golden brown. Makes 5 servings.

Was a prize-winner in the 1973 Baskin-Robbins Ice Cream Show-Off Recipe Contest.
MILLIE SNOW, SOUTHFIELD, MICHIGAN

DOUBLE CHOCOLATE CREPES

1 ounce unsweetened chocolate
2 eggs
1/4 cup sugar
1 teaspoon salt
1/4 teaspoon cinnamon
1 cup water
1/2 cup light cream

3/4 cup all-purpose flour
1 1/2 cups Chocolate Sauce
 (recipe below)
1 quart Baskin-Robbins Chocolate
 Almond or French Vanilla Ice
 Cream
Chopped walnuts, optional

Melt chocolate over hot water. Beat eggs until thick and light yellow. Slowly add sugar and salt to eggs, beating well after each addition. Stir in chocolate and cinnamon. Combine water and cream and add alternately with flour to chocolate mixture. To make crepes, pour about 2 table-spoons of batter onto a hot, greased griddle. Swirl batter out to make a thin crepe; cook and turn once to brown other side. Store crepes between pieces of waxed paper until ready to use. Makes 12 to 14 crepes.

To make Chocolate Sauce: Melt 1 cup semi-sweet chocolate bits and 1/2 ounce unsweetened chocolate over hot water. Stir in 1/2 cup dairy sour cream, 1/4 teaspoon cinnamon and 1/4 cup milk. Blend well. Serve warm.

To serve: Working quickly, spread a scoop of Ice Cream across the bottom edge of each crepe; roll tightly. Place filled crepes in freezer just until all are made. Place two filled crepes on each dessert plate, top with warm Chocolate Sauce, and, if desired, chopped nuts. Serve immediately. Makes 6 to 7 servings.

Was a prize-winner in the 1973 Baskin-Robbins Ice Cream Show-Off Recipe Contest.
LINDA J. CLAFF, BELMONT, MASSACHUSETTS

BAKE-OFF®
CONTEST

HOT ROLL TACO ROUND-UP

1 cup milk
3/4 cup cornmeal
2 envelopes taco seasoning mix
1 package Pillsbury Hot Roll
  Mix
1/4 cup warm water (105 degrees -
  115 degrees F.)

1 egg
1 1/2 pounds ground beef
1/2 cup water
2 cups (8 oz.) shredded Cheddar
  or American cheese
Shredded lettuce, cherry tomatoes,
  ripe olives, taco sauce

Heat milk; stir in cornmeal and 1 tablespoon seasoning mix, reserving remainder. Cool to lukewarm. In large bowl, dissolve yeast from hot roll mix in 1/4 cup water. Add cornmeal mixture, egg and 1 1/2 cups hot roll flour mixture; beat 2 minutes at medium speed. By hand, stir in remaining flour. Cover; let rise in warm place 30 to 45 minutes.

Brown ground beef; drain. Add remaining seasoning mix and 1/2 cup water; simmer 15 minutes. Cool to lukewarm.

Grease 12-cup fluted tube pan or 10-inch tube pan; sprinkle with 1 tablespoon cornmeal. Punch down dough; on well floured surface, knead until smooth and elastic, about 4 minutes.

Roll out dough on well floured surface to 15x12 inch rectangle. Spread with beef filling; sprinkle with 1 1/2 cups cheese. Starting with longer side, roll up tightly; seal edge. Place sealed edge down in prepared pan. Cover; let rise until doubled, 30 to 45 minutes.

Heat oven to 350 degrees F. Bake 40 to 45 minutes or until deep golden brown. Cool 5 minutes; invert onto serving plate. Sprinkle hot ring with remaining cheese. Serve with shredded lettuce, cherry tomatoes, ripe olives and taco sauce. Makes 10 to 12 servings.

High Altitude: No change.

Was a finalist in the 28th BAKE-OFF® contest.
MRS. BETTY NOEL, SPOKANE, WASHINGTON

DENVER BISCUIT SOUFFLE

1 (10 oz.) can Hungry Jack®
 Refrigerated Big Flaky Biscuits
3 eggs, separated
1 (3 oz.) package cream
 cheese, softened
1/4 cup chopped green pepper

1 tablespoon instant minced
 onion or 1/4 cup chopped onion
4 ounces (1 cup) shredded Cheddar
 cheese
1 (2 1/2 oz.) package sliced smoked
 ham, diced, or 1/2 cup diced
 cooked ham
Paprika

Heat oven to 350 degrees. Separate dough into 10 biscuits. Place in un-greased 8 or 9 inch round cake pan; press over bottom of pan to form crust. In small bowl, beat egg whites until stiff, but not dry; set aside. In medium bowl, beat egg yolks and cream cheese until smooth; stir in green pepper, onion, cheese and ham. Fold in beaten egg whites; spoon evenly over crust. Sprinkle with paprika.

Bake at 350 degrees F. for 35 to 45 minutes or until knife inserted near center comes out clean and deep golden brown. Cut into wedges to serve. Makes 6 servings.

Tips: To make ahead, prepare, cover and refrigerate up to 2 hours; bake as directed.

To reheat, cover loosely with foil; heat at 375 degrees F. for 10 to 15 min-utes.

High Altitude: No change.

Was a finalist in the 29th BAKE-OFF® contest.
PEGGY SANDERSON (MRS. WILLIAM), OVERLAND PARK, KANSAS

HAM'N SWISS ON BISCUITS

6 3/4 oz. can (1 cup) cooked
 ham, drained and flaked
2 tablespoons finely chopped
 onion or 1 teaspoon instant
 minced onion
1 to 3 teaspoons poppy seed, if
 desired
2 tablespoons margarine or
 butter, softened

1 to 2 tablespoons horseradish
 mustard or prepared mustard
1 (10 oz.) can Hungry Jack®
 Refrigerated Big Flaky Biscuits
5 (4x4 inch) slices Swiss or
 Mozzarella cheese

Heat oven to 375 degrees F. Combine first five ingredients; blend well. Reserve 1/3 cup. Separate biscuit dough into 10 biscuits; press or roll 5 biscuits to 3 1/2 inch circles and place on ungreased cookie sheet. Spoon about 1/4 cup ham mixture onto center of each flattened biscuit. Fold cheese slices into quarters; place on ham mixture, pressing slightly. Spoon remaining ham mixture over cheese. Press or roll remaining 5 biscuits to 4 inch circles; place over ham mixture. Do not seal. If desired, sprinkle with poppy seed.

Bake at 375 degrees F. for 10 to 15 minutes or until golden brown. Serve warm. Makes 5 sandwiches.

Tip: To reheat, wrap loosely in foil; heat at 375 degrees for 10 to 12 minutes.

High Altitude: No change.

Won $2,000 in the 28th BAKE-OFF® contest.
MRS. MARJORIE B. HOOPER, LAKELAND, FLORIDA

FRENCH ONION CRESCENT SQUARES

1 (8 oz.) can Pillsbury Refrigerated
  Quick Crescent Dinner Rolls
1 (3 oz.) can French Fried onions
1 1/2 cups (6 oz.) shredded Swiss
  or Monterey Jack cheese

4 eggs, slightly beaten
1/2 teaspoon salt
1/8 teaspoon cayenne or black
  pepper
1 (10 1/2 oz.) can condensed cream
  of onion soup

Heat oven to 375 degrees F. Separate crescent dough into two rectangles. Place in ungreased 13x9 inch pan; press over bottom and 1/2 inch up sides to form crust, sealing perforations. Sprinkle 1 cup onions and 1 cup cheese over dough. Combine eggs, salt, pepper and soup; pour evenly over cheese. Sprinkle with remaining cheese.

Bake at 375 degrees F. for 25 to 30 minutes or until crust is golden brown. Crush remaining onions; sprinkle over top. Bake 5 to 10 minutes or until onions are golden brown and filling is set. Makes 6 to 8 servings.

Tip: To make ahead, prepare, cover and refrigerate up to two hours; bake as directed.

To reheat, cover loosely with foil; heat at 375 degrees F. for 15 to 20 minutes.

High Altitude: No change.

Was a finalist in the 28th BAKE-OFF® contest.
JEAN W. SANDERSON, LEAWOOD, KANSAS

CHOCOLATE TOFFEE CRESCENT BARS

1 (8 oz.) can Pillsbury Refrigerated
    Quick Crescent Dinner Rolls
2/3 cup firmly packed brown sugar
2/3 cup butter or margarine

1 to 1 1/2 cups nut halves or
    chopped nuts
1 (6 oz.) package (1 cup) milk
    chocolate or semi-sweet chocolate
    pieces

Preheat oven to 375 degrees. Separate crescent dough into two (2) large rectangles. Place in ungreased 15x10 inch jelly roll pan. Gently press dough to cover bottom of pan; seal perforations. In small saucepan, combine brown sugar and butter; boil 1 minute. Pour evenly over dough. Sprinkle with nuts. Bake 14 to 18 minutes until golden brown. Remove from oven; immediately sprinkle with chocolate pieces. Slightly swirl pieces as they melt, leaving some pieces partially melted or whole. (Do not spread evenly; leave a mottled appearance.) Cool; cut into bars. Makes 3 to 4 dozen bars.

Was a finalist in the 26th BAKE-OFF® contest.
MRS. ALBERT VAN BUREN, WILLMAR, MINNESOTA

HOT ROLL BRAN BREAD

1 cup whole bran cereal
1/4 cup wheat germ
1/2 teaspoon salt
1 tablespoon butter or margarine
1 tablespoon honey

1/2 cup boiling water
1 package Pillsbury Hot Roll Mix
3/4 cup very warm water (105
    degrees - 115 degrees F.)
2 eggs

In large bowl, combine first six (6) ingredients; cool to lukewarm. Dissolve yeast from hot roll mix in very warm water. Add yeast, eggs and flour mixture to cereal mixture; blend well. Cover; let rise in warm place until light and doubled in size, 30 to 45 minutes. Generously grease 9x5 or 8x4 inch loaf pan. Stir down dough. Spoon into greased pan. Cover; let rise in warm place until light and doubled in size, 30 to 40 minutes. Preheat oven to 375 degrees. Bake 40 to 50 minutes or until deep golden brown. If loaf becomes too brown, cover with foil during last 10 minutes of baking. Immediately remove from pan. Makes 1 loaf.

High Altitude: 5200 feet, bake at 375 degrees, 35 to 45 minutes.

Won $5,000 in the 25th BAKE-OFF® contest.
MRS. EDNA BUCKLEY, COLLINS, NEW YORK

FRANKS AND BEANS CASSEROLE

3 tablespoons brown sugar
1 teaspoon dry mustard
3 tablespoons catsup
1 (21 oz.) can (2 1/4 cups)
  pork and beans

1 (15 oz.) can (1 2/3 cups) chili
  without beans
1 pound wieners, sliced
1 (3 oz.) can French fried
  onions

Topping:

1 1/4 cups Hungry Jack® Instant
  Mashed Potato Flakes
1 cup Pillsbury's Best® All
  Purpose or Unbleached Flour*
1 1/2 teaspoons baking powder
1/2 teaspoon salt

3/4 cup milk
2 tablespoons margarine or butter,
  melted
1 (8 oz.) can (1 cup) cream style
  corn
1 egg
1 tablespoon parsley flakes

Heat oven to 400 degrees F. Combine all ingredients except Topping in ungreased 3 quart casserole or 13x9 inch baking dish.

(Lightly spoon flour into measuring cup; level off.) Combine all Topping ingredients except parsley flakes; blend well. Drop by spoonfuls around edge of casserole; sprinkle with parsley flakes.

Bake at 400 degrees F. for 35 to 40 minutes or until Topping is light golden brown and meat mixture is bubbly. Makes 6 to 8 servings.

*If using Pillsbury's Best® Self-Rising Flour, omit baking powder and salt.

High Altitude: Above 3500 feet, add 3 tablespoons water to bean mixture.

Won $2,000 in the 28th BAKE-OFF® contest.
MRS. WILLIAM VAUGHAN, RICHMOND, VIRGINIA

CRESCENT DENVER SANDWICH SQUARES

1 (8 oz.) can Pillsbury Refrigerated
  Quick Crescent Dinner Rolls
1 cup (4 oz.) shredded Cheddar
  cheese
1 (10 3/4 oz.) can condensed
  cream of onion soup

4 eggs
1 (3 oz.) package (2/3 cup) sliced
  smoked ham, diced or 1 cup
  cooked, cubed ham
2 tablespoons chopped green
  pepper
Paprika

Preheat oven to 350 degrees F. Separate crescent dough into two rectangles. Place in ungreased 13x9 inch pan; press over bottom and 1/2 inch up sides to form crust, sealing perforations. Sprinkle cheese over crust. In medium bowl, beat soup and eggs; stir in ham and green pepper. Pour over crust; sprinkle with paprika. Bake 30 to 35 minutes until crust is golden brown and filling is set. Cut into squares; serve immediately. (Refrigerate any leftovers.) Makes 4 to 6 servings.

Tip: To make ahead, prepare, cover and refrigerate up to two hours; bake as directed.

To reheat, wrap loosely in foil; heat at 375 degrees F. for 15 to 20 minutes.

High Altitude: No change.

Was a finalist in the 27th BAKE-OFF® contest.
JEAN W. SANDERSON, LEAWOOD, KANSAS

CHEESY BISCUIT FINGER ROLLS

2 (8 oz.) cans Pillsbury Refrigerated Buttermilk or Country Style Biscuits
4 ounces American or Cheddar cheese, cut into 20 strips (3 x 1/4 x 1/4 inch)

2 tablespoons butter or margarine, melted
1/2 teaspoon Worcestershire sauce
1/4 teaspoon garlic salt
1/2 cup finely crushed potato chips

Preheat oven to 400 degrees. Grease 11x7 inch, or 8 or 9 inch square baking pan. Separate each can biscuit dough into 10 biscuits. Pat out each to about 3 1/2 inch oval. Place strip of cheese on each. Wrap dough around cheese strip, pressing all edges to seal. Place rolls in two rows in prepared pan. Combine butter, Worcestershire sauce and garlic salt; brush on tops of rolls. Sprinkle with potato chips; gently press into rolls. Bake at 400 degrees for 18 to 22 minutes until golden brown. Serve warm.

Tips: Reheat, loosely wrapped in foil, at 400 degrees for 8 to 10 minutes until warm. To make ahead, prepare, cover and refrigerate up to 2 hours before baking. Bake as directed.

High Altitude Adjustment: 5,200 feet. No change.

Was a finalist in the 22nd BAKE-OFF® contest.
MRS. PRUDENCE HILBURN, PIEDMONT, ALABAMA

CHICKEN ALA CRESCENTS

1/3 cup crushed herb seasoned croutons or bread stuffing
1/4 cup chopped walnuts or pecans
1 (3 oz.) package cream cheese with chives, softened*
2 tablespoons butter or margarine, softened
1/2 teaspoon lemon and pepper seasoning, if desired

1 to 2 (5 oz.) cans boned chicken, drained or 1 cup cubed cooked chicken
1/3 cup (2 oz. can) drained mushroom stems and pieces
1 (8 oz.) can Pillsbury Refrigerated Quick Crescent Dinner Rolls
3 tablespoons butter or margarine, melted

Sauce:

1 (5/8 oz.) package chicken gravy mix

1 to 2 tablespoons chopped chives

Heat oven to 375 degrees F. In small bowl, combine crushed croutons and walnuts; set aside. In medium mixing bowl, combine cream cheese, 2 tablespoons butter and seasoning; mix well. Stir in chicken and mushrooms; set aside. Separate crescent dough into 8 triangles; spread each with about 1/4 cup chicken mixture. Roll up; start at shortest side of triangle and roll to opposite point. Tuck sides and point under to seal completely. Dip rolls in melted butter; coat with crumb-nut mixture. Place on ungreased cookie sheet. Bake at 375 degrees F. for 15 to 20 minutes until golden brown. Serve with sauce. Makes 4 to 5 servings.

Sauce: Prepare gravy mix as directed on package. Stir in chives.

Tips: *1 (3 oz.) package cream cheese, softened and 1 1/2 teaspoons chopped chives can be used for cream cheese with chives.

To make ahead, prepare, cover and refrigerate up to 2 hours before baking. Bake at 375 degrees F. for 20 to 25 minutes.

Was a finalist in the 22nd BAKE-OFF® contest.
JEAN W. SANDERSON, LEAWOOD, KANSAS

ITALIAN ZUCCHINI CRESCENT PIE
A Distinctive Herb Blend Lends a Mellow Flavor

4 cups thinly sliced, unpeeled zucchini
1 cup coarsely chopped onion
½ cup margarine or butter
½ cup chopped parsley or 2 tablespoons parsley flakes
½ teaspoon salt
½ teaspoon black pepper
¼ teaspoon garlic powder
¼ teaspoon sweet basil leaves
¼ teaspoon oregano leaves
2 eggs, well beaten
8 oz. (2 cups) shredded Muenster or Mozzarella cheese
8 oz. can Pillsbury Refrigerated Quick Crescent Dinner Rolls
2 teaspoons Dijon or prepared mustard

Heat oven to 375° F. In 10-inch skillet, cook zucchini and onion in margarine until tender, about 10 minutes. Stir in parsley and seasonings. In large bowl, blend eggs and cheese. Stir in vegetable mixture.

Separate dough into 8 triangles. Place in ungreased 11-inch quiche pan, 10-inch pie pan or 12 x 8-inch baking dish; press over bottom and up sides to form crust. Spread crust with mustard. Pour vegetable mixture evenly into crust.

Bake at 375° F. for 18 to 20 minutes or until knife inserted near center comes out clean. (If crust becomes too brown, cover with foil during last 10 minutes of baking.) Let stand 10 minutes before serving. Cut into wedges to serve; serve hot. Makes 6 servings.

Tips: If using 12 x 8-inch baking dish, separate dough into 2 long rectangles; press over bottom and 1 inch up sides to form crust.

To reheat, cover loosely with foil; heat at 375° F. for 12 to 15 minutes.

High Altitude: No change.

Generic Term: Refrigerated crescent dinner rolls

Won the Grand Prize of $40,000 in the 29th Bake-Off® contest.
MRS. MILLICENT A. CAPLAN, TAMARAC, FLORIDA

SOUR CREAM APPLE SQUARES

2 cups Pillsbury's Best All
  Purpose or Unbleached
  Flour*
2 cups firmly packed brown
  sugar
½ cup butter or margarine,
  softened
1 cup chopped nuts

1 to 2 teaspoons cinnamon
1 teaspoon soda
½ teaspoon salt
1 cup dairy sour cream
1 teaspoon vanilla
1 egg
2 cups (2 medium) peeled,
  finely chopped apples

Preheat oven to 350°. (Lightly spoon flour into measuring cup; level off.) In large bowl, combine first 3 ingredients; blend at low speed until crumbly. Stir in nuts. Press 2¾ cups crumb mixture into ungreased 13 x 9 inch pan. To remaining mixture, add cinnamon, soda, salt, sour cream, vanilla and egg; blend well. Stir in apples. Spoon evenly over base. Bake 25 to 35 minutes until toothpick inserted in center comes out clean. Cut into squares; serve with whipped cream, if desired. Makes 12 to 15 squares.

*If using Pillsbury's Best Self-Rising Flour, omit soda and salt.

Won the Grand Prize of $25,000 in the 26th Bake-Off® contest.
MRS. LUELLA MAKI, ELY, MINNESOTA

NATIONAL BEEF COOK-OFF

BEEF "TOURNEDOS" SUPREME—BUDGET-STYLE

2 pounds beef round steak,
  cut in 6 pieces and run
  through cubing machine
6 slices French bread (about
  1/2 loaf, cut on diagonal
  1 inch thick)
6 tablespoons butter or margarine
  softened
2 tablespoons cooking oil
1/2 teaspoon seasoned salt
1/4 teaspoon seasoned pepper
1/2 cup beer

1 (10 1/2 oz.) can beef consomme
3 cups sliced onions
1/4 teaspoon garlic powder
1/2 pound fresh mushrooms,
  sliced
1 tablespoon flour
1 tablespoon butter or margarine
1 cup dairy sour cream, warmed
1 teaspoon prepared horseradish
1/4 teaspoon paprika
Parsley sprigs

Spread both sides of bread slices with 3 tablespoons butter. Brown bread in frying-pan on both sides and place in 13x9x2 inch baking dish. Sprinkle cubed steaks with seasoned salt and seasoned pepper. Heat remaining butter and oil in frying-pan. Fry cubed steaks over medium high heat in butter-oil mixture 2 minutes on each side or to desired doneness. Place a cubed steak on each slice of toasted bread; keep warm in 225 degree F. oven. Add beer to frying-pan and heat slowly, scraping pan to loosen any meat particles. Add consomme, onions and garlic powder. Increase heat and boil 5 minutes; add mushrooms and cook at slow boil 5 minutes. Cream flour with butter until crumbly; combine with vegetable mixture and heat, stirring until slightly thickened. Spoon sauce over cubed steaks. Combine sour cream and horseradish; spoon dollop on each serving. Sprinkle paprika over sour cream. Garnish with parsley and serve with remaining sour cream sauce. Makes 6 servings.

Was the Kansas State Finalist in the 1980 National Beef Cook-Off; sponsored by American National Cowbelles.
JEAN W. SANDERSON, KANSAS

RANCH-STYLE BEEF CREPES

2 pounds ground beef round steak
*Crepes
3/4 cup chopped onion
1/4 cup butter or margarine
1 pound fresh mushrooms, sliced
1/4 teaspoon salt
1/8 teaspoon pepper

1 (8 oz.) package cream cheese,
softened
1/2 cup dairy sour cream
2 tablespoons instant beef
bouillon
2/3 cup dairy sour cream
1 teaspoon prepared horseradish

Prepare crepe batter. Brown beef and onions in medium frying-pan. Pour off drippings. Melt butter or margarine in separate frying-pan; add mushrooms, sprinkle with salt and pepper and fry until done, stirring occasionally. Using mixer, blend cream cheese, 1/2 cup dairy sour cream and bouillon granules; stir into beef mixture. Reserve 1/2 cup mushrooms and stir remaining mushrooms into beef mixture. Prepare crepes from batter. Spoon beef mixture down center of each of 8 crepes, folding edges up to overlap in center. Place crepes, folded side up, in 13x9x2 inch baking pan. Combine 2/3 cup sour cream and horseradish and spoon over crepes. Place reserved mushrooms over sour cream. Cover and bake in moderate oven (375 degrees F.) for 20 to 25 minutes, until heated through. Makes 8 servings.

Note: Combine and warm additional 2/3 cup sour cream and 1 teaspoon prepared horseradish to serve as topping, if desired.

*Crepes

3 eggs
1 1/2 cups milk
1 1/4 cups flour

2 tablespoons butter or margarine
melted
1/8 teaspoon salt

Place eggs, milk, flour, butter or margarine and salt in blender or mixer bowl and beat well. Let batter stand while preparing filling. To cook crepes, hold heated pan in one hand and add 3 tablespoons of crepe batter, quickly rotating pan so that batter covers bottom in a thin even layer. Return pan to heat and cook 45 to 60 seconds. Brown 1 side only and remove crepe. Repeat until all batter is used. Use 8 crepes as directed and freeze remaining crepes for future use.

Note: If inverted crepe pan is used, cook crepes according to manufacturer's directions.

Was the Kansas State Finalist in the 1977 National Beef Cook-Off, sponsored by the American National Cowbelles.
JEAN W. SANDERSON, KANSAS

ZUBEEFI

2 1/2 pounds ground beef round	2 teaspoons salt
2 medium zucchini	1/2 teaspoon pepper
Salt and pepper	1 tablespoon oregano
1/2 cup olive oil	1 (6 oz.) can tomato paste
3 medium onions, sliced	1 cup small curd cottage cheese
1 green pepper, chopped	2 cups grated Mozzarella cheese
1/3 clove garlic, chopped	1/4 cup grated Parmesan cheese
3 tablespoons butter	4 stuffed green olives, sliced
	Butter

Slice one zucchini thinly, season with salt and pepper and fry in olive oil. Place zucchini in a buttered 3 quart casserole. Fry onions, green pepper and garlic in butter in large frying-pan; remove and add to zucchini. Brown beef in frying-pan, pour off drippings. Stir salt, pepper, oregano and tomato paste into meat and cook slowly 3 minutes. Add meat mixture to zucchini; cool 5 minutes. Add cottage cheese and mix well. Sprinkle Mozzarella cheese on top; cover and bake in a moderate oven (350 degrees F.) for 30 minutes. Remove cover, sprinkle with Parmesan cheese; place sliced olives on top and bake, uncovered, for 15 minutes, 6 to 8 servings.

To serve: Slice remaining zucchini, saute in butter and place on top of casserole.

Won Second Prize of $500 in the 1976 National Beef Cook-Off, sponsored by the American National Cowbelles.
DR. SAM G. TORNIK, OHIO

BEEF AND OYSTER SAUCE

3 pound beef rump roast	1 cup water
7 tablespoons peanut oil	3 tablespoons cornstarch
7 tablespoons soy sauce	Cooking oil
3 tablespoons cornstarch	2 medium onions, sliced
7 tablespoons soy sauce	1 green pepper, sliced
5 tablespoons oyster sauce	2 cloves garlic, crushed
2 tablespoons sesame seed oil	3 tablespoons chopped pimiento, if desired
	Cooked rice

Slice roast in thin strips across grain. Gradually add peanut oil and 7 tablespoons soy sauce to 3 tablespoons cornstarch in deep bowl, stirring to blend. Stir in beef strips, cover bowl and place in refrigerator to marinate 3 hours (overnight if desired). To prepare sauce, combine 7 tablespoons soy sauce, oyster sauce, sesame seed oil and water; add to 3 tablespoons cornstarch, stirring to blend; reserve. Remove meat from marinade and brown, a small amount at a time, in hot oil in large frying-pan; remove to absorbent paper. Add onions, green pepper and garlic to fat and fry until vegetables are tender but crunchy. Drain off any excess oil from pan. Return meat to pan and add pimiento strips, if desired. Pour sauce over meat and vegetables and cook slowly 15 minutes, stirring occasionally. Serve over hot rice. Makes 7 to 9 servings.

Was the Florida State Finalist in the 1977 National Beef Cook-Off, sponsored by American National Cowbelles.
MRS. JOHN BABINEC, FLORIDA

BEEF KIEV OLE

2 pounds beef round steak, cut in 6 pieces and run through a cubing machine
1 1/2 cups Cheddar cheese cracker crumbs
1 tablespoon taco seasoning mix
3/4 cup melted butter or margarine

1/2 pound Cheddar cheese, cut into 6 narrow strips
1/4 cup taco sauce
2 to 3 cups shredded lettuce
3/4 to 1 cup diced tomato
6 whole ripe olives
Taco sauce, if desired

Combine cracker crumbs and taco seasoning mix. Dip each piece of steak in butter or margarine then in cheese crumbs. Place a strip of cheese on center of each steak and cover each strip with 2 teaspoons taco sauce. Roll each steak, tucking in ends to completely enclose cheese; fasten with wooden picks. Place rolls, seam side down, in a 12x8x2 inch shallow baking dish. Drizzle remaining butter or margarine over top of each roll. Bake in a moderate oven (375 degrees F.) for 35 to 40 minutes or until tender. Remove picks and serve each roll on bed of shredded lettuce and diced tomato. Top each with a ripe olive and serve with taco sauce, if desired. Makes 6 servings.

Was the Kansas State Finalist in the 1975 National Beef Cook-Off, sponsored by the American National Cowbelles.
MRS. JEAN W. SANDERSON, KANSAS

SOUTHERN SPICY BEEF CUBES-FRIED BROWN RICE

2 pounds beef for stew, cut in
  3/4 inch pieces
1 tablespoon brown sugar
1/4 teaspoon ground ginger
2 cups cider
2 teaspoons whole cloves
1/2 cup flour
1 teaspoon salt
1/4 teaspoon pepper
1/4 teaspoon paprika
1/4 cup cooking fat
1/4 cup finely chopped onion
2 tablespoons margarine

2 1/2 cups cooked brown rice
  (cooked in beef broth)
2 tablespoons minced parsley
1/2 cup pecans, finely chopped
1/4 teaspoon basil
1/4 teaspoon ginger
1/4 teaspoon pepper
1/4 teaspoon salt
2 tablespoons cornstarch
1 teaspoon bottled brown sauce
  for gravy
1/2 cup Burgundy wine
Broiled tomato wedges
Parsley

Place beef cubes in casserole large enough to hold beef. Combine brown sugar, ginger, cider and whole cloves and pour over cubes. Cover and marinate beef in refrigerator overnight. Remove beef cubes from marinade. Discard cloves, reserve marinade. Combine flour, 1 teaspoon salt, 1/4 teaspoon pepper and 1/4 teaspoon paprika and dredge beef cubes. Brown beef in fat in heavy skillet. Place beef in casserole, add 1/4 cup marinade. Cover and bake in a slow oven (325 degrees F.) for 2 to 2 1/2 hours or until tender. Remove beef cubes to center of a hot serving platter and keep hot. Saute onion in margarine until transparent. Add onion to rice. Toss cooked rice with parsley, pecans, basil, ginger, 1/4 teaspoon pepper and 1/4 teaspoon salt until hot; keep hot while making gravy. To make gravy, blend cornstarch and 1/4 cup reserved marinade; cook, stirring constantly, until thickened, stir in brown sauce and wine. Surround beef cubes with hot rice. Drizzle spicy gravy over beef cubes. Garnish with broiled tomato wedges and parsley. Makes 6 servings.

Was the Mississippi Finalist in the 1975 National Beef Cook-Off, sponsored by the American National Cowbelles.
MRS. MARGIE F. TYLER, MISSISSIPPI

HEARTY PARTY BEEF TARTS

2 pounds boneless lean beef chuck,
  cut 1 inch thick
2 tablespoons flour
1/2 teaspoon salt
1/4 cup water
2 cups shelled pecans
1 cup seedless raisins
1/4 cup apricot brandy
1 cup freeze-dried diced
  pineapple
1 cup dark brown sugar

1 teaspoon ground cinnamon
1 cup apple juice
1 cup apple butter
16 three inch frozen tart shells
3 tablespoons sugar
1 teaspoon ground cinnamon
1 pint whipping cream
16 maraschino cherries with
  stems, if desired
48 pecan halves, if desired

Cut beef in 2x4 inch pieces. Mix flour and salt in brown paper bag; add beef and shake to coat. Place beef on rack in 12x8 inch baking pan. Add water to pan. Cook, uncovered, in hot oven (400 degrees F.) for 15 minutes, turning as needed to brown. Lower oven temperature to 325 degrees F., cover pan tightly and continue baking 45 minutes. Let beef cool. Lower oven temperature to 200 degrees F. and place pecans in shallow pan in oven for 20 minutes. Cover raisins with boiling water. Pour apricot brandy over pineapple. Put beef through food chopper, using medium coarse blade. Grind pecans to a meal. Combine brown sugar and 1 teaspoon cinnamon in large bowl. Add apple juice, apple butter, ground beef, pecans, raisins (drained) and pineapple with brandy, stirring to combine. Place frozen tart shells on baking sheet and pierce with fork. Bake in moderate oven (350 degrees F.) for 10 minutes, until golden brown. Combine 3 tablespoons sugar with 1 teaspoon cinnamon. Whip cream, gradually adding sugar mixture, until it stands in peaks. Fill each tart with 1/2 cup beef mixture and top with whipped cream. Garnish each tart with 1 cherry and 3 pecan halves, if desired.

Yield: 16 servings.

Won Second Prize of $750 in the 1978 National Beef Cook-Off, sponsored by the American National Cowbelles.
MISS RENA HEAD, OKLAHOMA

FIESTA CREPES EN CASSEROLE

2 pounds ground beef chuck
1/2 cup finely chopped onion
1/2 cup finely chopped celery
1 (17 oz.) can cream style corn
2 (8 oz.) cans tomato sauce

1 (1 1/2 oz.) envelope taco
  seasoning mix
Cornmeal Crepes*
4 ounces Cheddar cheese, shredded
1/3 cup sliced ripe olives

Brown beef, onion and celery in large frying pan. Pour off drippings Stir in corn. Combine tomato sauce and taco seasoning mix, stirring to blend. Add 1 1/3 cups tomato sauce mixture to meat and corn, mixing well. Spoon two tablespoons meat mixture onto each cornmeal crepe and roll to enclose filling. Spread remaining meat mixture in 13x9 inch baking dish. Place crepes, seam side down, on top of meat. Spoon remaining tomato sauce over crepes. Bake in a moderate oven (375 degrees F.) for 20 minutes. Sprinkle with cheese and top with olives. Makes 10 servings.

*Cornmeal Crepes

1 cup flour
1/2 cup yellow cornmeal
1 1/2 cups milk

3 eggs
Dash of salt
Oil

Combine flour, cornmeal, milk, eggs and salt; beat with rotary beater until smooth. For each crepe, pour 1/4 cup batter into hot lightly oiled crepe pan or small frying-pan; tilt pan to coat bottom evenly. Cook over medium heat until top is dull and underside is delicately browned. Turn; cook 10 to 15 seconds. Makes 10 crepes.

Won First Prize of $1,500 in the 1979 National Beef Cook-Off, sponsored by the American National Cowbelles.
MRS. MARKELL (LAVELLE) BRELAND, MISSISSIPPI

GERMAN BEEF SAUSAGE

5 pound beef chuck roast or
  pot roast
3 cups water
1 1/2 teaspoons salt

1/2 teaspoon pepper
2 teaspoons allspice
2 teaspoons salt

Place beef in pressure pan, add water and season with 1 1/2 teaspoons salt and pepper. Cook at 10 pounds pressure 30 to 45 minutes or until very tender.* Let beef cool in liquid. Skim off fat. Pour off liquid and reserve. Trim separable fat from beef and remove any bones. Put beef through food grinder; add reserved cooking liquid, allspice and 2 teaspoons salt. Add water, if necessary, until well moistened. Pack into freezer containers seal tightly and freeze. When ready to use, defrost and slice. Cook in frying-pan with a small amount of water until hot. Makes 20 servings.

*Beef may also be braised slowly in water in Dutch oven 3 to 4 hours or until very tender.

Serving suggestions:

With pancakes: Place 1/4 cup hot beef sausage on a pancake. Fold in half and top with butter and syrup. Garnish with strawberries.

Skillet dinner: Add 3 cups shredded raw potato and 1/4 cup minced onion to each 1 cup beef sausage. Heat in frying-pan until potatoes are done, adding water if necessary.

Sandwich: Place 1/4 cup hot beef sausage on bun. Top with onion and catsup.

Won Second Prize of $750 in the 1979 National Beef Cook-Off, sponsored by the American National Cowbelles.
MRS. NORMAN (DARLENE) DICKMAN, IOWA

FIESTA BEEF TORTA OLE

Beef Filling:

2 pounds ground beef round
1 package taco seasoning mix
2 tablespoons water

1/2 can (16 oz.) refried beans
2 ounces Monterey Jack cheese, grated

Dough:

2 1/2 cups unbleached flour
1/2 cup yellow cornmeal
1/4 cup brown sugar, packed
1 teaspoon garlic salt
1 teaspoon taco seasoning mix

1 package (1 tablespoon) active dry yeast
2/3 cup milk
1/3 cup water
1/4 cup (1/2 stick) margarine
2 eggs, beaten

Coating, Topping, Garnish:

2 tablespoons cornmeal
2 tablespoons reserved beaten egg
1 to 2 tablespoons pine nuts, if desired

2 (8 oz.) jars taco sauce, hot or mild, as preferred
Shredded lettuce, cherry tomatoes, ripe olives

Prepare dough as follows: In a large bowl, or electric mixer, mix 3/4 cup flour, cornmeal, brown sugar, garlic salt, 1 teaspoon taco seasoning and dry yeast. In saucepan, combine milk, water and margarine; heat over low heat until mixture is very warm (120 degrees F. to 130 degrees F.), margarine does not need to be melted. Add mixture gradually to dry ingredients and beat 2 minutes at medium speed, scraping bowl occasionally. Reserve 2 tablespoons beaten egg. Add remaining eggs and 1/3 cup flour; beat at high speed 2 minutes, scraping bowl occasionally. Stir in enough additional flour to make a stiff dough. Turn out on a lightly floured board; knead until smooth and elastic, 5 to 8 minutes.

While dough rises, prepare Beef Filling as follows: Brown ground beef slowly in frying pan until red color disappears; drain, if necessary, add remaining taco seasoning and water and simmer, stirring occasionally for 15 minutes. Stir in beans and cheese; blend well. Cool slightly.

Generously grease a 9-inch tube pan (with removable bottom) or spring-form pan. Fold a 30x6 inch piece of heavy foil in half lengthwise; fasten foil around top of pan to form a collar extending about 2 1/2 inches above rim of pan (as for a souffle); grease inside of foil also. *Dust bottom and sides of pan with cornmeal; discard excess. Punch down dough; divide into three pieces. Pat or roll each piece of dough to a round about 9 inches. Fit first round into prepared pan and press at edge to form a slight rim. Spoon in half of the Beef Filling spreading evenly almost to edge of pan. Top with a second round of dough; then remaining Beef Filling. Place third round of dough on top; cover and let rise in a warm place until light, 25 to 35 minutes. Preheat oven to moderate temperature (350 degrees F.). Score top of torta with a sharp knife into 8 pie-shaped wedges. Brush with reserved egg and sprinkle with pine nuts, if desired. Bake 60 minutes, or until a deep golden brown. When almost ready to serve, heat taco sauce in a small saucepan.

To serve: Place torta on a large platter or plate. Surround with a ring of shredded lettuce, garnished with cherry tomatoes and ripe olives. Place the heated taco sauce in a gravy boat to spoon over torta after it is cut and served. Cut in wedges as indicated. Makes 8 servings.

Won First Prize of $1,000 in the 1976 National Beef Cook-Off, sponsored by the American National Cowbelles.
MRS. ALEXANDER DE SANTIS, PENNSYLVANIA

ZESTY BEEF SALAD

2 1/2 pound beef chuck arm pot roast, cut 1 inch thick	4 medium tomatoes, thinly sliced
1 1/2 tablespoons sugar	1 large red onion, thinly sliced
1 teaspoon salt	1 bunch green onions, chopped
1/8 teaspoon pepper	Italian salad dressing
6 ounces raw peanuts	
1 large head lettuce, torn in bite-sized pieces	

Partially freeze beef for easy slicing. Remove any fat and bone. Cut beef into thin strips (1/8 inch or thinner) about 3 inches in length. Sprinkle sugar, salt and pepper over beef strips and let stand at least 1 hour in refrigerator. Fry peanuts in large frying-pan at medium heat until lightly brown. (They will form their own oil.) Remove peanuts from frying-pan and remove skins. Place lettuce on 6 individual serving plates; top with tomato and red onion slices. Fry green onions until transparent in oil remaining in pan; add beef strips and continue frying about 3 minutes on high heat, stirring constantly. Spoon hot beef mixture on top of tomato and onion slices. Sprinkle peanuts on beef mixture and top with salad dressing. Serve immediately. Makes 6 servings.

Won Third Prize of $500 in the 1978 National Beef Cook-Off, sponsored by the American National Cowbelles.
MRS. JESSE (KIM) LANDHUIS, IOWA

CRESCENT CARAMEL SWIRL

½ cup butter or margarine
½ cup chopped nuts
1 cup brown sugar

2 tablespoons water
2 cans (8 oz. each) Pillsbury
Refrigerated Quick Crescent
Dinner Rolls

Preheat oven to 375° F. (350° F. for colored fluted tube pan). In small saucepan, melt butter. (Do not use pan with removable bottom.) Coat bottom and sides of 12-cup fluted tube pan with 2 tablespoons of the melted butter; sprinkle pan with 3 tablespoons of the nuts. Add remaining nuts, brown sugar and water to butter; heat to boiling, stirring occasionally. Remove crescents from cans in rolled sections; do not unroll. Cut each section into four slices. Arrange eight slices in prepared pan, separating each pinwheel slightly to allow sauce to penetrate. Spoon half the caramel sauce over dough. Repeat with remaining dough, topping slices in pan; pour remaining caramel sauce over dough. Bake 25 to 30 minutes (30 to 35 minutes for colored fluted tube pan) until deep golden brown. Cool three minutes, turn onto serving platter or wax paper. Makes a 10-inch ring coffee cake.

High Altitude: No change.

Won the Grand Prize of $25,000 in the 27th Bake-Off® contest.
MRS. BERT GROVE, SAN ANTONIO, TEXAS

SWEET MEAT BARS

2 pounds ground beef chuck
1 (16 oz.) can whole berry
  cranberry sauce
1½ cups brown sugar
1 cup seedless raisins
¾ cup coarsely chopped
  walnuts
½ cup orange marmalade
½ cup orange juice

2 tablespoons orange peel
  (commercial or fresh)
1 teaspoon salt
4 cups flour
2 tablespoons baking powder
2 teaspoons salt
1⅓ cups milk
⅔ cup oil
Glaze*

Place ground chuck, cranberry sauce, brown sugar, raisins, walnuts, orange marmalade, orange juice, orange peel and 1 teaspoon salt in Dutch oven. Cook over medium heat until mixture boils; continue cooking 20 minutes, stirring constantly. Cool. Combine flour, baking powder and 2 teaspoons of salt; add milk and oil, all at once, stirring until flour is moistened. Place dough on waxed paper and knead about 10 times; divide in half. Roll half the dough between two sheets of waxed paper to fit 17 x 10-inch jelly roll pan. Peel off top sheet of waxed paper and invert dough onto jelly roll pan. Carefully peel off other piece of waxed paper; press dough to fit over bottom and up sides of pan. Spoon cooled filling mixture over dough. Roll second half of dough into 17 x 10-inch rectangle. Remove top sheet of waxed paper and invert dough on top of filling. Remove second sheet of paper. Press top and bottom crust edges together to seal. Make 4 slashes in top crust. Bake in hot oven (425° F.) 25 to 30 minutes or until crust is golden brown. Cool slightly and drizzle with Glaze. Cut into 24 bars.

*Glaze:
1½ cups confectioners sugar

3 tablespoons milk
1 tablespoon rum

Combine confectioners sugar, milk and rum; mix until smooth.

Won First Prize of $1,500 in the 1981 National Beef Cook-Off, Sponsored by the American National Cowbelles.
CONSTANCE BECKWITH, CONNECTICUT

BAKED BEEF BRISKET

4 pound boneless beef brisket
2 teaspoons salt
½ teaspoon black pepper
1 clove garlic, minced

3 medium onions, thickly sliced
1 cup hot water
2 tablespoons cornstarch
1 cup cold water
Garnishes, as desired

Place brisket, fat side up, in 10 x 13-inch roasting pan. Season brisket with salt and pepper, sprinkle with garlic and place onions on top. Bake in moderate oven (350° F.) 1 hour, or until the onions turn brown. Add hot water, cover with aluminum foil and seal tight. Reduce oven heat to 300° F. and continue cooking 2 hours. Remove brisket and onions to warm platter. To make gravy, combine 2 tablespoons cornstarch, dissolved in 1 cup cold water, with cooking liquid and cook, stirring until boiling and thickened. Makes 12 servings.

Note: Garnish with parsley, cherry tomatoes, pickled peppers, turnips or stuffed olives.

Won First Prize of $1,500 in the 1980 National Beef Cook-Off, Sponsored by the American National Cowbelles.
MRS. H.D. (LUCILLE) ROACH, MISSOURI

SEAGRAM'S V.O. ONE DISH SUPPER CONTEST

COMIN' THROUGH THE RYE

1 broiler-fryer chicken (3 1/2 lb.)
1 teaspoon salt
Pepper
2 tablespoons butter
2 tablespoons olive oil
1/4 cup Seagram's V.O.
3 links sweet Italian sausage
1 cup coarsely chopped onion
2 chicken gizzards, coarsely chopped

2 chicken hearts, coarsely chopped
2 chicken livers, coarsely chopped
1 cup sliced mushrooms
1 cup converted rice
3 tablespoons grated Parmesan cheese
3 chicken bouillon cubes
2 1/2 cups boiling water

Cut chicken into 8 pieces, sprinkle with salt and pepper. Heat butter and oil in flameproof casserole, brown chicken, skin down first, about 16 minutes. Remove chicken to platter, sprinkle with Seagram's V.O. Let stand, turning occasionally to season evenly.

Pour off all but 4 tablespoons fat from casserole. Discard sausage casings, cut sausage into small chunks. Cook in casserole with onion until onion is wilted, stirring briskly. Add gizzards and hearts, cook, stirring, 5 minutes. Add chicken livers and mushrooms, cook 3 minutes, stirring. Stir in rice. Push rice to sides of casserole, return chicken to center, pour juices from platter over chicken. Cover with rice, sprinkle with cheese. Dissolve bouillon cubes in boiling water, add. Bring to a boil, cover, simmer 25 minutes. Makes 4 servings.

Won the Grand Prize of a two week trip to visit Gourmet Capitals of Europe and $1,500 in the 1975 Seagram's V.O. One Dish Supper Recipe Contest.
MRS. LUCIA T. MAGGIANI, NEW YORK, NEW YORK

PIQUANT ITALIAN LAMB WITH SQUASH

1 1/2 pounds Italian sausage
2 pounds lamb, in 1 inch cubes
2 tablespoons flour
1/2 onion, sliced
2 cups beef broth
1 cup dry red wine
1 (1 lb. 12 oz.) can peeled
   tomatoes
1 teaspoon paprika
1/2 teaspoon thyme
2 bay leaves
1/2 teaspoon rosemary

1 teaspoon salt
1 teaspoon ground pepper
1 garlic clove, minced
1 tablespoon basil
1 teaspoon ginger,
1 butternut squash, peeled,
   in 1 inch cubes
2 zucchini squash, in 1/2 inch
   slices
1/2 pound sliced mushrooms
Grated Romano cheese

Sour Cream Mint Sauce:

1 cup sour cream

1/2 cup mint jelly, melted

Discard casing from sausage, cut into 1 1/2 inch lengths, saute in Dutch oven until brown. Remove sausage, drain off all but 2 tablespoons fat. Brown lamb cubes, sprinkle with flour, cook, stirring, until flour browns. Add onion, cook until onion is translucent. Return sausage to Dutch oven with remaining ingredients except squash, mushrooms and cheese. Simmer over low heat, covered, 1 1/2 hours. Add the butternut squash, simmer 30 minutes. Add the zucchini squash, simmer 30 minutes. Add the mushrooms, simmer 5 to 10 minutes longer. Sprinkle with grated cheese, serve with sour cream mixed with melted mint jelly. Makes 6 servings.

Was a prize-winner in the 1975 Seagram's V.O. One Dish Supper Recipe Contest.
DR. BENJAMIN E. GREER, DENVER, COLORADO

CREOLE CHILI AND CORNBREAD PIE

1/2 pound pork suet, diced
1 teaspoon finely chopped garlic
2 pounds boneless beef round,
   cut in 1/2 inch cubes, lightly
   floured
1 teaspoon crumbled bay leaves
1 onion, coarsely chopped
1 green pepper, coarsely chopped
2 whole dried red chilies, seeded
2 cups boiling beef bouillon
1 cup dry red wine
2 teaspoons oregano
1 tablespoon cumin, toasted and
   crushed

3 tablespoons paprika
1 teaspoon salt
1 teaspoon sugar
1/2 teaspoon ground coriander
1/4 teaspoon ground cloves
1/4 teaspoon cayenne pepper
1/4 teaspoon freshly ground black
   pepper
1 cup cooked kidney beans, rinsed
Cornbread Topping (below)
2 cups coarsely grated mild
   Cheddar cheese
4 ripe tomatoes, sliced thickly

Render suet in a heavy, flameproof 3 to 4 quart bake and serve casserole. Discard suet and all but 1/3 cup fat. Add garlic to casserole, cook 3 minutes. Add beef, brown lightly. Add bay leaf, onion, green pepper and chilies. Cook for a moment, stirring gently to avoid crumbling the chilies. Add stock and half the wine. Cover casserole, cook in a moderate oven (350 degrees F.) about 1 hour, or until the beef is tender. Discard the chilies. Add remaining seasonings and beans. Add remaining wine, if sauce seems too thick. Blend well, adjust seasoning. Keep warm over low heat while you prepare the Cornbread Topping.

Sprinkle with grated cheese and tomato slices, cover all but center with cornbread batter. Bake in a hot oven (400 degrees F.) about 20 minutes, or until the cornbread is well browned and tests done. Makes 6 to 8 servings.

Cornbread Topping:

1 egg
1 cup milk
1/4 cup melted butter, cooled
6 tablespoons melted vegetable
   shortening, cooled
1 cup white corn meal

3/4 cup flour
1/4 cup sugar
1 teaspoon salt
2 tablespoons double-acting
   baking powder

Beat egg, add milk, melted butter and shortening, blend well. Toss dry ingredients to mix, add to egg mixture, stir to blend.

Was a prize-winner in the 1975 Seagram's V.O. One Dish Supper Recipe Contest.
FREIDA JOHNSON, WASHINGTON, D.C.

SEAGRAM'S V.O. INTERNATIONAL DESSERT CONTEST

ANGEL STRAWBERRY SUPREME

1 cup cake flour
1 3/4 cups sugar
12 egg whites
1 1/2 teaspoons cream of tartar
1/4 teaspoon salt
1 1/2 teaspoons vanilla
1/2 teaspoon almond flavoring
2 tablespoons unflavored gelatin
1/4 cup cold water

1 cup boiling water
1/2 cup orange juice
Juice of 1 lemon
1/2 cup Seagram's V.O.
1 cup sugar
1/8 teaspoon salt
2 pints whipped cream
2 cups strawberries

Sift flour and 3/4 cup sugar together three times. Beat egg whites, cream of tartar, salt, vanilla, and almond flavoring until stiff but not dry. Gradually add remaining sugar. Beat until meringue holds stiff peaks. Fold in flour and sugar mixture gently but quickly. Pour batter into ungreased 10-inch tube pan. Bake in moderate oven (375 degrees F.) 30 minutes, until top springs back when lightly touched. Invert on funnel. Cool completely and unmold. Soften gelatin in water. Add boiling water, stir until dissolved. Add fruit juices, Seagram's V.O., sugar, and salt. Mix well and chill until partially jelled. Fold in 1 cup whipped cream. Line a large mixing bowl with plastic wrap. Break cake into 2-inch pieces. Put a layer of cake pieces into bowl, then some pudding mixture, then more cake pieces, alternating until all is used. Refrigerate until set. Unmold onto serving tray. Ice with remaining whipped cream. Garnish with sliced strawberries. Makes 10-12 servings.

Was a prize-winner in the 1976 Seagram's V.O. International Dessert Recipe Contest.
AUDREY M. O'NEIL, SIERRA VISTA, ARIZONA

BUCHE AUX MARRONS
(Yule Log With Chestnuts)

3 eggs, separated
1 1/4 cups superfine sugar
1/4 cup cold water
2 teaspoons vanilla
2 1/4 cups sifted flour
2 teaspoons baking powder

1 egg white
1/2 cup Sugar Syrup (below)
4 cups Chestnut Butter Cream
  (below)
12 marrons glaces or candied
  violets for garnish

Beat together egg yolks and sugar until light and creamy. Beat in water and vanilla. Sift together flour and baking powder and fold into egg mixture. Beat 4 egg whites stiff and fold into batter, gently but quickly. Butter an 11x16 inch baking sheet or jelly roll pan. Line with wax paper and butter again. Spread batter evenly over bottom of pan and bake in a moderate oven (325 degrees F.) 20 minutes or until sides of cake shrink away from pan. Invert warm cake onto a moist kitchen towel, peel off wax paper. Moisten cake with Sugar Syrup, roll up, and cool. Cut off ragged cake ends on the bias and ice with Chestnut Butter Cream to simulate the bark of a tree. Surround with marrons glaces or candied violets. Makes 10 - 12 servings.

Sugar Syrup:

1/2 cup sugar
1/4 cup water

2 tablespoons rum

Stir sugar and water in a saucepan over medium heat until sugar dissolves. Raise heat and boil syrup, stirring, 10 minutes or until a candy thermometer registers 220 degrees F. Cool syrup and stir in rum.

Chestnut Butter Cream:

1 pound sweet butter
1 cup superfine sugar
2 tablespoons rum

1 (15 1/2 oz.) can unsweetened
  chestnut puree

Cream butter until light and fluffy. Add chestnut puree, sugar, and rum and beat until mixture is smooth.

Won the Grand Prize of $5,000 in the 1976 Seagram's V.O. International Dessert Recipe Contest.
MRS. CLAIRE WAGNER, LITTLE NECK, NEW YORK

MOCHA SWIRL CHEESECAKE

3/4 cup unbleached flour
2 tablespoons sugar
1/4 teaspoon salt
1/4 cup butter
1 tablespoon sugar
1 tablespoon instant coffee
3 tablespoons boiling water

6 ounces semi-sweet chocolate
2 pounds cream cheese
1 1/2 cups sugar
1/4 cup unbleached flour
2 teaspoons vanilla
6 eggs
1 cup sour cream

Mix together flour, sugar, and salt. Cut in butter with a pastry cutter. Mix sugar with instant coffee, and stir in boiling water to dissolve. In top of double boiler, heat, stirring, coffee mixture and chocolate until chocolate is melted. Add 2 tablespoons mocha mixture to the flour dough and blend with pastry cutter until color is uniform. Press batter evenly over bottom of a greased 9 inch springform pan. Bake in moderately hot oven (400 degrees F.) 10 minutes. Mix cream cheese, sugar, flour, and vanilla until smooth. Beat in eggs, one at a time, until all are incorporated. Beat in sour cream. Combine 2 cups cream cheese mixture with remaining mocha mixture. Pour 1/2 plain cheese mixture over baked crust. Top with mocha mixture. Cover with remaining plain cheese mixture. Gently cut through batter and swirl the two mixtures. Set in a 400 degree F. oven, reduce temperature to 300 degrees F., and cook 1 hour. Turn oven off. Do not open door, let cheesecake cool 1 hour in oven. Remove cake and cool 2-3 hours. Remove springform mold and chill 8 hours. Makes 16 servings.

Was a prize-winner in the 1976 Seagram's V.O. International Dessert Recipe Contest.
DEAN M. GOTTEHRER, MIDDLETOWN, CONNECTICUT

SEAGRAM'S V.O. INTERNATIONAL HOR'S D'OEUVRE CONTEST

GOLDEN GREEKS

1/4 cup light soy sauce
1/4 cup dry Sherry
1 tablespoon honey
2 tablespoons Chinese oyster
  sauce
3 cloves star anise
3 thin slices fresh ginger root

2 scallions, cut in 1 inch
  sections
4 boned chicken breasts (2
  chickens)
1/4 pound melted butter
1/2 pound phyllo dough or strudel
  leaves

Combine soy, Sherry, honey, oyster sauce, spices and scallions in a saucepan, simmer 5 minutes. Add chicken breasts, bring liquid to a boil. Cover the pan, reduce the heat, and simmer chicken gently for 20 minutes. Remove cover, cook 15 minutes longer, turning chicken often to color evenly. Cut into thin crosswise slices.

Melt butter. Cut phyllo into strips 2 inches wide by 10 to 12 inches long. For each serving, brush two strips lightly with melted butter. Lay 2 or 3 slices of chicken in a corner of one strip. Fold the corner over the chicken to form a triangle. Continue to fold in uniform triangles until the chicken is completely wrapped with the first strip of phyllo. Lay the wrapped chicken in the corner of the second strip of phyllo and repeat the process.

Arrange the triangles well apart on an ungreased baking sheet. Bake in a hot oven (425 degrees F.) 12 to 15 minutes, until golden brown. Serve warm. Makes 30 to 36 triangles. Figure on 2 to 3 per person.

The prepared triangles may be stored in the regrigerator for 24 hours before baking, or for about 1 month in the freezer.

Won the Grand Prize of a 14 day gourmet tour of Europe and $1,500 in the 1974 Seagram's V.O. International Hors d'Oeuvre Recipe Contest.
MARY BYRNE CONRY, KANSAS CITY, MISSOURI

CAMEMBERT WALKER

7 ounces Camembert cheese
1/2 cup butter
2 egg yolks
1/4 teaspoon salt
Pinch of cayenne pepper
2 tablespoons Cognac
2 tablespoons boiling water

2 tablespoons heavy cream
2 tablespoons chopped black
  walnuts
1 teaspoon minced red onion
75 medium canned or cooked
  mushroom caps (or blanched
  fresh mushroom caps)

Trim rind from Camembert, cut cheese into small cubes. Melt butter, cool slightly. With a whisk, beat egg yolks light in the top pan of a double boiler. Beat in salt, cayenne and Cognac. Add melted butter in a thin stream, whisking constantly. Beat in boiling water.

Put the pan over boiling water and cook, whisking constantly, until the sauce is thick and smooth. Continue to whisk for a few minutes after removing the pan from the heat. Stir in cheese, cream, walnuts and onion. Cool to room temperature. Use to stuff mushroom caps. Makes about 2 cups filling, enough for 75 medium mushrooms.

Was a prize-winner in the 1974 Seagram's V.O. International Hors d'-Oeuvre Recipe Contest.
E. BRUCE WALKER, NEW ORLEANS, LOUISIANA

SOUTHERN EGGPLANT CANAPES

1 large eggplant	1 teaspoon oregano
1/3 cup olive oil	1 1/2 teaspoons salt
1 cup finely chopped celery	1/2 teaspoon sweet basil
1 cup finely chopped onion	1/4 teaspoon crushed red pepper
4 cloves garlic, minced	1/4 teaspoon ground black pepper
1 cup finely chopped green pepper	1 tablespoon finely chopped
1/2 cup tomato paste	parsley
1 cup finely chopped cooked ham	1/4 cup dry bread crumbs

Peel eggplant, cut into 1 inch cubes. Soak in salted water 20 minutes, drain, rinse, drain again. Heat oil in 10 inch skillet. Add vegetables, saute 10 minutes over medium heat, stirring constantly from the bottom. Add tomato paste, ham and all seasonings except parsley. Cover skillet and simmer slowly for 20 minutes.

Add parsley and bread crumbs, mash well to make paste. Cool. Spread on thin toast rounds. Makes 4 cups, enough for 120 canapes.

Was a prize-winner in the 1974 Seagram's V.O. International Hors-d'Oeuvre Recipe Contest.
MRS. ALLIE A. LANGLOIS, PORT ALLEN, LOUISIANA

LA CHOY
SWING AMERICAN
CONTEST

TROPICAL CRAB SALAD

1 cup uncooked long-grain rice
1 1/2 cups water
1 cup unsweetened pineapple juice
1 teaspoon salt
1 teaspoon butter
1 (16 oz.) can LaChoy Fancy
  Mixed Chinese Vegetables,
  rinsed, drained

1 (12 oz.) package frozen crabmeat,
  thawed, drained
1 (8 oz.) can LaChoy Water
  Chestnuts, drained, sliced
1 1/3 cups mayonnaise
1/4 cup sliced green onions
1 1/2 teaspoons curry powder
2/3 cup half and half
Crisp salad greens

In large saucepan, combine rice with water, pineapple juice, salt and butter; heat to boiling. Cover; simmer for 15 minutes. Let stand, covered, for 10 minutes; chill. Toss chilled rice with Chinese vegetables, crabmeat and water chestnuts. In medium bowl, blend mayonnaise with onion and curry powder. Gradually stir in half and half; mix well. Fold dressing into rice mixture. Chill; serve on crisp salad greens. Makes 8 servings.

Won First Prize of $1,000 plus Samsonite luggage in the 1978 LaChoy Swing American Recipe Contest.
BARBARA L. WEINBERG, BLOOMINGTON, INDIANA

CHINESE MEAT PIES

1 1/2 cups LaChoy Chow Mein Noodles
1 teaspoon garlic salt
2 tablespoons butter, melted
1 pound lean ground beef
1/2 cup sliced green onions
1/4 cup mayonnaise

1 tablespoon prepared mustard
1 teaspoon salt
1 teaspoon prepared horseradish
Apricot Pea Pod Filling
Pimiento strips
Fresh parsley

Apricot Pea Pod Filling:

1 (6 oz.) package LaChoy Frozen Chinese Pea Pods
1/2 cup sliced green onions
1/2 teaspoon salt
1 tablespoon butter
1 (17 oz.) can apricot halves, well drained

1/2 cup seedless raisins
1/4 cup packed brown sugar
1/4 cup catsup
1 teaspoon prepared mustard
1/2 cup reserved noodle mixture
2 ounces Cheddar cheese, cut into 8 thin strips

In medium bowl, toss chow mein noodles with garlic salt and butter. Reserve 1/2 cup noodle mixture for Apricot Pea Pod Filling. Mix remaining noodles with beef, onions, mayonnaise, mustard, salt and horseradish. Shape into 4 balls; place in 9 inch square baking pan. Make deep well in center of each meatball. Bake at 450 degrees for 10 minutes. Remove from oven; spoon off excess fat. Reduce oven temperature to 350 degrees.

For filling, combine pea pods, onions and salt. Cook in butter 1 minute, stirring constantly. Drain off excess liquid. Stir in apricots and raisins. Mix brown sugar with catsup and mustard; stir into pea pod mixture. Spoon filling into meat shells; top with noodles. Return to oven for 5 minutes. Place cheese strips over noodles; continue heating for 3 to 5 minutes or until pies are heated through and cheese is melted. Garnish with pimiento strips and sprigs of parsley. Makes 4 servings.

Won First Prize of $1,000 plus Samsonite luggage in the 1978 LaChoy Swing American Recipe Contest.
GWEN GRIFFEN, LAKE FOREST, ILLINOIS

CURRIED ORIENTAL TIDBITS

2 (3 oz.) can LaChoy Chow
  Mein Noodles
1 (8 oz.) can LaChoy Water
  Chestnuts, drained, sliced
1 cup whole, unblanched almonds

1/4 cup grated Parmesan cheese
1/4 cup butter, melted
1 tablespoon LaChoy Soy Sauce
1 teaspoon curry powder
1/4 teaspoon seasoned salt

In large bowl, combine noodles with water chestnuts and almonds. Mix remaining ingredients; add to noodle mixture, tossing lightly until well blended. Spread mixture evenly on ungreased 15x10x1 inch baking pan. Bake at 325 degrees for 15 minutes, stirring occasionally. Serve warm. Yield: About 6 cups.

Won the Grand Prize of a Lincoln Continental car plus Samsonite luggage in the 1978 LaChoy Swing American Recipe Contest.
MRS. MAURINE VAUGHAN, RICHMOND, VIRGINIA

CANTONESE CAKE

3 eggs
1 (16 oz.) can LaChoy Bean
  Sprouts, rinsed, drained
2 cups sugar
1 cup oil
2 cups sifted all-purpose flour
2 teaspoons soda
1/2 teaspoon baking powder

1 teaspoon salt
1 teaspoon cinnamon
1 teaspoon ginger
1 (8 oz.) can LaChoy Water
  Chestnuts, drained, chopped
1 tablespoon vanilla
2 tablespoons butter, melted
2 tablespoons dark corn syrup

In large mixer bowl, beat eggs. Add bean sprouts, sugar and oil; mix well. Gradually add sifted dry ingredients, mixing well after each addition. Stir in water chestnuts and vanilla. Pour batter into greased and floured 13x9x2 inch baking pan. Bake at 350 degrees for 45 to 50 minutes. Brush warm cake with a glaze made by boiling butter and corn syrup for 3 minutes. Makes 12 to 15 servings.

Won First Prize of $1,000 plus Samsonite luggage in the 1978 LaChoy Swing American Recipe Contest.
SARAH REED, WICHITA, KANSAS

CHOW MEIN CHEWS

1 (8 oz.) bar milk chocolate
1/4 cup creamy peanut butter

1 (3 oz.) can LaChoy Chow
  Mein Noodles
1 cup salted peanuts

In medium saucepan, melt chocolate and peanut butter over low heat. Add noodles and peanuts; stir until well mixed. Drop mixture by rounded teaspoonfuls onto waxed paper-lined cookie sheet. Refrigerate until firm. Keep refrigerated. Makes 24 pieces.

Won First Prize of $1,000 plus Samsonite luggage in the 1978 LaChoy Swing American Recipe Contest.
BESS E. MILLER, TAMPA, FLORIDA

SNOW PEA CREAM SOUP

2 cups chicken broth
1 (6 oz.) package frozen LaChoy
  Chinese Pea Pods
1 cup half and half

1/2 cup thinly sliced celery
1/4 cup thinly sliced carrots
1/4 teaspoon salt
1/2 cup LaChoy Bean Sprouts,
  rinsed, drained

In medium saucepan, heat chicken broth to boiling. Add pea pods; simmer for 1 minute. In blender container put pea pods, 1/2 cup of hot broth, and half and half. Blend until pea pods are finely chopped. Add celery, carrots and salt to remaining broth in saucepan. Simmer, covered, for 10 minutes. Stir in pea pod mixture and bean sprouts; heat to serving temperature (do not boil). Makes 4 servings.

Won First Prize of $1,000 plus Samsonite luggage in the 1978 LaChoy Swing American Recipe Contest.
JOYCE W. PRESTON, NORMAL, ILLINOIS

NATIONAL FARM-RAISED CATFISH COOKING CONTEST

FARM-RAISED CATFISH VERMOUTH
BAKED WITH OYSTER-MUSHROOM STUFFING

2 pan-dressed farm-raised catfish
(1 lb. each after dressing), fresh
or frozen
1 teaspoon salt
1/8 teaspoon pepper

1/4 cup margarine, melted
1 cup corn flakes crumbs
Oyster-Mushroom Stuffing
1/4 cup Parmesan cheese
Lemon slices

Thaw fish if frozen. Season with salt and pepper. Dip fish in margarine and roll in crumbs. Place fish on a well-greased shallow baking tray and chill for 1 to 2 hours to set coating. Stuff fish with the Oyster-Mushroom Stuffing. Place a small piece of aluminum foil over stuffing to keep it from drying out. Sprinkle fish with Parmesan cheese. Bake in a moderate oven, 350 degrees F., for 1 hour. Garnish with lemon slices. Makes 4 servings.

Oyster-Mushroom Stuffing:

1/2 pint stewing oysters, drained
8 ounces fresh mushrooms,
chopped
1 clove garlic, minced
2 tablespoons cooking oil
2 tablespoons margarine

1 cup dry bread crumbs
1 tablespoon dry Vermouth
1 tablespoon chopped parsley
1/2 teaspoon seafood seasoning
1/4 teaspoon ground oregano
1/4 teaspoon lemon pepper

Cook mushrooms and garlic in oil and margarine until tender. Add oysters and simmer for 1 to 2 minutes. In a large bowl combine cooked oyster-vegetable mixture with remaining ingredients; mix well. Makes approximately 2 cups stuffing.

Won Runner-up Prize of $125 in the 1980 National Catfish Cooking Contest.
MS. CHRIS EVERITT, COVINGTON, GEORGIA

FARM-RAISED CATFISH IN A RICE RING

1 1/2 pounds farm-raised catfish fillets, fresh or frozen
2 tablespoons mayonnaise
3 cloves garlic, sliced
1/2 cup finely chopped onion
1/2 cup finely chopped celery
1/4 cup finely chopped bell pepper, red or green

1 (10 3/4 oz.) can cream of mushroom soup
3 tablespoons dry white wine
1/2 teaspoon crushed Italian seasoning
2 teaspoons paprika
1/4 teaspoon salt
1/4 teaspoon pepper
Rice Ring

Thaw fish if frozen. Cut fish into 3 inch cubes. Heat mayonnaise in a 10 inch skillet. Add garlic and cook until garlic and mayonnaise are lightly browned. Discard garlic. Add onion, celery, and bell pepper to mayonnaise. Cook until vegetables are soft, but still crisp. Add soup, wine, and Italian seasoning. Bring to a boil; reduce heat and let simmer 10 to 15 minutes. Add cubed fish. Lower heat, cover and simmer for 12 to 15 minutes or until fish is done. Stir in paprika, salt and pepper. Spoon into Rice Ring. Garnish as desired. Makes 6 servings.

Rice Ring:

1/2 cup mayonnaise
1/2 cup chopped onion
1/4 cup finely chopped bell pepper
2 tablespoons finely chopped green onion tops
2 tablespoons finely chopped parsley

4 cups white cooked rice
1 large ripe tomato, seeded and chopped fine
1 cup cubed mild Cheddar cheese or pasteurized process cheese spread

Heat 1 tablespoon of the mayonnaise in a saucepan. Add onion and bell pepper and cook until vegetables are soft, but still crisp. Add onion tops and parsley and cook for 1 to 2 minutes longer. In a large mixing bowl combine remaining mayonnaise, rice, tomato, cheese and vegetables. Toss to mix thoroughly. Pack rice mixture into a hot water rinsed 5-cup ring mold. Turn out on a hot platter. Fill with farm-raised catfish mixture.

Won Third Prize of $250 in the 1980 National Catfish Cooking Contest.
MRS. AMSON CORNER, ABBEVILLE, LOUISIANA

FARM-RAISED CATFISH SESAME
WITH LEMON PARSLEY SAUCE

2 pounds farm-raised catfish fillets,
  fresh or frozen
1 teaspoon salt
1/4 teaspoon white pepper
1/4 cup all-purpose flour
1 egg, beaten

2 tablespoons milk
1/2 cup finely crushed saltine
  cracker crumbs
3 tablespoons sesame seed
Cooking oil for frying
Lemon Parsley Sauce

Thaw fish if frozen. Season fish with salt and pepper. Coat lightly with flour. Combine egg and milk. Combine cracker crumbs and sesame seed. Dip fish into egg mixture and roll in crumb mixture. Place fish in a single layer in hot oil in a large fry pan. Fry at a moderate heat, 360 degrees F., approximately 4 to 5 minutes. Turn carefully and cook 4 to 5 minutes longer or until brown and fish flakes easily when tested with a fork. Drain on absorbent paper. Serve Lemon Parsley Sauce over fish. Makes 6 servings.

Lemon Parsley Sauce:

1/3 cup finely chopped onion
1/4 cup finely chopped parsley

1/4 cup lemon juice

Combine all ingredients in saucepan. Heat to boiling. Serve over fish.

Won Second Prize of $500 in the 1980 National Catfish Cooking Contest.
MR. BILL ORANSKY, RICHBORO, PENNSYLVANIA

BURK'S FARM-RAISED CATFISH FRY

6 pan-dressed farm-raised
  catfish (3/4 to 1 lb. each)
1 cup buttermilk
2 tablespoons salt
1 tablespoon black pepper

1 1/2 cups self-rising corn meal
1/2 cup self-rising flour
1 1/2 to 2 quarts peanut oil
  for deep frying

Thaw fish if frozen. Cut thick part of each side of fish diagonally, approximately 1/8 inch deep. Place fish in a deep container. Add buttermilk, salt and pepper. Stir to coat fish evenly. Let fish marinate in refrigerator

4 to 6 hours (or overnight). Drain marinade from fish. Roll fish in meal-flour mixture, coating evenly. Place a few fish at a time in cooker. Fry in deep oil, 370 degrees F., until fish is golden brown, stirring constantly during cooking process. For doneness test cooked fish with tongs by squeezing upper neck. If fish "cry water," cook a few minutes longer. Drain cooked fish on absorbent paper. Transfer fish to pan with a wire rack. Place in a warm oven to keep fish crisp. Makes 6 servings.

Note: Serve fish with coleslaw, hush puppies or tater tots, lemon slices, catsup or cocktail sauce.

An outdoor gas deep-fat cooker may be used for cooking large quantities of fish. Oil may be used several times by straining and storing in refrigerator.

Won First Prize of $1,000 in the 1980 National Catfish Cooking Contest.
MRS. W. F. BURK, SR., ROME, GEORGIA

STUFFED FARM-RAISED CATFISH ALMONDINE

8 small pan-dressed farm-raised
  catfish, fresh or frozen
10 medium cooked shrimp,
  chopped
1 (6 oz.) can crabmeat, drained
  well
1/2 cup white wine
1 tablespoon chopped onion

1/2 teaspoon salt
1/4 teaspoon pepper
3/4 cup margarine or butter
1 (4 oz.) package sliced almonds
1 tablespoon lemon juice
Cherry tomatoes, parsley sprigs,
  lemon slices (garnish)

Thaw catfish if frozen. Clean thoroughly and dry with absorbent paper. Combine shrimp, crabmeat, wine, onion, and pepper and let marinate for 30 minutes. Drain and reserve liquid. If the cavity of the fish is small, enlarge cavity by cutting a small pocket along the backbone. Stuff each fish with the shrimp and crabmeat mixture. Sprinkle fish with salt. Fry fish in margarine until brown on both sides and fish is done and flakes easily when tested with a fork. Remove fish from pan to a warm platter. Add almonds, lemon juice and reserved marinate to fry pan; cook until almonds are brown. Spread over catfish. Garnish with tomatoes, parsley and lemon slices. Makes 4 servings.

Won First Prize of $500 in the 1978 National Catfish Cooking Contest.
MRS. ROSE McCORKLE, MEMPHIS, TENNESSEE

SAVORY FARM-RAISED CATFISH QUICHE

2 cups cooked, flaked farm-raised
  catfish
1 frozen 9 inch unbaked pastry
  shell, defrosted
1 1/2 cups shredded Swiss cheese
3 eggs
1 (10 3/4 oz.) can condensed cream
  of onion soup

1 (2 oz.) can mushroom stems and
  pieces, drained and chopped
1/4 teaspoon liquid smoke
1 tablespoon instant minced onion
3/4 teaspoon lemon-pepper
  seasoning
1/8 teaspoon paprika
Parsley sprigs (garnish)

Sprinkle 1 cup cheese over bottom of pastry shell. Using mixer, beat eggs and soup together. Stir in flaked catfish, mushrooms, liquid smoke, minced onion and lemon-pepper seasoning. Pour into pastry shell. Sprinkle with remaining 1/2 cup cheese and paprika. Place on a baking sheet. Bake in a moderate oven, 375 degrees F., on lowest oven shelf for 35 to 40 minutes or until golden brown and filling is set, cool 10 minutes before serving. Garnish with parsley sprigs. Makes 6 servings.

Flaked Farm-Raised Catfish:

1 1/2 pounds farm-raised
  catfish fillets, fresh or frozen

1 quart boiling water
1 tablespoon salt

Thaw fish if frozen. Place fillets in boiling, salted water. Cover and return to the boiling point. Reduce heat and simmer for 10 minutes or until fish flakes easily when tested with a fork. Drain and flake. Yields 2 cups flaked fish.

Won Second Prize of $250 in the 1978 National Catfish Cooking Contest. JEAN W. SANDERSON, LEAWOOD, KANSAS

DELUXE FARM-RAISED CATFISH AND FRESH SPINACH SALAD

2 pounds skinned farm-raised
  catfish fillets, fresh or frozen
1 quart boiling water
1 tablespoon salt
1 lemon, cut in half
1 tablespoon lemon juice
1 pound fresh spinach, washed
  and drained
1 cup sliced red onion
1/2 cup sliced pitted ripe olives

1 cup sliced fresh mushrooms
3 slices bacon, diced
1 teaspoon all-purpose flour
1/4 cup red wine vinegar
1/4 cup water
1 teaspoon sugar
1 teaspoon salt
1/4 teaspoon pepper
1/4 teaspoon dijon mustard
2 hard-cooked eggs, cut into fourths

Thaw fish if frozen. Combine boiling water, 1 tablespoon salt and lemon. Place fillets in water. Cover and return to the boiling point. Reduce heat and simmer for 8 to 10 minutes or until fish flakes easily when tested with a fork. Drain. Flake fish into bite sized pieces and sprinkle with lemon juice. Remove large stems from spinach and break into bite sized pieces. In a large salad bowl combine fish, spinach, onion, olives and mushrooms. Fry bacon until crisp. Blend flour into bacon and drippings. Add vinegar, water, sugar, 1 teaspoon salt, pepper and mustard, stirring constantly until slightly thick. Pour sauce over fish mixture and toss. Garnish with egg. Makes 6 servings.

Won Runner-up Prize of $75 in the 1979 National Farm-Raised Catfish Cooking Contest.
MRS. ELIZABETH McMILLAN, JACKSON, MISSISSIPPI

DOWN HOME FARM-RAISED CATFISH ROLLS

2 pounds farm-raised catfish
  fillets, fresh or frozen
1 1/2 teaspoons salt
1/4 teaspoon pepper
1/4 teaspoon basil
1 cup prepared stuffing mix
1 egg, beaten

1 tablespoon lemon juice
1 (10 3/4 oz.) can condensed
  Manhatten clam chowder
1/2 cup dairy sour cream
1/2 teaspoon paprika
Parsley sprigs and lemon wedges
  (garnish)

Thaw fish if frozen. Clean fillets and dry with absorbent paper. Cut fillets in half lengthwise. Combine salt, pepper and basil; sprinkle over fillets. Roll up jelly-roll fashion, allowing about 1 1/2 inch diameter center for stuffing. Combine prepared stuffing mix, egg and lemon juice. Mix and spoon into center of rolls. Combine soup and sour cream; pour over rolls. Sprinkle with paprika. Bake in a moderate oven, 350 degrees F., for 20 - 25 minutes or until fish flakes easily when tested with a fork. Garnish serving platter with lemon wedges and parsley. Makes 6 servings.

Won Third Prize of $100 in the 1978 National Catfish Cooking Contest.
MRS. LORRAINE WALMANN, KANSAS CITY, MISSOURI

FARM-RAISED CATFISH -- KIEV STYLE

2 pounds skinned farm-raised
catfish fillets, fresh or frozen
1 teaspoon onion salt
1 (3 oz.) package cream cheese
with chives
2 tablespoons margarine or butter

1 teaspoon lemon pepper seasoning
1 (4 oz.) can mushroom stems
and pieces, drained and chopped
1/2 cup melted margarine or butter
1 1/3 cups seasoned crouton
crumbs
Parsley sprigs

Thaw fish if frozen. Divide fillets into 12 strips about 6x2 inches. Press slightly to flatten fish; sprinkle with onion salt. In a medium bowl combine cream cheese, 2 tablespoons margarine and lemon pepper seasoning. Stir in mushrooms. Divide cheese mixture into 12 portions. Place a portion of cheese mixture at one end of each strip of fish. Roll fish around cheese and secure with a toothpick. Dip rolls into melted margarine and roll in crumbs. Place rolls in a well-greased baking dish, 13x9x2 inches. Drizzle with remaining margarine. Bake, uncovered, in a moderate oven, 350 degrees F., for 25 to 30 minutes or until fish flakes easily when tested with a fork and crumbs are golden brown. Remove toothpicks. Garnish with parsley. Makes 6 servings.

Won First Prize of $500 in the 1979 National Farm-Raised Catfish Cooking Contest.
JEAN W. SANDERSON, LEAWOOD, KANSAS

DILLY CREAMED FARM-RAISED CATFISH DELIGHT

6 skinned pan-dressed farm-raised
catfish, fresh or frozen
1/2 cup mayonnaise or salad
dressing
1 1/2 tablespoons all-purpose flour
2 (8 oz.) cartons sour cream with
chives

3 tablespoons chopped pimiento
stuffed green olives
1 teaspoon celery salt
1/2 teaspoon paprika
1/2 teaspoon pepper
1/4 teaspoon ground thyme
1 teaspoon dill weed
Lemon wedges and parsley sprigs

Thaw fish if frozen. Clean, wash and dry fish. Place fish in a well-greased baking dish, approximately 13x9x2 inches. Combine mayonnaise and flour. Add sour cream, olives, celery salt, paprika, pepper and thyme. Spread sauce over fish. Sprinkle with dill weed. Bake in a moderate oven, 350 degrees F., for 25 to 35 minutes or until fish flakes easily when tested with a fork. Garnish with lemon wedges and parsley sprigs. Makes 6 servings.

Note: Plain yogurt may be substituted in place of the sour cream.

Won Second Prize of $250 in the 1979 National Farm-Raised Catfish Cooking Contest.
MRS. JOAN K. VAN BUREN, WILLMAR, MINNESOTA

FARMERS FARM-RAISED CATFISH DINNER

6 farm-raised catfish steaks or fillets 3/4 inch thick and 3 - 3 1/2 inches in diameter (approximately 2 - 2 1/2 lb.)
1/2 teaspoon salt
1 (6 oz.) packet Italian salad dressing seasoning mix
6 tablespoons bottled Creamy Italian dressing
1/4 cup butter or margarine

6 medium tomato slices, 1/4 inch thick
6 medium bell pepper rings, 1/4 inch thick
1/2 cup cooked rice (this can be leftover rice)
2 tablespoons each, chopped fresh parsley and green onion tops
6 medium onion slices, 1/4 inch thick
6 slices mild cheese

Season catfish with salt and salad dressing mix and 3 tablespoons of the bottled Creamy Italian dressing. Heat butter or margarine in a 9x13x2 inch baking pan or dish. Place fish in melted butter; top each piece of fish with a tomato slice, then top with a bell pepper ring. Combine rice, 2 tablespoons of the Creamy dressing, onion tops and parsley. Mix well and spoon rice mixture into bell pepper rings. Top each with an onion slice. Brush onion slices with remaining dressing. Cover with foil and bake in 350 degree oven for 35 to 45 minutes, until fish flakes easily with a fork. Turn off oven and top each stack with a slice of cheese. Let stand in oven only until cheese begins to melt down sides, about 1/2 minute. Transfer catfish to warm serving platter and garnish as desired. Makes 6 servings.

Won Runner-up Prize in the 1977 National Catfish Cooking Contest.
MRS. AMSON CORNER, ABBEVILLE, LOUISIANA

CRISP FRIED FARM-RAISED CATFISH

6 small farm-raised catfish or
  slices of larger fish
1 teaspoon salt
1/4 teaspoon pepper

1 (2 oz.) bottle Tabasco sauce
2 cups self-rising corn meal in
  brown paper bag
1 quart corn oil (or more)

Sprinkle fish over lightly with salt and pepper; let marinate in Tabasco hot sauce for 1 or 2 hours in refrigerator. When ready to cook, drop pieces into bag of meal to cover completely.

Use a deep pot or skillet filled half full with cooking oil. Heat fat until just under "smoking hot." Place each piece into fat separately. Cook on high until the fish floats to top and reaches a golden brown. Drain well and place on paper towel. Serve hot.

The Tabasco sauce will not make the fish hot; it enhances color and flavor. Makes 6 servings.

Won Second Prize in the 1977 National Catfish Cooking Contest.
MS. LOIS O. WARD, LOUISVILLE, MISSISSIPPI

FARM-RAISED CATFISH ELDORADO DE COLORADO

6 skinned, pan-dressed
  farm-raised catfish
Lard or bacon drippings
1 medium white onion, diced
1 large clove garlic, minced
1 green bell pepper, diced
1 (28 oz.) can tomatoes
3 dashes Tabasco sauce (or
  to taste)
1 tablespoon Worcestershire sauce
1/3 cup (generous) beer

1/2 teaspoon basil
1 bay leaf
1/2 teaspoon salt
1/8 teaspoon pepper
3 eggs
4 tablespoons white flour
2 (4 oz.) cans green chili strips,
  roasted and peeled (pit,
  white core, and seeds removed)
6 ounces Monterey Jack cheese
  (or Longhorn Cheddar), shredded
  coarsely

Saute onion, garlic and bell pepper in 1 or 2 tablespoons lard until soften-ed. Add tomatoes and simmer for 5 minutes. Add Tabasco sauce, Worcestershire sauce, beer, basil, bay leaf, salt and pepper. Simmer, stirring occasionally for 10-15 minutes, (or a little longer if desired.) While simmering sauce, prepare catfish. Preheat oven to 350 degrees.

Melt lard in a frying pan to lightly cover bottom. Separate egg yolks and whites. Beat egg whites until fluffy. Fold in beaten egg yolks and stir egg mixture briskly in bowl. Wash catfish in cold water. Dredge fish, one by one, in flour. Holding fish by tail, dip in egg mixture and cover completely. Place fish immediately in moderately heated frying pan (350 degrees). Brown lightly on each side. Remove fish from frying pan and place in non-greased baking dish. Lay 3 1/2 inch wide green chili strips lengthwise on each fish. Cover fish with tomato sauce. Bake in oven about 20 to 25 minutes or until fish flakes easily when tested with fork. Sprinkle grated cheese over each fish during last 5 minutes of baking. Allow cheese to melt. Serves 6. (Enameled saucepan and non-metallic baking dish are recommended for best flavor.)

Won First Prize in the 1977 National Catfish Cooking Contest.
MISS KAREN SPUHLER, BOULDER, COLORADO

CHEESY FARM-RAISED CATFISH SOUP

6 (2 lbs.) farm-raised catfish fillets
3 (10 3/4 oz.) cans chicken broth
1/2 cup water
1/2 cup carrots, grated
1/2 cup celery, finely chopped
1 cup green onions, finely chopped
1 medium white onion, chopped
1/2 cup butter or margarine

1 cup flour
3 soup cans milk
1 1/3 cups pasteurized process cheese spread
1/2 teaspoon salt
1 teaspoon black pepper
1/4 teaspoon cayenne pepper
1 tablespoon prepared mustard
1/4 cup sherry

Cut catfish into 2 inch pieces. Boil catfish in 1 1/2 cans of chicken broth and 1/2 cup water for 10 minutes. Boil carrots, celery, and green onions in remaining chicken broth for 5 minutes. Saute onion in butter until tender. Add flour and blend well. Add milk and cook until mixture thickens. Add cheese, salt, pepper and cayenne pepper. Stir in mustard and boiled vegetables. Cook an additional 5 minutes. Add catfish mixture. Add sherry. Heat until hot enough to serve. Serves 8.

Won Third Prize in the 1977 National Catfish Cooking Contest.
MRS. JEAN FRIEDRICKS, BATON ROUGE, LOUISIANA

MANDARIN FARM-RAISED CATFISH AMANDINE

4 pan-dressed farm-raised
   catfish (10 to 12 oz. each),
   fresh or frozen
1 can (11 oz.) Mandarin orange
   sections (reserve juice)
2 eggs, beaten
2 tablespoons reserved orange
   juice

1½ cups fine dry bread crumbs
1 teaspoon salt
½ teaspoon grated lemon rind
6 tablespoons margarine or
   butter, melted
Mandarin-Almond Cream
   Sauce

Thaw fish if frozen. In a shallow dish combine eggs and orange juice. In another shallow dish combine bread crumbs, salt and lemon rind. Dip fish in egg mixture, then roll in crumb mixture. Place fish on a wire rack to dry slightly. Pour margarine in a baking dish approximately 15 ½ x 10 ½ x 1 inches. Place fish in dish; turn over to coat both sides with margarine. Bake in a moderate oven, 350° F, for 35-40 minutes or until fish flakes easily when tested with a fork. Serve with Mandarin-Almond Cream Sauce. Garnish as desired. Makes 4 servings.

Note: To prevent fish tails from browning too much, wrap in aluminum foil which has been oiled.

Mandarin-Almond Cream
Sauce:
¼ cup sliced almonds
¼ cup margarine or butter,
   melted
⅔ cup reserved orange juice*

1 tablespoon cornstarch
½ cup diced Mandarin orange
   sections
1 tablespoon lemon juice
⅛ teaspoon salt
¼ cup sour cream

In a medium-size saucepan cook the almonds in margarine until lightly browned. Remove almonds from margarine and set aside. Combine juice, cornstarch; add to margarine. Stir in orange sections, lemon juice and salt. Cook over low heat until mixture thickens, stirring constantly. Remove from heat and allow to cool slightly. Stir in sour cream; blend well. Serve sauce over fish; sprinkle with almonds. Makes approximately 1 ¼ cups sauce.

*If necessary, add enough water to the reserved juice to make ⅔ cup.

Won First Prize of $1,000 in the 1981 National Catfish Cooking Contest.
MRS. PRUDENCE HILBURN, PIEDMONT, ALABAMA

BAKED ELEGANCE OF FARM-RAISED CATFISH

4 pan-dressed farm-raised
  catfish (1 to 1½ lb. each),
  fresh or frozen

2 teaspoons seasoned salt
2 cups water
Sauce Jerrold

Thaw fish if frozen. Rinse, then pat fish dry inside and outside, with paper towels. Score fish on one side only at 1-inch intervals making a diamond shaped pattern. Pour water in the bottom of a broiler pan, approximately 13 x 17 inches. Place broiler rack on top of pan; oil well. Sprinkle seasoned salt on both sides of fish. Place fish, scored side up, on broiler rack; put into a preheated 350° oven and bake for 20 minutes. Baste with Sauce Jerrold. Continue to cook an additional 20 minutes or until fish flakes easily when tested with a fork. Just before fish is done, baste again with Sauce Jerrold. Serve fish with remaining sauce; heated. Makes 4 servings.

Sauce Jerrold:
2 teaspoons lemon juice
2 tablespoons mayonnaise
2 tablespoons prepared
  mustard
2 teaspoons onion juice

2 teaspoons garlic juice
2 teaspoons cream style
  prepared horseradish
½ teaspoon liquid hot pepper
  sauce
1 cup margarine or butter

In a small saucepan combine mayonnaise and mustard. Add onion juice, garlic juice, lemon juice, horseradish and liquid hot pepper sauce. Blend into a smooth mixture. Place over low heat and add margarine, a small amount at a time, stirring it into mayonnaise mixture as it melts. Makes approximately 1 ½ cups sauce.

Won Second Prize of $500 in the 1981 National Catfish Cooking Contest.
JERROLD L. CARPENTER, SR., DENHAM SPRINGS, LOUISIANA

FRENCH'S RECIPES HUNT CONTEST

TACO EL PLATO

Meat Sauce:

1 pound ground beef
1 envelope French's Taco
  Seasoning Mix

2 cups water
3/4 cup packaged pre-cooked
  rice

Salad:

1 small head lettuce, shredded
  (about 4 cups)

2 or 3 tomatoes, diced
1/3 cup prepared French dressing

Toppings:

Chopped onion
Shredded Cheddar cheese

Prepared bottled taco sauce, if
  desired

Brown beef in skillet, stirring to crumble; pour off excess fat. Stir in contents of seasoning mix envelope, water, and rice. Bring to a boil, reduce heat, and simmer 10 to 15 minutes, stirring occasionally. Combine lettuce, tomatoes, and dressing; toss lightly. Serve salad mixture on plates and top with hot meat sauce. Pass onion, cheese, and taco sauce to add as desired. Makes 6 servings.

Won First Prize of $2,500 in the 1975 French's Recipe Hunt Contest. JOYCE TRUESDELL, CLARK, MISSOURI

EGGS BENEDICT SOUFFLES

4 eggs
1/4 cup heavy cream
1 teaspoon salt
Dash of pepper
1/2 to 1 cup finely diced
  cooked ham

1/2 cup shredded Swiss cheese
1 envelope French's Hollandaise
  Sauce Mix
4 English muffins, split, toasted,
  and buttered

Beat together until frothy eggs, cream, salt, and pepper; stir in ham and cheese. Pour into 4 well-buttered custard cups. Place in pan filled with hot water; bake at 250 degrees for 50 to 60 minutes, or until knife inserted in center comes out clean. Prepare sauce mix as directed on envelope. Remove eggs from custard cups, turning upside down on English muffins. Serve topped with hot Hollandaise sauce. Makes 4 servings.

Won First Prize of $2,500 in the 1975 French's Recipe Hunt Contest.
SUSAN EISENMAN, DEL MAR, CALIFORNIA

SAUCY SHRIMP QUICHE

1 (4 or 5 oz.) can shrimp,
  drained and rinsed
1 frozen 9-inch unbaked pastry
  shell, thawed
1 1/2 cups shredded Swiss cheese
1 envelope French's Sour Cream
  Sauce Mix

1 cup heavy cream
3 eggs, beaten
1 teaspoon grated lemon rind
1/2 teaspoon salt
Paprika

Arrange shrimp in bottom of pastry shell; sprinkle with 1 cup cheese. Combine contents of envelope of sauce mix with cream, stirring with a fork until smooth. Stir in eggs, lemon rind, and salt; pour into pastry shell. Sprinkle with remaining 1/2 cup cheese and a little paprika. Place on cookie sheet; bake on lowest oven shelf at 375 degrees for 20 to 25 minutes, or until knife inserted in center comes out clean. Makes 6 servings.

Won First Prize of $2,500 in the 1975 French's Recipe Hunt Contest.
SHARON L. SCHUBERT, MENTOR, OHIO

V. I. PIZZA

1 pound ground beef
1 tablespoon chopped onion
1 envelope French's Seasoning
  Mix for Sloppy Joes
1 1/4 cups water
1 (6 oz.) can tomato paste
1 (3 or 4 oz.) can mushrooms,
  drained and chopped

2 tablespoons chopped green
  pepper
Pizza crust (recipe below)
1 to 2 cups shredded Mozzarella
  or Cheddar cheese
1/2 cup pitted ripe olives, sliced
Tomato slices, if desired

Brown beef with onion in large skillet, stirring to crumble; pour off excess fat. Stir in contents of seasoning mix envelope, water, tomato paste, mushrooms, and pepper. Simmer 10 minutes, stirring occasionally. Prepare pizza crust as directed below. Spoon pizza sauce over crust and top with cheese and olives. Bake at 400 degrees for 12 to 15 minutes, until crust is deep golden brown. Garnish with tomatoes, if desired. Makes 2 or 3 pizzas (8 to 10 servings).

Pizza Crust: Soften 1 package active dry yeast in 3/4 cup warm water. Add 2 1/2 cups biscuit mix; beat vigorously 2 minutes. Knead on floured surface until smooth, about 25 strokes. Roll or pat out dough to make two 12 inch or three 9 inch rounds; crimp edges.

Won First Prize of $2,500 in the 1975 French's Recipe Hunt Contest.
CHERYL K. THOM, EUGENE, OREGON

TRI-COLOR TUNA CASSEROLE

6 ounces uncooked spinach
  noodles
2 envelopes French's Hollandaise
  Sauce Mix
2/3 cup water
2/3 cup dry sherry or other
  dry white wine
2 (7 oz.) cans chunk style
  tuna, drained
1 cup pitted ripe olives, sliced

1 (3 or 4 oz.) can sliced mushrooms,
  drained
3 tablespoons chopped pimiento
2 green onions, chopped
1/2 cup shredded Mozzarella
  cheese
1 teaspoon paprika
1/4 teaspoon chili powder

Cook noodles until tender as directed on package; drain. Combine contents of both sauce mix envelopes, water, and wine in saucepan; heat to boiling, stirring frequently. Combine sauce mixture with tuna, olives, mushrooms, pimiento, onions, and noodles; mix lightly. Spoon into greased 2 quart casserole. Sprinkle with cheese. Mix together paprika and chili powder; sprinkle over cheese. Bake at 350 degrees for 25 to 30 minutes, until bubbling hot. Makes 6 to 8 servings.

Won First Prize of $2,500 in the 1975 French's Recipe Hunt Contest. VIRGINIA DOOLEY, TAOS, NEW MEXICO

EAST INDIAN MOUSSE

2 (3 oz.) packages lemon flavor
  gelatin
1 cup boiling water
1/2 cup cold water
1 teaspoon curry powder
1 envelope French's Sour Cream
  Sauce Mix
1/3 cup chutney, chopped
1 (10 3/4 oz.) can chicken broth

1 (10 3/4 oz.) can cream of
  chicken soup
1/3 cup mayonnaise
1 1/4 cups diced cooked or
  canned chicken
1/4 cup chopped macadamia
  nuts
Lettuce

Dissolve 1 package gelatin in boiling water. Add cold water and 1/2 teaspoon curry powder; cool slightly. Prepare sauce mix according to package directions; blend into gelatin mixture. Chill until slightly thickened; stir in chutney. Pour into oiled 1 1/2 quart mold; chill until set. Bring chicken broth to a boil in saucepan. Add remaining package of gelatin and stir until dissolved. Stir in soup, mayonnaise, and remaining 1/2 teaspoon curry powder. Chill until partially thickened. Stir in chicken and nuts; pour on top of "set" gelatin mixture in mold. Chill until firm. Loosen edges and turn out onto lettuce-lined serving plate. Makes 6 servings.

Won First Prize of $2,500 in the 1975 French's Recipe Hunt Contest. STEVEN SACKS, PENLLYN, PENNSYLVANIA

POP-OVER PIZZA

1 pound ground beef
1 large onion, chopped
1 envelope French's Spaghetti
Sauce Mix

1 (15 oz.) can tomato sauce
1/2 cup water
1 (8 oz.) package sliced
Mozzarella cheese

Popover Batter:

2 large eggs
1 cup milk
1 tablespoon oil

1 cup all-purpose flour
1/2 teaspoon salt
1/2 cup grated Parmesan cheese

Brown beef with onion in large skillet, stirring to crumble; pour off excess fat. Add contents of sauce mix envelope, tomato sauce, and water; simmer 10 minutes. Spoon into greased 13x9 inch baking pan. Top with Mozzarella cheese. Place in 400 degree oven to keep hot. To prepare popover batter, beat together eggs, milk, and oil with rotary beater. Add flour and salt; beat until smooth. Pour over hot pizza filling, being careful to cover filling completely. Sprinkle with Parmesan cheese. Bake at 400 degrees for 30 minutes, until puffed and deep golden brown. Cut into squares and serve immediately. Makes 6 to 8 servings.

Won First Prize of $2,500 in the 1975 French's Recipe Hunt Contest. HELEN F. BOLLEN, SPOKANE, WASHINGTON

HUNGARIAN GOULASH

1/4 cup flour
1 teaspoon seasoning salt
Dash of pepper
1 1/2 pounds stewing beef or
chuck steak, cut in 1 inch
strips
3 tablespoons fat
1 envelope French's Beef
Stew Seasoning Mix
1 cup water

6 carrots, cut diagonally in
1 inch pieces
6 stalks celery, cut diagonally
in 1 inch pieces
1/2 pound fresh mushrooms,
sliced
1 cup dairy sour cream
1/2 cup red wine
Cooked noodles or rice

Combine flour, seasoning salt, and pepper in paper or plastic bag. Add beef; shake until well coated. Heat fat in large skillet or Dutch oven. Add beef and brown on all sides. Add contents of seasoning mix envelope, water, carrots, celery, and mushrooms. Cover and simmer 2 to 3 hours, until tender, stirring occasionally. Stir in sour cream and wine; heat gently. Serve over noodles or rice. Makes 6 servings.

Won First Prize of $2,500 in the 1975 French's Recipe Hunt Contest. ARDITH R. HARTLEY, FOUNTAIN VALLEY, CALIFORNIA

EMPRESS PORK

1 pork roast, 4 to 5 pounds
1 (6 oz.) can frozen orange juice
  concentrate, undiluted
1 envelope French's Gravy Mix
  for Pork
1 cup water

1/2 teaspoon ground ginger
1/4 teaspoon freshly ground
  pepper (or use more for a
  highly seasoned, exotic flavor)
1 (11 oz.) can mandarin
  oranges, drained

Place roast on rack in foil-lined roasting pan. Roast at 325 degrees for 2 to 2 1/2 hours, until tender and well done (170 degrees on meat thermometer). Combine half the orange juice concentrate with 1 tablespoon from contents of gravy mix envelope. Brush over roast two or three times during last 15 minutes of roasting. Combine water, ginger, and pepper with remaining orange juice concentrate and remaining gravy mix; simmer 2 minutes, stirring occasionally. Add oranges; heat 2 to 3 minutes longer. Makes 8 to 10 servings.

Won First Prize of $2,500 in the 1975 French's Recipe Hunt Contest. DOROTHY L. STODDARD, FAIRHAVEN, MASSACHUSETTS

SIMPLE BUT ELEGANT SOLE

2 pounds fillet of sole
Salt
1 envelope French's Chicken
  Gravy Mix
1/2 cup water
1 (10 3/4 oz.) can cream of
  celery soup

2 tablespoons sherry
1 cup seedless green grapes, cut
  in half
Paprika
Thin slices of orange
2 tablespoons vodka

Dry fish with paper towels; sprinkle with salt. Roll up, jelly roll style, and place, seam-side down, in greased shallow baking dish. Combine contents of gravy mix envelope with water until smooth; stir in soup and sherry. Spoon over fish. Cover and bake at 375 degrees for 30 minutes, until fish flakes easily when pierced with a fork. Sprinkle with grapes and paprika; bake, uncovered, 5 minutes longer. Garnish with orange slices. Gently heat vodka in small pan. Ignite and pour flaming vodka over fish. Serve as soon as flames die. Makes 4 to 6 servings.

Note: For Simple But Elegant Chicken, use 3 or 4 chicken breasts, split and boned, instead of sole. Increase baking time to 40 minutes.

Won First Prize of $2,500 in the 1975 French's Recipe Hunt Contest.
GAIL PEARSON FEASTER, SPRINGFIELD, VIRGINIA

NATIONAL CHICKEN COOKING CONTEST

SUNSHINE CHICKEN PIE

1 whole broiler-fryer chicken
2 cups water (about)
3 celery tops
1 tablespoon salt
1 bay leaf
1 cup light cream
7 tablespoons flour
1/2 teaspoon Worcestershire
 sauce

1/8 teaspoon pepper
1/8 teaspoon ground mace
7 tablespoons butter
12 small onions, cooked
1 (10 oz.) package frozen peas,
 cooked, seasoned, buttered
Carrot Biscuits: recipe follows

In deep saucepan place chicken. Add water, celery, salt, and bay leaf. Cover and simmer about 45 minutes or until fork can be inserted in chicken with ease. Cool. Strain and reserve broth, add water, if needed, to measure 2 cups liquid. Separate meat from bones. Discard bones and skin. Cut chicken in bite-sized pieces and place in large baking pan or casserole. In small bowl mix together cream, flour, Worcestershire sauce, pepper, and mace; reserve. In medium saucepan make sauce by placing butter and melt over medium heat. Gradually add reserved flour mixture and reserved 2 cups chicken broth. Cook, stirring, about 7 minutes or until mixture is thick and bubbly. Pour sauce oven chicken; top with onions; then biscuits. Bake, uncovered, in 425 degree F. oven about 20 minutes or until biscuits are golden. To serve, place spoonful of peas in center of each biscuit. Makes 4 servings.

Carrot Biscuits: In large bowl place 2 cups biscuit mix and 1/2 cup raw grated carrot. Add milk according to package directions and mix until soft dough forms. On hard floured surface roll out dough to 1/2 inch thickness. Cut with doughnut cutter dipped in flour. Brush top with light cream.

Won Fifth Prize of $1,000 in the 1980 National Chicken Cooking Contest. MARY LOU BERNDT, GLASCO, KANSAS

CHICKEN CHABLIS

1 broiler-fryer chicken, cut in parts
3 tablespoons butter
2 teaspoons Beau Monde seasoning
4 small white onions, quartered
1 (16 oz.) can artichoke hearts, drained and halved
1 tablespoon freshly shredded parsley
2 tablespoons water
1 teaspoon Italian seasoning
1/8 teaspoon garlic powder
1 tomato, chopped
1/4 cup Chablis wine
1/4 cup grated Parmesan cheese

In large fry pan place butter and heat to medium temperature. Add chicken and cook, turning, about 10 minutes or until brown on all sides. Sprinkle Beau Monde on chicken while it is cooking. Remove chicken to a medium baking pan or casserole. In same fry pan place onion, artichokes, parsley, water, Italian seasoning, and garlic powder; cook, stirring occasionally, over medium heat about 5 minutes or until onion is tender and brown bits in fry pan have dissolved. Stir in tomato and wine; pour over chicken. Cover and bake in 350 degree F. oven for about 50 minutes or until fork can be inserted in chicken with ease. Remove cover, sprinkle with cheese, and return to oven for 5 minutes or until cheese melts. Makes 4 servings.

Was the California State Finalist in the 1980 National Chicken Cooking Contest.

BECKY STYLES, WALNUT CREEK, CALIFORNIA

PUFFED RICOTTA CHICKEN

2 whole broiler-fryer chicken breasts, halved, boned, skinned
1/2 teaspoon salt
1/4 teaspoon white pepper
3 tablespoons butter
1/2 cup ricotta cheese
1/4 cup orange juice
2 teaspoons grated orange peel
1/2 teaspoon rosemary leaves
1 sheet frozen puff pastry, defrosted according to package directions
1 egg, beaten

Sprinkle chicken with salt and pepper. In fry pan place butter and melt over medium heat. Add chicken and cook, turning, about 3 minutes on each side or until fork can be inserted in chicken with ease. In small bowl mix together Ricotta cheese, orange juice, orange peel, and rosemary.

On lightly floured board unfold pastry sheet; cut into 4 equal squares. Roll out each square large enough to enclose chicken breast. Make chicken puff by placing a piece of chicken on each pastry square; spread each with 1/4 cheese mixture. Carefully wrap pastry around chicken; pinch edges closed to seal. Place on ungreased baking sheet; brush with egg. Bake in 350 degree F. oven for about 20 minutes or until golden brown. Makes 4 servings.

Was the Illinois State Finalist in the 1980 National Chicken Cooking Contest.
MRS. WILLIAM DANIELS, CHICAGO, ILLINOIS

CHICKEN HAWAIIAN

1 broiler-fryer chicken, cut in
  parts
1 teaspoon salt
1 egg beaten
1/3 cup frozen pineapple-orange
  juice concentrate, thawed

1 cup corn flake crumbs
1/2 cup shredded coconut
1/2 teaspoon curry powder
1/4 cup butter, melted

In large dish place chicken. Sprinkle salt on chicken. In bowl mix egg and juice. Pour over chicken. Marinate 1 hour, turning pieces once. In shallow dish mix together crumbs, coconut and curry. Remove chicken from marinade and drain slightly. Dip chicken, one piece at a time, in coconut mixture, turning to coat. In large shallow baking pan place chicken, skin side up, in single layer. Drizzle melted butter over chicken. Bake, uncovered, in 350 degree F. oven about 1 hour or until fork can be inserted in chicken with ease. Makes 4 servings.

Won Fifth Prize of $1,000 in the 1978 National Chicken Cooking Contest.
ALICE ALBERTSEN, WAYNE, NEBRASKA

PICKLED PEPPER CHICKEN

1 broiler-fryer chicken, cut in
  parts
1 teaspoon Accent flavor enhancer
1/3 cup flour
1/4 cup Mazola corn oil

1 (12 oz.) bottle chili sauce
1 (16 oz.) jar sweet cherry peppers,
  drained, liquid reserved
1/4 cup liquid from peppers
1/2 cup sherry

Sprinkle chicken with flavor enhancer. Coat with flour. Heat corn oil in fry pan over medium heat. Add chicken and brown on all sides.

Add chili sauce, liquid from peppers and sherry. Cover; simmer 45 minutes or until fork can be inserted with ease. Remove chicken to serving dish. Distribute peppers attractively over and around chicken. Reheat sauce and pour over chicken. Makes 4 servings.

Won Third Prize of $3,000 in the 1976 National Chicken Cooking Contest.
MRS. ELLA MARIE MALLOY, VANCOUVER, WASHINGTON

SWEET SURPRISE CHICKEN

3 whole broiler-fryer chicken
  breasts, halved
1 (16 oz.) can jellied cranberry
  sauce

1 (8 oz.) bottle creamy French
  dressing
1 (1.4 oz.) envelope onion soup
  mix

In shallow greased baking pan place chicken, skin side up, in single layer. In medium bowl mix together cranberry sauce, French dressing, and onion soup mix. Pour over chicken. Bake, uncovered, in 250 degree F. oven about 2 hours or until fork can be inserted in chicken with ease. Makes 6 servings.

Was the Maine State Finalist in the 1980 National Chicken Cooking Contest.
PRISCILLA B. AUSTIN, NEWCASTLE, MAINE

CHICKEN LITTLE'S POPPY SEED - CHICKEN FEED

1 broiler-fryer chicken, cut in
  serving pieces
1 (10 oz.) box Cheddar cheese
  flavored crackers, crushed to
  make fine crumbs

2 tablespoons poppy seed
3/4 cup Mazola margarine
  melted

Mix crumbs and poppy seed. Dip chicken pieces in margarine to cover well. Generously coat each piece with crumb mixture. Place chicken on flat shallow baking sheet (about 15x10x1 inches) so that pieces are not touching. Bake, uncovered, in 350 degree F. (moderate) oven 1 hour or until chicken is brown and tender. Makes 4 servings.

Was the Junior Kansas State Finalist in the 1970 National Chicken Cooking Contest.
MISS ANN SANDERSON, LEAWOOD, KANSAS

CHICKEN MAHARANI

4 whole broiler-fryer chicken
  breasts, halved, skinned, boned,
  flattened to 1/4 inch thickness
2 teaspoon Accent flavor
  enhancer
1 teaspoon salt
1/4 teaspoon pepper
8 ounces Cheddar cheese, shredded
  (about 2 cups)
8 ounces cream cheese, softened
1/4 cup Mazola corn oil
1 (10 oz.) jar chutney, chopped

Sprinkle chicken with flavor enhancer, salt and pepper. Beat cheeses in mixer until light. Refrigerate until firm. Smooth out chicken on board. Place portion of cheese mixture in center of each piece of chicken, leaving a 1/2 inch edge all around. Roll up each breast, tucking in ends; secure with food picks. Place in baking pan. Brush on all sides with corn oil. Bake in 350 degree oven, uncovered, about 40 minutes. Remove picks. Spoon chutney over chicken and continue cooking about 20 minutes or until fork can be inserted with ease and sauce is warm. Serve on rice. Garnish with parsley. Makes 8 servings.

Won Fifth Prize of $1,000 in the 1976 National Chicken Cooking Contest.
MRS. NANCY ANN THOMPSON, BANGOR, MAINE

CHEESY CHICKEN MANICOTTI STYLE

4 whole broiler-fryer chicken
  breasts, halved, boned, skinned
  and flattened
1 egg, beaten
2 tablespoon chopped parsley
1/2 cup grated Parmesan cheese
1 (4 oz.) package shredded
  Mozzarella cheese, divided
1/3 cup Ricotta cheese
1 teaspoon sugar
1 teaspoon Accent flavor
  enhancer
1/3 cup Mazola corn oil
2 tablespoons bottled Italian
  salad dressing
1 1/3 cups seasoned crouton
  crumbs
1 (15 1/2 oz.) jar prepared
  spaghetti sauce

In small bowl mix together egg, parsley, Parmesan cheese, 1/2 cup of the Mozzarella cheese and the Ricotta cheese. Stir in sugar and flavor enhancer. Smooth chicken on work surface. Divide cheese mixture into 8 portions placing one portion in center of each breast. Roll up, tucking in ends and fasten with food picks. Mix corn oil and salad dressing. Dip chicken rolls in corn oil mixture turning to coat all sides; then roll in crumbs covering well. Place rolls in baking pan, drizzle remaining corn oil mixture over rolls. Bake in 375 degree oven, uncovered, about 30 minutes or until fork can be inserted with ease. Remove picks. Heat spaghetti sauce and serve over chicken. Sprinkle remaining Mozzarella cheese over warm sauce. Makes 8 servings.

Was the Kansas State Finalist in the 1976 National Chicken Cooking Contest.
JEAN W. SANDERSON, LEAWOOD, KANSAS

FRIED GINGER CHICKEN THIGHS

12 broiler-fryer chicken thighs
6 tablespoons dry vermouth
6 tablespoons soy sauce
6 tablespoons sugar
1 teaspoon Accent flavor
  enhancer

1/4 cup Mazola corn oil
6 slices ginger root, 1/4 inch
  thick, 1 inch wide and 1 1/2
  inches long
1 stalk scallion, cut 2 inches
  long and shredded

Mix together vermouth, soy sauce, sugar and flavor enhancer. Heat corn oil in large fry pan over medium heat. Add chicken, skin side down. Add ginger and brown chicken on all sides. Remove oil from fry pan leaving only 2 tablespoons. Pour seasoning mixture over chicken. Cover and cook about 7 minutes or until sauce is thickened and fork can be inserted in chicken with ease. Stir and mix well. Remove ginger. Sprinkle shredded scallion over chicken. Makes 6 servings.

Won Second Prize of $4,000 in the 1976 National Chicken Cooking Contest.
MS. ROSE CHANG ALEXANDER, SAN FRANCISCO, CALIFORNIA

MEXICAN CHICKEN KIEV

4 whole broiler-fryer chicken breasts, halved, boned and skinned
1/4 cup Mazola margarine
1/4 cup sharp Old English cheese (from 5 oz. jar)
2 tablespoons chopped green chilies
2 teaspoons instant minced onion
2 teaspoons Accent
1 teaspoon salt
1/4 cup flour
2 eggs, beaten with 1 tablespoon water
1 cup fine dry bread crumbs
4 1/2 teaspoons taco seasoning mix
3 cups Mazola corn oil
4 to 5 cups shredded lettuce
2 tomatoes, peeled and diced
1/2 cup chopped pitted ripe olives
Bottled taco sauce, heated

Cream together margarine and cheese; mix in chilies and onion. Freeze while preparing chicken. Place chicken breasts between 2 pieces of Alcoa Wrap aluminum foil and pound to flatten. Sprinkle inside of each breast with Accent and salt. Divide cheese mixture into 8 portions and place one portion in center of each breast. Roll up, tucking in ends, and fasten with food picks. Dip chicken rolls in flour, then in beaten egg, then in bread crumbs mixed with taco seasoning mix. Chill rolls 1 hour. Pour corn oil into Wear-Ever 3 quart saucepan; heat to 360 degrees F. Fry rolls 10 to 15 minutes, turning occasionally. To serve, remove picks and place rolls on bed of lettuce and tomatoes. Garnish with olives and serve with taco sauce. Makes 8 servings.

Was the Kansas State Finalist in the 1972 National Chicken Cooking Contest.
JEAN W. SANDERSON, LEAWOOD, KANSAS

FARMER BROWN'S CHICKEN CASSEROLE

1 broiler-fryer chicken, cut in parts, with giblets
1 tablespoon cooking oil
1 tablespoon butter
6 small onions, peeled
2 cups sliced fresh mushrooms
4 medium potatoes, peeled
4 large carrots, peeled, sliced lengthwise, cut in 1 inch chunks
3 ribs celery, cut in 1 1/2 inch lengths
1 cup chicken broth
1 teaspoon salt
1/4 teaspoon pepper
4 small garlic buds
1/2 cup heavy cream
1 tablespoon lemon juice
2 tablespoons flour

In fry pan place oil and butter and heat until melted at medium temperature. Add chicken and cook, turning, about 10 minutes or until brown on all sides. Remove chicken to large, shallow, baking pan. In fry pan place onions, mushrooms and giblets and saute about 5 minutes or until lightly browned. To chicken in baking pan add this mixture; also add potatoes, carrots, celery, broth, salt and pepper. Cover and bake in 350 degree F. oven about 1 1/2 hours. Add garlic buds and bake 30 minutes longer or until fork can be inserted in chicken with ease. Remove garlic buds. Place chicken and vegetables on platter. Drain liquid from baking pan into saucepan. Add cream and remaining juice. Add flour, stir constantly; cook until thickened. Pour sauce over chicken and vegetables. Makes 4 servings.

Won Fourth Prize of $2,000 in the 1978 National Chicken Cooking Contest.
ROBERT A. BROWN, PITTSFIELD, NEW HAMPSHIRE

COOKOUT BARBECUED CHICKEN

1 broiler-fryer chicken, quartered	1 tablespoon Worcestershire sauce
1/2 cup margarine, melted	1 tablespoon vinegar
1 cup catsup	1 teaspoon salt
1 1/2 cups water	1 teaspoon celery salt
2 tablespoons lemon juice	1/8 teaspoon Tabasco sauce
1 tablespoon soy sauce	3 tablespoons honey

*Add wet hickory chips to briquettes in charcoal grill.

Brush margarine on both sides of chicken. Place chicken on grill over hot coals, skin side up, about 8 inches from heat. Cook, turning and basting with margarine, about 30 minutes or until chicken is lightly browned. In saucepan mix together catsup, water, lemon juice, soy sauce, Worcestershire, vinegar, salt, celery salt and Tabasco. Boil 5 minutes. Brush chicken with catsup mixture and continue to cook, turning and basting every 5 minutes with catsup mixture, 30 minutes longer. Add honey to catsup mixture. Brush on chicken and cook about 10 minutes longer or until fork can be inserted in chicken with ease. Heat remaining sauce and pour over chicken when serving. Makes 4 servings.

*Instead of using wet hickory chips, the contestant used 1 tablespoon liquid smoke in the catsup mixture.

Won Third Prize of $3,000 in the 1978 National Chicken Cooking Contest.
JUNE R. GRAYSON, ENID, OKLAHOMA

CHICKEN SPINACH SOUFFLE

1 broiler-fryer chicken, cut
  in parts
1 1/2 teaspoons salt, divided
1/2 cup Mazola corn oil
1 (8 oz.) package mild Cheddar
  cheese, shredded
1/4 pound butter
2 tablespoons snipped chives
1 1/2 cups warmed buttermilk
1/4 cup hot water

2 chicken bouillon cubes, crushed
1 teaspoon Accent flavor
  enhancer
1/4 teaspoon garlic salt
1/8 teaspoon cayenne pepper
1 cup frozen chopped spinach,
  thawed, pressed dry
4 eggs, slightly beaten
8 regular slices day-old bread,
  crusts removed, cut in 1/2 inch
  cubes

Sprinkle chicken with 1 teaspoon of the salt. Heat corn oil in fry pan over medium heat. Add chicken and cook about 30 minutes or until fork can be inserted with ease. Cool, cut in cubes, there should be 2 cups. In top of double boiler placed over boiling water, melt cheese and butter. Add chives, buttermilk, hot water, chicken bouillon cubes, flavor enhancer, garlic salt, remaining 1/2 teaspoon salt, cayenne pepper, spinach and eggs. Stir to blend. Place bread cubes and chicken in medium-sized greased casserole. Pour on sauce mixture and mix lightly. Refrigerate several hours or overnight. Bake in 350 degree oven, in pan of water, uncovered, about 1 1/4 hours. Makes 6 servings.

Won Fourth Prize of $2,000 in the 1976 National Chicken Cooking Contest.
MS. LAURALEE A. FUGAZZI, DENVER, COLORADO

CHICKEN WITH SHRIMP

1 broiler-fryer chicken, cut in
  serving pieces
2 teaspoons Accent flavor
  enhancer
1 medium onion, thinly sliced
6 tablespoons Mazola corn oil,
  divided
1/4 cup dry white wine

1 clove garlic, crushed
1 bay leaf
1/4 teaspoon thyme
1/2 cup chicken broth
1/2 teaspoon salt
1 (4 oz.) can tomato sauce
1/2 pound mushrooms, sliced
Juice of 1/2 lemon
1 cup cooked shrimp

Rub chicken pieces with flavor enhancer. Saute onion until delicately colored in 4 tablespoons of the corn oil in fry pan over medium heat.

Remove onion slices. Add chicken and brown on all sides, turning as needed. Add wine, garlic, bay leaf, thyme, chicken broth, salt and tomato sauce. Cover and simmer 1/2 hour or until chicken is done. Remove chicken; strain sauce and reduce about 5 minutes over medium heat. Saute mushrooms in separate fry pan over medium heat in remaining 2 tablespoons of corn oil. Add lemon juice. Place chicken, onion slices, shrimp and mushrooms in deep baking dish. Add sauce and heat in 350 degree oven. Garnish with parsley and serve with rice. Makes 6 servings.

Won Fifth Prize of $1,000 in the 1974 National Chicken Cooking Contest. MRS. CHARLES EVANS, PORTLAND, OREGON

WINE GLAZED CHICKEN AND VEGETABLES

1 broiler-fryer chicken, quartered
1 teaspoon Accent flavor
  enhancer
1/2 teaspoon salt
1/4 teaspoon ground pepper
1/4 cup Mazola corn oil
2 tablespoons flour
1 teaspoon sugar
1/8 teaspoon dry thyme leaves

1/8 teaspoon dry rosemary
2 tablespoons lemon juice
1 (6 oz.) can mushrooms with
  liquid
1/2 cup chicken broth
1/2 cup red Burgundy wine
12 small onions, peeled
1 pound baby carrots
Parsley

Sprinkle chicken with flavor enhancer, salt and pepper. Heat corn oil in fry pan or Dutch oven over medium heat. Add chicken, brown lightly, turning as needed. Remove chicken. Mix together flour, sugar, thyme and rosemary. Stir into pan drippings to make a smooth paste. Add lemon juice, mushroom liquid, broth; cook stirring until it boils. Add wine, onions, carrots, mushrooms and chicken. Reduce heat; cover and simmer 30 minutes. Remove cover and continue cooking at a higher heat until most liquid is evaporated and chicken and vegetables are coated with thick, rich glaze. Garnish with parsley. Makes 4 servings.

Won Third Prize of $3,000 in the 1974 National Chicken Cooking Contest. MRS. LENORE SWANK, CASSOPOLIS, MICHIGAN

PERSIAN CHICKEN KABOBS

4 whole broiler-fryer chicken
  breasts, halved, boned, skinned,
  cut into skewer pieces
1 teaspoon Accent flavor
  enhancer
2 teaspoons salt, divided
1/4 cup Mazola corn oil
1/4 cup tarragon wine vinegar
1/2 teaspoon dry mint leaves

1/4 teaspoon dry rosemary
1 clove garlic, crushed
1/4 teaspoon hot pepper sauce
4 medium tomatoes, quartered
16 small white onions, peeled
2 green peppers, seeded, cut
  into skewer pieces
16 small to medium fresh
  mushrooms caps

Sprinkle chicken with flavor enhancer and 1 teaspoon of the salt. Stir together corn oil, vinegar, mint, rosemary, garlic and hot pepper sauce. Pour over chicken in flat dish or bowl. Cover; marinate in refrigerator at least 2 hours or overnight, if possible, turning once or twice. Drain marinade from chicken, reserving marinade to use as brushing sauce. Thread chicken on skewers alternating with vegetables. Brush with marinade; sprinkle with remaining 1 teaspoon salt. Cook on outdoor grill about 6 inches from heat, 30 minutes or until chicken is done. Turn and baste while cooking. Serve with rice pilaf or plain rice. Makes 6 servings.

Won Second Prize of $4,000 in the 1974 National Chicken Cooking Contest.
DR. HAROLD TARA, WAYNE, NEW JERSEY

LINDOS CHICKEN

1 broiler-fryer chicken, cut in
  serving pieces
1/3 cup Mazola corn oil
1 large clove garlic, minced
1 1/2 teaspoons Accent flavor
  enhancer, divided
1 cup dairy sour cream
1 (10 3/4 oz.) can cream of
  chicken soup
1 tablespoon lemon juice

1 teaspoon thyme
1 1/2 cups sliced fresh mushrooms
1/2 cup sliced green onion
  (Use some of the green top.)
1/2 cup sliced pitted black olives,
  well drained
1/4 teaspoon celery salt
6 slices bacon, cut in halves
Garnish, parsley

Heat corn oil in fry pan over medium heat. Add garlic and brown lightly. Add chicken; sprinkle with 1 teaspoon flavor enhancer. Cook over medium heat, turning as needed, to brown nicely on all sides. In a mixing bowl, stir together sour cream, chicken soup, lemon juice, thyme, mushrooms, onion, olives, celery salt and remaining flavor enhancer. Place the browned chicken in large flat casserole; cover with bacon pieces. Bake, uncovered, in 425 degree oven 25 minutes or until bacon is crisp. Remove excess fat. Spoon prepared sauce over chicken, covering each piece entirely. Reduce heat to 375 degrees; bake 25 minutes or until sauce bubbles, mushrooms are tender and chicken is done. Garnish with parsley. Makes 6 servings.

Won Fourth Prize of $2,000 in the 1974 National Chicken Cooking Contest.
MISS CARA BERGGREN, STATE COLLEGE, PENNSYLVANIA

SHIRLEY'S CHICKEN AND MACARONI

1 broiler-fryer chicken, cut in parts	1/4 cup sherry wine
1/2 cup flour	3 teaspoons salt
2 teaspoons seasoned salt	1 teaspoon freshly ground black pepper
1/2 cup cooking oil	2 tablespoons prepared grated horseradish
5 green onions, green and white parts included, chopped	1 1/2 teaspoons dry mustard
1 cup chopped green pepper	1/2 teaspoon tarragon
1 pound mushrooms, sliced	2 chicken bouillon cubes
1 (28 oz.) can tomatoes, drained, coarsely chopped, liquid reserved	1 cup water, (plus additional)
	2 cups uncooked macaroni

In bag mix flour and seasoned salt. Add chicken, a few pieces at a time, and shake to coat. In fry pan, place oil and heat to medium temperature. Add chicken and cook, turning, about 15 minutes or until brown on all sides. Remove chicken from fry pan and set aside. In same fry pan, place green onions and green peppers and saute about 5 minutes or until soft. Add mushrooms and saute 2 minutes. Add tomatoes, wine, salt, black pepper, horseradish, mustard and tarragon and stir. Remove from heat.

In small bowl place bouillon cubes; add 1 cup water and stir until dissolved; add to tomato mixture. In measuring cup place reserved tomato juice; add water to make 2 cups; add to tomato mixture. In large shallow pan spread macaroni. Arrange chicken, skin side up, in single layer on macaroni. Pour tomato mixture over all. Cover and bake in 350 degree F. oven about 40 minutes or until fork can be inserted in chicken with ease. Makes 4 servings.

Won Third Prize of $3,000 in the 1979 National Chicken Cooking Contest. SHIRLEY MISKA, WESTON, CONNECTICUT

GINGERED PEAR CHICKEN AND WALNUTS

2 whole broiler-fryer chicken breasts, halved and skinned	3/4 cup ginger ale
3 tablespoons margarine	1/4 cup brown sugar
1/4 teaspoon salt	3 tablespoons soy sauce
1 (16 oz.) can pear halves, drained, each half cut in 2 wedges, juice reserved	2 teaspoons cornstarch
	1/4 cup water
	1/4 teaspoon powdered ginger
	1/4 cup walnuts, coarsely broken

In fry pan, place margarine and melt over medium heat. Add chicken and cook, turning, about 10 minutes or until brown on both sides. Sprinkle salt on chicken. Place pear juice in measuring cup. If necessary, add water to make 3/4 cup. In bowl, mix together pear juice, ginger ale, brown sugar and soy sauce; pour over chicken. Cover and cook over medium heat, turning occasionally, 25 minutes or until fork can be inserted in chicken with ease. Remove chicken from fry pan and place, in single layer, in large shallow baking pan. Place pear wedges around chicken. In small bowl, mix cornstarch with water, stirring until smooth; add ginger and stir. Pour cornstarch mixture, stirring, to remaining liquid in fry pan. Cook, stirring, about 5 minutes or until thick. Pour thickened mixture over chicken and pears. Sprinkle walnuts on top. Bake, uncovered, in 350 degree F. oven about 10 minutes or until pears are heated through. Makes 4 servings.

Won Second Prize of $4,000 in the 1979 National Chicken Cooking Contest. FRAN C. FOSTER, EASLEY, SOUTH CAROLINA

CHICKEN MUSHROOM DINNER

1 whole broiler-fryer chicken
1 teaspoon salt
4 slices bacon
4 tablespoons margarine
1/2 pound fresh mushrooms, sliced
1/2 teaspoon monosodium glutamate
1/4 teaspoon white pepper
2 tablespoons finely chopped parsley

3 tablespoons flour, divided
1 teaspoon paprika
1 teaspoon oregano
1 teaspoon caraway seed
2 medium potatoes, pared and cut in thick slices
1/2 cup white cooking wine
1 cup chicken broth, divided

Rub salt on chicken and set aside. In fry pan, place bacon and cook about 5 minutes or until crisp. Drain and crumble. In a saucepan, place margarine and melt over medium heat. Add mushrooms, monosodium glutamate and white pepper; cook, stirring, 5 minutes. Add parsley; remove from heat and cool. Add 2 tablespoons flour and bacon. Stir well. Place mushroom mixture in cavity of chicken. Place chicken in ovenproof fry pan. Sprinkle paprika, oregano and caraway seed on chicken. Arrange potatoes around chicken. Add wine and 1/2 cup of the broth. Roast, uncovered, in 350 degree F. oven, basting occasionally, 1 hour or until leg moves freely when lifted or twisted. In small bowl, place remaining flour. Add remaining broth and stir well. Add to chicken and potatoes in fry pan. Cook 5 more minutes. Makes 4 servings.

Won Fourth Prize of $2,000 in the 1979 National Chicken Cooking Contest.
BARBARA M. ZOLLIKOFER, TOWSON, MARYLAND

CHICKEN ESCALOPE GOURMET

2 whole broiler-fryer chicken breasts, halved, boned, skinned
2 tablespoons plus 1 teaspoon lemon juice, divided
1/16 teaspoon ground white pepper
8 tablespoons butter, divided
1/2 teaspoon salt

1/4 pound fresh mushrooms, sliced
2 small shallots, minced
2 tablespoons flour
1 cup dry white wine
1 cup chicken stock
1 teaspoon tarragon leaves
1 teaspoon thyme leaves
1 cup heavy cream

152

On hard surface with meat mallet or similar flattening utensil pound chicken to 1/4 inch thickness. Rub with 1 teaspoon of the lemon juice; sprinkle with salt and pepper. In fry pan place 3 tablespoons of the butter and melt over medium heat. Add chicken and cook, turning, about 3 minutes or until firm and opaque and fork can be inserted in chicken with ease. Remove to heated serving dish, cover, and keep warm. In same fry pan add 2 tablespoons of the butter drippings and melt. Add mushrooms, shallots, and remaining 2 tablespoons lemon juice. Cook about 2 minutes or until tender; spoon mushrooms and shallots over chicken. Make sauce in same fry pan by adding remaining 3 tablespoons butter; melt over medium heat. Add flour, stirring, until absorbed. Stir in wine, chicken stock, tarragon, and thyme; cook, stirring, until mixture boils and becomes thick. Simmer, uncovered, over low heat about 9 minutes. Gradually stir in cream and cook until sauce reduces to about 1 1/2 cups. Pour sauce over chicken to serve. Makes 4 servings.

Won Fourth Prize of $2,000 in the 1980 National Chicken Cooking Contest.
BILL CALIGARI, RALEIGH, NORTH CAROLINA

CREAMY LEMON CHICKEN

3 whole broiler-fryer chicken
  breasts, halved
1/2 cup flour
1/2 teaspoon paprika
1/2 teaspoon salt
1/2 teaspoon pepper
1 egg, beaten
1 1/2 cups seasoned crouton
  crumbs

1/2 cup butter
1/4 cup chicken consomme
1/2 cup slivered almonds
3 tablespoons chopped chives
3/4 cup whipping cream, whipped,
  salted to taste
1 lemon, sliced thin

In a shallow dish mix together flour, paprika, salt, and pepper. In another shallow dish place egg; and in a third shallow dish place crumbs. Add chicken one piece at a time to flour mixture, dredging to coat. Then dip chicken in egg and roll in crumbs. In a heavy fry pan place butter and melt over medium heat. Add chicken and cook, turning, about 10 minutes or until brown on all sides. Add consomme and almonds; cover and simmer about 25 minutes or until fork can be inserted in chicken with ease. Fold chives into the salted whipped cream and chill until time to serve. When chicken is done, remove to a warm serving platter and place a lemon slice on each piece of chicken and then top with a spoonful of cream. Makes 6 servings.

Won Second Prize of $4,000 in the 1980 National Chicken Cooking Contest.
HEDY PENNEY, SALT LAKE CITY, UTAH

CAPITAL CHICKEN CASSEROLE

1 broiler-fryer chicken,
  cut in parts
4 tablespoons butter
1 tablespoon cooking oil
1 (8 oz.) package fresh
  mushrooms, sliced
1 tablespoon flour
1 (11 oz.) can cream of chicken
  soup
1 cup dry white wine
1 cup water

1/2 cup cream
1 teaspoon salt
1/4 teaspoon tarragon leaves
1/4 teaspoon pepper
1 (15 oz.) can artichoke hearts,
  drained
6 green onions, green and white
  parts included, chopped
2 tablespoons chopped
  parsley

In large fry pan place butter and oil and heat to medium temperature, until butter melts. Add chicken and cook, turning, about 10 minutes or until brown on all sides. Remove chicken and place in baking pan or casserole. In same fry pan saute mushrooms about 5 minutes or until tender. Stir in flour. Add soup, wine, and water; simmer, stirring, about 10 minutes or until sauce thickens. Stir in cream, salt, tarragon, and pepper; pour over chicken. Bake, uncovered, in 350 degree F. oven for 60 minutes. Mix in artichoke hearts, green onions, and parsley. Bake about 5 more minutes or until fork can be inserted in chicken with ease. Makes 4 servings.

Won First Prize of $10,000 in the 1980 National Chicken Cooking Contest.
SHEILA M. HOBAN, WASHINGTON, D.C.

CHICKEN ZUCCHINI PARMESAN

2 whole broiler-fryer chicken
  breasts, halved, boned, skinned
6 tablespoons olive oil, divided
1 medium onion, diced
2 cloves garlic, minced
2 (10 3/4 oz.) cans tomato
  puree
1 1/4 teaspoons salt
1/4 teaspoon pepper

1/8 teaspoon ground oregano
1 egg, beaten
1/4 cup dry bread crumbs
1/4 cup plus 3 tablespoons grated
  Parmesan cheese
8 ounces Mozzarella cheese, sliced
  thin, divided
1 pound zucchini, sliced

In medium saucepan make sauce by placing 3 tablespoons of the olive oil and heat to medium temperature. Add onion and garlic and cook about 5 minutes or until onion is translucent. Add puree, salt, pepper, and oregano; stir. Cover and simmer over low heat, stirring occasionally, for 1/2 hour. In shallow dish place egg. In another shallow dish mix bread crumbs and 1/4 cup of the Parmesan cheese. Dip chicken in egg, then in bread-crumb mixture, one piece at a time, turning to coat. In large fry pan place remaining 3 tablespoons oil and heat to medium temperature. Add chicken and cook, turning, about 8 minutes or until brown on both sides. Place chicken in large shallow baking pan. Spread with 1/2 tomato sauce; then with 1/2 Mozzarella cheese. Arrange zucchini over all. Spread remaining 1/2 tomato sauce; then remaining 1/2 Mozzarella cheese. Sprinkle with remaining 3 tablespoons Parmesan cheese. Bake, uncovered, in 375 degree F. oven for 30 minutes. Makes 4 servings.

Won Third Prize of $3,000 in the 1980 National Chicken Cooking Contest.
CATHERINE ROOKER, JONESBORO, ARKANSAS

CHICKEN 'N SWISS EXTRAORDINAIRE

2 whole broiler-fryer chicken
  breasts, halved, skinned,
  boned
1 teaspoon Accent flavor
  enhancer
1/2 cup flour
1/4 cup Mazola corn oil
4 thick slices French bread

4 slices Swiss cheese
1 tablespoon margarine
1/2 pound mushrooms, sliced
2/3 cup dry white wine
1 teaspoon salt
1/4 teaspoon pepper

Sprinkle chicken with flavor enhancer. Roll in flour. Heat corn oil in fry pan over medium heat. Add chicken and brown on all sides. Reduce heat; cover tightly and cook about 15 minutes or until fork can be inserted with ease. Place bread topped with cheese slices on baking sheet. Heat in 200 degree F. oven while preparing mushrooms. Remove chicken from fry pan. Add margarine to fry pan; add mushrooms and cook over low heat about 3 minutes. Push mushrooms aside; add wine and stir to loosen browned bits. Add salt and pepper. Return chicken to fry pan and simmer until sauce is slightly thickened. Place chicken piece on top of each bread slice and spoon mushrooms and sauce over chicken. Makes 4 servings.

Won First Prize of $10,000 in the 1975 National Chicken Cooking Contest.
MRS. CAROLINE GRAEFE, COUNCIL, IDAHO

CHICKEN ASPARAGUS CASSEROLE

2 whole broiler-fryer chicken
  breasts, skinned and boned
1 teaspoon Accent flavor
  enhancer
1/8 teaspoon pepper
1/4 cup Mazola corn oil
1 (10 oz.) package frozen
  asparagus

1 (10 3/4 oz.) can condensed cream
  of chicken soup
1/3 cup real mayonnaise
1 teaspoon lemon juice
1/2 teaspoon curry powder
1/4 cup shredded Cheddar
  cheese

Cut each breast into lengthwise strips (2x4 inch). Sprinkle with flavor enhancer and pepper. Heat corn oil in fry pan over medium heat. Add chicken and brown. Cook asparagus 3 to 4 minutes following package directions. Drain. Stir together soup, mayonnaise, lemon juice and curry powder. Place asparagus in single layer in shallow baking pan. Place chicken over asparagus. Spoon on sauce. Sprinkle with cheese. Cover with foil. Bake in 375 degree F. oven 30 minutes or until bubbly. Makes 4 servings.

Won First Prize of $10,000 in the 1973 National Chicken Cooking Contest.
MR. R. CLEMENT HOLLEY, WILMINGTON, DELAWARE

HOT CHINESE CHICKEN SALAD

8 broiler-fryer chicken thighs,
skinned, boned, cut into
1 inch chunks
1/4 cup corn starch
1/4 cup Mazola corn oil
1/8 teaspoon garlic powder
1 large ripe tomato, cut into
chunks
1 (4 oz.) can water chestnuts,
drained, sliced

1 (4 oz.) can sliced mushrooms,
drained
1 cup coarsely chopped green
onion
1 cup slant sliced celery
1 teaspoon Accent flavor enhancer
1/4 cup soy sauce
2 cups finely shredded iceberg
lettuce

Roll chicken in cornstarch. Heat corn oil in fry pan or wok over medium high heat. Add chicken; quickly brown. Sprinkle with garlic powder. Add tomato, water chestnuts, mushrooms, onion and celery. Stir. Sprinkle with flavor enhancer. Add soy sauce. Stir. Cover, reduce heat to simmer and cook 5 minutes. Lightly toss chicken-vegetable mix with lettuce. Serve hot with rice. Makes 4 servings.

Won First Prize of $10,000 in the 1974 National Chicken Cooking Contest.
MRS. FAYNE LUTZ, TAOS, NEW MEXICO

CHICKEN POT-AU-FEU

1/4 cup Mazola corn oil
1 broiler-fryer chicken, cut
in parts
1 quart water
1 onion, halved
2 carrots, sliced
2 ribs celery, sliced
2 chicken bouillon cubes

3 sprigs parsley
1 1/2 teaspoons salt
1 teaspoon Accent flavor
enhancer
1 small head cabbage, cut in
eighths
1 (10 oz.) package frozen peas
1 tablespoon cornstarch
1 tablespoon water

Heat corn oil in Dutch oven over medium heat. Add chicken and brown on all sides. Add water, onion, carrots, celery, bouillon cubes, parsley, salt and flavor enhancer. Cover and simmer about 30 minutes or until fork can be inserted with ease. Remove parsley. Add cabbage and peas.

Cover and simmer 15 minutes or until vegetables are tender. Remove chicken and vegetables; keep warm. Stir together cornstarch and water. Add to juices in Dutch oven. Bring to boil; boil 1 minute, stirring constantly. Return chicken and vegetables to Dutch oven and heat thoroughly. Makes 4 servings.

Won First Prize of $10,000 in the 1972 National Chicken Cooking Contest.
MRS. CAROL PFEIFFER, LEWES, DELAWARE

CHICKEN PIZZA

2 whole broiler-fryer chicken breasts, halved, boned, skinned and cut in 1 inch pieces
1 package (8 rolls) refrigerated crescent rolls
1/4 cup cooking oil
1 large onion, sliced into thin rings
1 large green pepper, seeded, cut into thin rings
1/2 pound fresh mushrooms, sliced
1/2 cup pitted ripe olives, sliced
1 (10 1/2 oz.) can pizza sauce with cheese
1 teaspoon garlic salt
1 teaspoon oregano
1/4 cup Parmesan cheese
2 cups shredded Mozzarella cheese

Unroll crescent dough into 8 triangles. Into lightly oiled 12 inch pizza pan, press dough, especially at perforations, to seal. In fry pan place oil and heat to medium temperature. Add chicken, onion, green pepper, mushrooms and olives and cook, stirring, about 5 minutes or until fork can be inserted in chicken with ease. Spread pizza sauce over crust. Spoon chicken mixture evenly over sauce. Sprinkle garlic salt, oregano and Parmesan cheese on all. Top with Mozzarella cheese. Bake, uncovered, in 425 degree oven 20 minutes or until crust is done. Cut into wedges to serve. Makes 4 servings.

Won First Prize of $10,000 in the 1978 National Chicken Cooking Contest.
MARY G. CERAMI, OJAI, CALIFORNIA

CHICKEN RATATOUILLE

1/4 cup Mazola corn oil
2 whole broiler-fryer chicken
  breasts, skinned, boned and
  cut in 1 inch pieces
2 small zucchini squash,
  unpared and thinly sliced
1 small eggplant, peeled and
  cut into 1 inch cubes
1 large onion, thinly sliced
1 medium green pepper, seeded
  and cut in 1 inch pieces

1/2 pound mushrooms, sliced
1 (16 oz.) can tomato wedges
2 teaspoons garlic salt
1 teaspoon Accent flavor
  enhancer
1 teaspoon dried sweet basil,
  crushed
1 teaspoon dried parsley
1/2 teaspoon black pepper

Heat corn oil in large fry pan. Add chicken and saute about 2 minutes on each side. Then add zucchini, eggplant, onion, green pepper and mushrooms. Cook, stirring occasionally about 15 minutes or until tender crisp. Add tomatoes stirring carefully. Add garlic salt, flavor enhancer, basil, parsley and pepper. Simmer about 5 minutes or until fork can be inserted in chicken with ease. Serve chicken on large platter with mound of rice in center. Makes 4 servings.

Won First Prize of $10,000 in the 1977 National Chicken Cooking Contest.
ANN E. COSTA, ATLANTA, GEORGIA

DIPPER'S NUGGETS CHICKEN

2 whole broiler-fryer chicken
  breasts, skinned, boned
1 egg, beaten
1/3 cup water
1/3 cup flour
2 teaspoons sesame seed

1 teaspoon Accent flavor
  enhancer
1/2 teaspoon salt
1 pint Mazola corn oil
Nippy Pineapple Sauce (recipe
  below)

Cut breast pieces into 1 x 1 x 1/2 inch nuggets. Mix egg and water. Add flour, sesame seed, flavor enhancer and salt to make batter. Pour corn oil into heavy saucepan or deep fryer, filling utensil no more than 1/3 full. Dip nuggets into batter; drain off excess batter. Carefully add nuggets, a few at a time. Fry about 3 to 5 minutes or until golden brown and fork can be inserted with ease. Drain on paper towels. Serve with Nippy Pineapple Sauce. Makes 4 servings.

Nippy Pineapple Sauce: In small saucepan, stir together 1/2 cup pineapple preserves, 2 tablespoons prepared mustard and 2 tablespoons horseradish. Heat over low heat. Makes 3/4 cup.

Won First Prize of $10,000 in the 1971 National Chicken Cooking Contest.
NORMA YOUNG, SEARCY, ARKANSAS

CREAM PUFF TOPPED CHICKEN PIE

2 whole broiler-fryer chicken
  breasts, halved, boned, skinned,
  cut in 1 inch chunks
1 teaspoon salt
1/4 teaspoon white pepper
3 tablespoons butter
1 cup chicken broth
1 1/2 cups frozen mixed
  vegetables

1/4 cup water
2 tablespoons cornstarch
3 tablespoons cooking sherry
1/3 cup sour cream
3/4 cup shredded Cheddar
  cheese
Cream Puff Topping (recipe
  follows)

Sprinkle salt and pepper on chicken. In fry pan place butter and melt over medium heat. Add chicken and saute, stirring, about 8 minutes or until chicken is opaque and fork can be inserted in chicken with ease. Add broth and mixed vegetables. Cover and simmer 10 minutes. In bowl mix water and cornstarch, stirring to blend. Add cornstarch mixture to chicken; add sherry and sour cream and stir. In deep baking pan place chicken mixture. Sprinkle cheese on chicken mixture. Drop cream puff topping by teaspoon in mounds on chicken mixture. Bake, uncovered, in 425 degree F. oven 20 minutes. Reduce heat to 350 degrees F. Bake about 15 minutes longer or until puffs are done and brown. Makes 4 servings.

Cream Puff Topping: In saucepan mix together 1/2 cup water, 1/4 cup butter and 1/8 teaspoon salt and bring to boil. Reduce heat and add 1/2 cup flour all at once. Beat until dough forms a ball and leaves sides of pan. Remove from heat and beat in 2 eggs, one at a time, until mixture is smooth and glossy.

Was the Pennsylvania Finalist in the 1978 National Chicken Cooking Contest.
JUDY REYNOLDS, EDINBORO, PENNSYLVANIA

SUNSHINE CHICKEN

6 broiler-fryer chicken thighs
6 broiler-fryer chicken
  drumsticks
1 teaspoon salt
1 teaspoon basil
1 teaspoon Accent flavor
  enhancer
1/4 teaspoon freshly ground
  pepper

1/2 cup soy sauce
1/2 cup ketchup
1/4 cup honey
1/4 cup Mazola corn oil
2 cloves garlic, crushed
Poached Oranges (recipe
  follows)

Sprinkle chicken with salt, basil, flavor enhancer and pepper. Mix together soy sauce, ketchup, honey, corn oil and garlic. Place chicken skin side up in shallow baking pan. Baste with sauce. Bake in 350 degree F. oven, basting frequently, 1 hour or until tender. Serve with Poached Oranges and remaining basting sauce, mixed with sauce from Poached Oranges. Makes 4 to 6 servings.

Poached Oranges: Mix together 3/4 cup water, 1 1/2 cups sugar, 3 tablespoons slivered orange peel. Cook until slightly thickened. Add 3 cups fresh orange sections. Cook about 3 minutes. Add 2 tablespoons orange liqueur.

Won First Prize of $10,000 in the 1976 National Chicken Cooking Contest.
TOM C. PARVIS, UPPER MONTCLAIR, NEW JERSEY

CHICKEN AND RICE OLE'

1 broiler-fryer chicken, cut in
  parts
1/2 cup margarine, melted,
  divided
1 (11 oz.) can condensed Cheddar
  cheese soup
1 (10 3/4 oz.) can condensed
  tomato soup
2/3 cup water
1 (1.25 oz.) envelope taco
  seasoning mix, divided

1 (4 oz.) can green chilies, seeded,
  drained, chopped
2 medium tomatoes, drained,
  coarsely chopped
2/3 cup long grain rice
1 egg, beaten
1/2 cup flour
1/2 cup yellow corn meal
1 onion, sliced

In large shallow baking pan, place 2 tablespoons of the margarine; spread to coat bottom and side surfaces. In bowl mix together, cheese soup, tomato soup, water, all except 1 tablespoon of the taco mix, chiles, tomatoes, and rice. Pour in baking pan. In shallow dish, mix egg and remaining margarine. In another shallow dish, mix together flour, corn meal and remaining taco mix. Dip chicken, first in egg mixture, turning to coat; then in flour mixture, dredging to coat. Place chicken skin side up in single layer, larger pieces toward outside, on top of rice mixture, Cover and bake in 350 degree F. oven 1/2 hour; remove cover and continue baking about 1 hour, or until fork can be inserted in chicken with ease. Separate onion into rings; dip first in remaining egg mixture; then in remaining flour mixture. On ungreased baking sheet, place onion slices in single layer. Bake, uncovered, in 350 degree F. oven 30 minutes. To serve, arrange onion slices on chicken. Makes 4 servings.

Was the Kentucky Finalist in the 1979 National Chicken Cooking Contest. TIMOTHY E. TROENDLE, LEXINGTON, KENTUCKY

COUNTRY SUNSHINE CHICKEN

2 broiler-fryer chickens, cut in parts
1 teaspoon salt
1 teaspoon Accent flavor enhancer
1/4 cup Mazola corn oil
1 1/2 cups chicken broth
1/2 cup cider vinegar
1/3 cup sugar
1/3 cup brown sugar
1 (13 oz.) can pineapple chunks, drained, juice reserved

1 (11 oz.) can mandarin oranges, drained, juice reserved
1 cup reserved pineapple and orange juice
1 thinly sliced red onion
3 tablespoons cornstarch
2 tablespoons water
1 tablespoon soy sauce
1 (3 oz.) can sliced mushrooms
1 small green pepper, cut in 1 inch squares

Sprinkle chicken with salt and flavor enhancer. Dip in corn oil. Place in single layer in large shallow baking pan. Bake in 400 degree oven, uncovered, 20 minutes. In saucepan place broth, vinegar, sugar, brown sugar, pineapple, mandarin oranges, reserved juices, and onion. Bring to boil. Stir together cornstarch, water and soy sauce. Add to sauce and stir until thickened. Place mushroom slices on chicken pieces. Top with green pepper. Spoon over about 1/2 the sauce. Reduce oven temperature to 350 degrees. Bake chicken, uncovered, about 30 minutes. Spoon on remaining sauce, basting well. Continue baking about 30 minutes or until fork can be inserted with ease. Makes 8 servings.

Was the Wyoming Finalist in the 1976 National Chicken Cooking Contest. MRS. C.B. PLATT, CASPER, WYOMING

CHICKEN BREASTS ROCKEFELLER

2 whole broiler-fryer chicken breasts, halved, boned, skinned and flattened
1/2 teaspoon seasoned salt
1/8 teaspoon paprika
1 (10 oz.) package frozen, chopped spinach, thawed and well drained
1/2 cup minced green onions

1 cup shredded sharp Cheddar cheese
1 (10 3/4 oz.) can cream of chicken soup
2 tablespoons light cream
1 tablespoon Worcestershire sauce
2 tablespoons toasted buttered breadcrumbs

*Sprinkle seasoned salt and paprika on chicken. In bowl mix spinach and green onions. Place 1 tablespoon spinach mixture on each chicken breast half. Place 1 tablespoon cheese on top of spinach mixture. Roll chicken, jelly-roll fashion, and secure with wooden picks. In large shallow glass baking dish mix together soup, cream, Worcestershire, remaining cheese and remaining spinach mixture. Microwave at high 2 minutes; stir; microwave about 2 minutes longer or until cheese is melted. Place chicken breast rolls in glass dish in soup mixture. Spoon soup mixture over chicken; top with crumbs. Sprinkle paprika on top of crumbs. Cover with wax paper. Microwave, turning dish every 5 minutes, about 20 minutes or until fork can be inserted in chicken with ease. Let stand, covered, 5 minutes. Makes 4 servings.

*For conventional oven mix sauce ingredients in saucepan and cook, stirring, over medium heat about 5 minutes or until cheese is melted. Follow procedures with chicken as listed. Bake, uncovered, in 350 degree F. oven about 50 minutes or until fork can be inserted in chicken with ease.

Was the Missouri Finalist in the 1978 National Chicken Cooking Contest.
BETTY STAUFENBIEL, AFFTON, MISSOURI

BARBARA LONG'S CURRIED CHICKEN ROLLS

2 whole broiler-fryer chicken
  breasts, halved, boned and
  skinned
1/2 teaspoon salt
1/8 teaspoon pepper
1 tablespoon margarine
1/2 onion, finely chopped
3/4 cup cooked rice
1/4 cup raisins
1 tablespoon chopped parsley

1 teaspoon curry powder
1/2 teaspoon poultry seasoning
1 teaspoon brown sugar
1/16 teaspoon garlic powder
1 tablespoon cooking oil
1/2 cup white wine
1 teaspoon granulated chicken
  bouillon

On hard surface with meat mallet or similar flattening utensil, pound chicken to 3/8 inch thickness. Sprinkle salt and pepper on chicken. In fry pan, make stuffing by placing margarine and melting over medium heat. Add onion and saute about 3 minutes or until soft. Add rice, raisins, parsley, curry powder, poultry seasoning, brown sugar and garlic powder. Stir until well mixed. Divide stuffing in 4 portions. Place one portion on each piece of chicken. Roll and fasten with wooden picks. In another fry pan, place oil and heat to medium temperature. Add chicken rolls and cook, turning, about 15 minutes or until brown on all sides. Add wine and bouillon. Cover and simmer about 30 minutes or until fork can be inserted in chicken with ease. Makes 4 servings.

Won First Prize of $10,000 in the 1979 National Chicken Cooking Contest.
BARBARA LONG, LARAMIE, WYOMING

CHICKEN BOURGINON

1/2 cup flour
1 teaspoon Accent flavor
  enhancer
1/4 teaspoon black pepper
1 broiler-fryer chicken, cut
  in parts
1/4 cup Mazola corn oil
6 small onions
2 (4 1/2 oz.) cans sliced
  mushrooms

4 carrots, halved
1 cup chicken broth
1 cup red burgundy wine
1 clove garlic, crushed
1 teaspoon salt
1/2 teaspoon dried thyme leaves
1 bay leaf
2 sprigs parsley

Mix flour, flavor enhancer and pepper. Coat chicken. Heat corn oil in large fry pan over medium heat. Add chicken and brown on all sides. Drain off excess pan drippings. Add onion, mushrooms, carrots, broth, wine, garlic, salt, thyme, bay leaf and parsley. Simmer, covered, about 1 hour or until fork can be inserted with ease. Makes 4 servings.

Was the New Hampshire Finalist in the 1977 National Chicken Cooking Contest.
VIRGINIA McMAHON, DOVER, NEW HAMPSHIRE

GRILLED YOGURT-LEMON CHICKEN

1 broiler-fryer chicken, cut
   in parts
1 (8 oz.) carton plain yogurt
1/4 cup wine vinegar
1 tablespoon lemon juice
1 clove garlic, minced
1 teaspoon ground coriander

1 teaspoon powdered mustard
1/2 teaspoon freshly ground
   pepper
1/2 teaspoon ground ginger
1/8 teaspoon ground cloves
5 drops Tabasco sauce

In large bowl mix together yogurt, vinegar, lemon juice, garlic, coriander, mustard, pepper, ginger, cloves, and Tabasco sauce. Add chicken, turning to coat, and marinate in refrigerator about 1 1/2 hours; reserve marinade. Place chicken skin side up, on grill over hot coals about 7 inches from heat. Cook, turning and basting with reserved marinade, about 1 hour or until fork can be inserted in chicken with ease. Makes 4 servings.

Was the Virginia State Finalist in the 1980 National Chicken Cooking Contest.
JOAN McCORMICK, TABB, VIRGINIA

IMPOSSIBLE CHICKEN PIE

1 broiler-fryer chicken, cut in
   parts
2 cups water
2 teaspoons salt, divided
1 cup shredded Mozzarella
   cheese, divided
1 can (6 oz.) tomato paste
1 teaspoon oregano leaves

½ teaspoon basil leaves
½ cup small curd cottage
   cheese
⅔ cup prepared biscuit mix
1 cup milk
2 eggs
¼ teaspoon pepper

In deep saucepan, place chicken. Add water and 1 teaspoon of the salt. Cover and simmer about 45 minutes or until fork can be inserted in chicken with ease. Cool. Separate meat from bones. Discard bones and skin. Cut chicken in bite-size pieces and place in large bowl; add ½ cup of the Mozzarella cheese, tomato paste, oregano and basil; stir to mix and set aside. In a lightly greased large quiche dish or deep-dish pie pan, place cottage cheese and spread evenly. Place chicken mixture evenly over cottage cheese. In bowl, place biscuit mix, milk, eggs, pepper and remaining 1 teaspoon salt; beat 1 minute with hand mixer. Pour over chicken mixture. Bake in 350° F. oven about 30 minutes or until brown and a knife inserted in middle comes out clean. Remove from oven and sprinkle with the remaining ½ cup of Mozzarella cheese. Let set 5 minutes before serving. Makes 4 servings.

Won First Prize of $10,000 in the 1981 National Chicken Cooking Contest.
JUNE HERKE, HOWARD, SOUTH DAKOTA

ISLAND CHICKEN WITH VEGETABLES

8 broiler-fryer chicken thighs,
  boned, halved
¼ cup soy sauce
2 tablespoons sugar
2 tablespoons water
1/16 teaspoon salt
1½-inch cube fresh ginger,
crushed

1 clove garlic, crushed
4 green onions, cut in 1-inch
  pieces, white and green parts
  divided
1¾ cups sliced cabbage

In large saucepan, make sauce by mixing together soy sauce, sugar, water, salt, ginger and garlic. Cook, stirring over high temperature about 1 minute or until sauce boils. Add chicken, onion and white pieces of the green onions; stir. Bring to a boil. Reduce heat to low and simmer chicken mixture for 10 minutes. Stir to coat chicken with sauce and continue cooking about 15 minutes longer or until fork can be inserted in chicken with ease. Add cabbage and green top pieces of the green onions. Cook, stirring about 5 minutes or until vegetables are tender-crisp. Makes 4 servings.

Won Fourth Prize of $2,000 in the 1981 National Chicken Cooking Contest.
RITSUKO NISHIDA, AIEA, HAWAII

BREAST OF CHICKEN IN CHEESE

2 whole broiler-fryer chicken
  breasts, halved, boned
1 can (4 oz.) whole green
  chilies, seeded
1 egg
1 teaspoon olive oil

1/16 teaspoon salt
1/2 cup grated Parmesan cheese
1/2 cup fresh bread crumbs
1 cup margarine, divided
1 tablespoon lemon juice

Place chicken, skin-side down, on a flat surface; place strip of chili in center of each breast. Fold and fasten with a wooden pick. In shallow dish, mix together egg, oil and salt. In another shallow dish, mix Parmesan cheese and bread crumbs. Dip chicken first in egg mixture and then in bread crumb mixture, one piece at a time, turning to coat. Refrigerate for 20 minutes. In frypan, place 1/2 cup of the margarine and melt over medium heat. Add chicken and cook, turning, about 10 minutes or until light brown. Reduce temperature to low and continue cooking about 10 minutes longer or until fork can be inserted in chicken with ease. In small saucepan, place remaining 1/2 cup margarine and melt over low heat; add lemon juice, stir. Place chicken on warm platter. Pour lemon mixture over chicken. Makes 4 servings.

Won Fifth Prize of $1,000 in the 1981 National Chicken Cooking Contest. MRS. WINIFRED LOGUE, ROGERS, ARKANSAS

CHICKEN BREAST PIQUANT

2 whole broiler-fryer chicken
  breasts, halved, boned,
  skinned
1 can (8 oz.) crushed pineapple
  in unsweetened juice
1 can (6 oz.) frozen limeade,
  thawed

1 1/2 ounces light rum
3 whole cloves
1/3 cup flour
2 teaspoons salt
1/4 cup cooking oil
1/3 cup slivered almonds

On hard surface with meat mallet or similar flattening utensil, pound chicken to 1/4-inch thickness. In shallow bowl, make marinade by mixing together pineapple, including juice, limeade, rum and cloves; stir. Add chicken, turning to coat. Cover and marinate at room temperature 30 minutes; remove chicken and drain, reserving marinade. In shallow dish, mix flour and salt. Add chicken, one piece at a time; dredging to coat. In frypan, place oil and heat to medium temperature. Add chicken and cook, turning, about 10 minutes or until brown on all sides. Remove chicken and place in single layer in large shallow greased baking pan. Pour reserved marinade over chicken; sprinkle with almonds. Bake, uncovered in 400° F. oven, basting twice, about 25 minutes or until fork can be inserted in chicken with ease. To serve, place chicken on serving platter and pour sauce over chicken. Makes 4 servings.

Won Second Prize of $4,000 in the 1981 National Chicken Cooking Contest.
HILDA PARSONS, BENNINGTON, NEW HAMPSHIRE

CHICKEN OLÉ

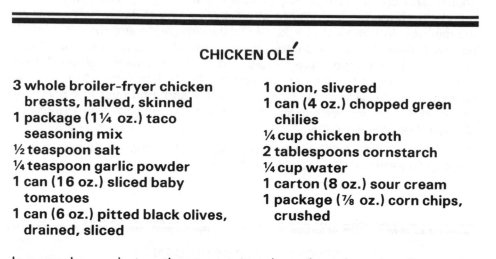

3 whole broiler-fryer chicken breasts, halved, skinned
1 package (1¼ oz.) taco seasoning mix
½ teaspoon salt
¼ teaspoon garlic powder
1 can (16 oz.) sliced baby tomatoes
1 can (6 oz.) pitted black olives, drained, sliced

1 onion, slivered
1 can (4 oz.) chopped green chilies
¼ cup chicken broth
2 tablespoons cornstarch
¼ cup water
1 carton (8 oz.) sour cream
1 package (⅞ oz.) corn chips, crushed

In paper bag, mix together taco seasoning mix, salt and garlic powder. Add chicken, one piece at a time, shaking to coat. In large shallow greased glass baking dish, place chicken. Cover with wax paper. Microwave on high 5 minutes. Turn. Uncover and cook 5 minutes longer. Place tomatoes, olives, onion and chilies over chicken; pour chicken broth over all. Cover and microwave, turning once, on high about 12 minutes. Remove from oven; let stand, covered, about 5 minutes. Return to oven for additional cooking if fork cannot be inserted in chicken with ease when testing for doneness. Remove chicken to serving platter. In small bowl, mix cornstarch and water; add to vegetables in baking dish and microwave about 3 minutes, stirring every minute, or until thick. To serve, pour sauce over chicken; top with sour cream; sprinkle with corn chips. Makes 6 servings.

Won Third Prize of $3,000 in the 1981 National Chicken Cooking Contest.
MARILYN BEACH, SANTEE, CALIFORNIA

LAWRY'S WORLD'S GREATEST HAMBURGER CONTEST

LAWRY'S LUSCIOUS LUAU BURGER

2 pounds lean ground beef
1/4 cup water
1 teaspoon Lawry's Seasoned Salt
1 teaspoon Lawry's Onion Salt
1/4 teaspoon Lawry's Lemon
   Pepper Marinade

1 tablespoon Worcestershire sauce
1/4 cup minced or finely grated
   green pepper
1 (20 oz.) can sliced pineapple (10
   slices) drained and juice reserved
8 tablespoons cheese spread

Mustard Sauce:

1 cup mayonnaise
1/4 cup Dijon-style mustard
1/4 cup reserved pineapple juice

1/8 teaspoon Lawry's Lemon
   Pepper Marinade
4 English muffins, split

Combine ground beef, water, seasoned salt, onion salt, lemon pepper marinade, Worcestershire sauce and green pepper; mix well. Shape into 16 equal sized balls and flatten into patties 1/2 inch larger than pineapple slice. Place a pineapple slice on 8 patties and place 1 tablespoon cheese spread on top of pineapple slice. Cover with remaining patties, sealing securely by pressing edges of patties together. Set aside. Prepare Mustard Sauce: Blend together mayonnaise, mustard, reserved pineapple juice and lemon pepper marinade. Brush a little on each muffin half and brown under broiler. Keep warm. Broil hamburger patties 8 inches from heat, 10 to 12 minutes or until done, turning once. Place hamburgers on prepared muffin halves and top with remaining Mustard Sauce. Garnish with broiled pineapple slices quartered. Makes 8 servings.

Won First Prize of $5,000 in the 1977 Lawry's World's Greatest Hamburger Recipe Contest.
CATHERINE BUGNITZ, FLORISSANT, MISSOURI

LAWRY'S REUBEN BURGER

1 1/2 pounds lean ground beef
1 tablespoon caraway seeds
1/2 teaspoon Lawry's Garlic Salt
1/2 teaspoon Lawry's Lemon
  Pepper Marinade
6 slices bacon

1 small onion, finely chopped
1 (16 oz.) can sauerkraut,
  well drained
6 slices Swiss cheese
12 slices rye bread

Combine ground beef, caraway seeds, garlic salt and lemon pepper marinade; mix well. Shape into 6 patties and set aside. In a skillet, fry bacon until crisp; remove and crumble. Saute onion in bacon fat until golden brown. Add sauerkraut and mix thoroughly; keep warm. Broil patties 7 minutes, turn and continue broiling 5 minutes more. Place each patty on a slice of rye bread and top with sauerkraut, crumbled bacon, a slice of cheese and another slice of bread. Makes 6 servings. Serve with your favorite condiments.

Won Second Prize of $500 in the 1977 Lawry's World's Greatest Hamburger Recipe Contest.
MRS. RITA RISHE, BRISTOL, RHODE ISLAND

LAWRY'S WORLD'S GREATEST HAMBURGER

1 pound lean ground lamb
1 1/2 teaspoon Lawry's Lemon
  Pepper Marinade
1 teaspoon ground coriander
1/2 teaspoon crushed mint flakes
8 slices French bread (1/2 inch
  thick)

1 tablespoon fresh lemon juice
1 (6 oz.) jar marinated artichoke
  hearts, drained and cut into
  small pieces
4 tomato slices
1/2 teaspoon Lawry's Garlic Salt

Combine lamb, lemon pepper marinade, coriander and mint flakes; mix well. Shape into 4 patties. Broil or grill to desired degree of doneness. For each serving, place a patty on a slice of bread; sprinkle with lemon juice and top with 1/4 of artichoke hearts and 1 slice of tomato. Sprinkle with garlic salt and top with another slice of bread. Makes 4 servings.

Won Second Prize of $500 in the 1977 Lawry's World's Greatest Hamburger Recipe Contest.
MRS. MARLENE BUCK, LITTLETON, COLORADO

PECAN BURGERS

1/4 cup Worcestershire sauce
1/2 teaspoon Lawry's Lemon
  Pepper Marinade
1 tablespoon butter or margarine
1 cup pecan pieces or halves

2 pounds lean ground beef
1 teaspoon Lawry's Seasoned Salt
12 English muffins, split and
  toasted

Combine Worcestershire sauce, lemon pepper marinade and butter in a small saucepan; heat until butter melts. Remove from heat and add pecans. Stir until pecans absorb sauce and are well coated, about 5 minutes. Mix together pecans, ground beef and seasoned salt; shape into 12 patties. Broil patties 4 inches from heat, 6 minutes. Turn and continue broiling 4 minutes for medium. Serve patties on English muffins. Makes 12 servings.

Won Second Prize of $500 in the 1977 Lawry's World's Greatest Hamburger Recipe Contest.
MR. JACK SILCOTT, LAKEWOOD, COLORADO

GOURMET OLÉ BURGERS

2 pounds lean ground beef
1 (1 1/4 oz.) package Lawry's
  Taco Seasoning Mix
1/2 cup white wine
1 teaspoon Lawry's Seasoned
  Salt
1/2 teaspoon Lawry's Seasoned
  Pepper
1 (4 oz.) can diced green chiles

1 large tomato, coarsely chopped
4 green onions, chopped, including
  tops
1 cup shredded, Cheddar
  cheese
1/2 teaspoon Lawry's Seasoned
  Salt
Shredded lettuce, optional
Sliced ripe olives, optional

In large bowl, mix together ground beef, taco seasoning mix, white wine, seasoned salt, seasoned pepper and diced green chiles. Shape into 6 large patties; let stand at least 5 minutes before cooking. Grill patties to desired degree of doneness. Meanwhile combine chopped tomato, green onion, Cheddar cheese and 1/2 teaspoon seasoned salt; toss lightly to combine. Spoon some tomato mixture over each grilled patty and press lightly on top. Return to heat, just long enough to melt cheese. Serve on buns with shredded lettuce and sliced ripe olives, if desired. Makes 6 servings.

Won Second Prize of $500 in the 1977 Lawry's World's Greatest Hamburger Recipe Contest.
MRS. LOUISE ROSS, SONORA, CALIFORNIA

LAWRY'S SEASONING/SAUCE OR GRAVY MIXES CONTEST

CHICKEN DOUBLE CHICK

6 broiler-fryer chicken legs
  with thighs attached
1 (1 oz.) package Lawry's
  Chicken Gravy Mix
1 tablespoon paprika

1 tablespoon Lawry's Lemon
  Pepper Marinade
1/3 cup corn oil
6 pieces of heavy duty foil
  large enough to cover chicken
  leg and seal edges in

Mix paprika and lemon pepper marinade with the dry Lawry's Chicken Gravy Mix. Wipe chicken legs dry with paper towel. Using pastry brush cover chicken well with corn oil, working on the foil. Sprinkle both sides of leg and thigh with chicken gravy mixture. Place each piece of chicken skin side up in center of foil. Fold edges securely sealing chicken in. Do not press foil down on top of chicken. Bake in preheated 350 degree oven 60 minutes. Remove chicken from foil. Makes 6 servings.

Won "Husband's Weight in Groceries" in the 1972 Lawry's Seasoning/ Sauce or Gravy Mixes Recipe Contest.
JEAN W. SANDERSON, LEAWOOD, KANSAS

GENERAL ELECTRIC MICROWAVE COOKING AWARD CONTEST

SHERRIED SHRIMP ROCKEFELLER

2 (10 oz.) packages frozen
chopped spinach
1 pound medium to large raw
shrimp, peeled, deveined
1 (10 1/2 oz.) can condensed
cream of shrimp soup

1 cup (4 oz.) shredded sharp
Cheddar cheese
3 tablespoons cooking sherry
2 medium slices fresh bread
3 tablespoon butter

In 10 inch square casserole or 12x8x2 inch dish place unwrapped, frozen blocks of spinach. Microwave at defrost 10 minutes. Break up blocks. Microwave at high 3 to 4 minutes more, until just completely thawed. With hands, squeeze out as much juice as possible. Spread over bottom of casserole. Distribute shrimp evenly over spinach.

In 1 quart glass measure stir together undiluted soup, cheese and sherry. Microwave at high 4 minutes, stirring after 2 minutes, until cheese is melted. Set aside while preparing crumb topping.

Break bread in tiny bits or coarsely crumb in blender. Place in small glass bowl and add butter.

Microwave at high 1 minute, stirring after 1/2 minute, until butter is distributed among crumbs. Pour hot sauce over casserole and distribute crumbs over top. Sprinkle with paprika, if desired.

Microwave at high 12 to 14 minutes, uncovered, rotating dish 1/2 turn after 5 minutes. Let stand, covered, 5 minutes before serving. Makes 4 servings.

Won $5,000 in the 1975 General Electric Microwave Cooking Award Recipe Contest.
MRS. GENE HUNGATE, STERLING, ILLINOIS

HONEY DRIZZLE CAKE

5 eggs
1/4 cup sugar
1/8 teaspoon salt
1/2 cup sugar
1 teaspoon vanilla

1 1/2 cups chopped pecans
1 1/2 cups fine vanilla wafer
  crumbs
1 1/2 teaspoons baking powder
1/2 teaspoon cinnamon

Separate eggs, placing whites into large mixer bowl and yolks into small mixer bowl. Beat egg whites, until foamy, then gradually beat in 1/4 cup sugar and salt to make a fluffy meringue.

To egg yolks add 1/2 cup sugar and vanilla. Beat until thick and pale.

Pour yolk mixture over meringue, fold together until evenly mixed. Stir together pecans, wafer crumbs, baking powder and cinnamon and sprinkle over top. Fold all ingredients together thoroughly.

Pour batter into greased 8 inch square dish. Cook in microwave oven on high 10 to 12 minutes, giving dish half turn after 5 minutes. While cake is cooking mix Honey Syrup (below). Remove cake from oven and cook syrup. Carefully pour hot syrup over hot cake. Serve warm or cold with whipped cream.

Honey Syrup: Stir together, 2 cups water, 1 1/2 cups sugar and 2/3 cup honey in 2 quart casserole. Cook syrup 5 minutes.

Makes 1 (8 inch square) cake.

Won $5,000 in the 1973 General Electric Microwave Cooking Award Recipe Contest.
ALEX ANDREA ALLARD, SAN ANTONIO, TEXAS

FIESTA CHICKEN KIEV

4 whole chicken breasts, halved,
  boned and skinned
3 tablespoons butter
3 tablespoons old English-style
  sharp cheese spread
2 teaspoons instant minced
  onion
1 teaspoon salt
1 teaspoon monosodium
  glutamate (MSG or Accent)

2 tablespoons chopped green
  chiles
1/4 cup butter, melted
1 cup crushed Cheddar cheese
  crackers
1 1/2 tablespoons taco seasoning
  mix
Shredded lettuce
Diced tomatoes
Chopped ripe olives

174

Pound each raw chicken piece with mallet or foil-covered brick to flatten. Beat together butter and cheese spread until well blended. Mix in onion, salt, monosodium g'itamate and chiles. Divide mixture equally among the 8 flattened chicken pieces, placing a portion towards one end of each piece. Roll up each piece, tucking in ends to completely enclose filling. Fasten rolls with toothpicks. Dip each roll in melted butter to cover, then coat with mixture of cheese crackers and taco seasoning mix. Arrange rolls in 12x8x2 inch dish. Cover with wax paper. Place dish in microwave oven and cook 10 to 12 minutes. Power level: High.

Serve Chicken Kiev on a bed of shredded lettuce and diced tomatoes. Top with chopped olives. If desired, serve with additional whole olives, tomato wedges and favorite taco sauce. Makes 8 servings.

Won $5,000 in the 1974 General Electric Microwave Cooking Award Recipe Contest.
JEAN W. SANDERSON, LEAWOOD, KANSAS

APRICOT-GLAZED GRAHAM CAKE

½ cup all-purpose flour
1 teaspoon baking powder
½ teaspoon baking soda
¼ teaspoon salt
1½ cups graham cracker crumbs

In a small bowl, mix together flour, baking powder, baking soda, salt and cracker crumbs. Set aside.

½ cup butter, softened
1 cup brown sugar
½ cup granulated sugar
2 eggs
1 teaspoon vanilla extract
1 cup (8 oz.) plain yogurt
1 cup walnuts, chopped

In a large mixing bowl, cream butter with brown sugar and granulated sugar; beat in eggs and vanilla until fluffy.

To beaten butter-sugar mixture, add flour mixture alternately with yogurt, mixing just to blend. Stir in nuts. Pour into greased microwave-safe 12-cup fluted tube pan. Microwave at High (10) 12 to 14 minutes, rotating ¼ turn every 3 minutes. Let stand 10 minutes before turning out.

Apricot Glaze:
¼ cup brown sugar, packed
1 tablespoon cornstarch
1 (16 oz.) can apricot halves, drained, reserving ½ cup juice
¼ cup apricot preserves or jam
2 tablespoons butter

Combine sugar and cornstarch in 1 ½ -quart glass casserole dish. Stir in reserved juice and apricot preserves. Microwave at High (10) 4 to 5 minutes; stirring after 2 minutes, until thickened. Stir in butter until melted. Slice apricot halves and arrange evenly on top of cake. Spoon apricot glaze over hot cake. Makes 10 to 12 servings.

Power Level: High (10) Microwave time: 16 to 19 Minutes, Total

Won the $10,000 Grand Prize in the 1981/1982 General Electric Microwave Cooking Contest.
MAURINE VAUGHAN, RICHMOND, VIRGINIA

TACO-FLAVORED CHICKEN PLATTER

1 package (1 ¼ oz.) taco
  seasoning mix
½ teaspoon salt

¼ teaspoon garlic powder
3 whole chicken breasts,
  boned, skinned and cut in
  quarters

In a pie plate or shallow dish, combine taco seasoning, salt and garlic powder. Coat chicken pieces with taco seasoning mixture and arrange in a 12 x 8 x 2-inch dish. Cover with plastic wrap, turning back one corner to vent. Microwave at High (10) 10 minutes, rotating dish ½ turn after 5 minutes.

*1 (16 oz.) can sliced baby
  tomatoes
1 (6 oz.) can pitted ripe olives,
  drained and sliced

¼ cup chopped green onions
1 (4 oz.) can green chilies,
  drained and chopped
¼ cup chicken broth

Arrange tomatoes, olives (reserve a few for garnish), onions and green chilies over chicken. Pour broth over all and recover with plastic wrap. Microwave at High (10) 12 to 14 minutes, rotating dish ½ turn after 6 minutes. Remove from oven and place chicken pieces on a serving platter.

2 tablespoons cornstarch

¼ cup chicken broth

Combine cornstarch and chicken broth; stir into vegetables and liquid in 12 x 8 x 2-inch dish. Microwave at High (10) 3 to 5 minutes, until thickened. Pour sauce over chicken.

1 cup (8 oz.) sour cream
1 cup (4 oz.) crushed tortilla
  chips

¼ cup shredded Cheddar
  cheese

Top with sour cream. Sprinkle with crushed tortilla chips and cheese. Garnish with reserved olive slices. Makes 4 to 6 servings.

*1 can (14½ oz.) whole tomatoes can be substituted by using only ¼ cup tomato juice and cutting the tomatoes in quarters.

Power Level: High (10)   Microwave Time: 25 to 29 Minutes, Total

Won the $5,000 Prize as Best "Meal in a Dish" in the 1981/1982 General Electric Microwave Cooking Contest.
NILA WALKER, HOUSTON, TEXAS

CAMPBELL SOUP COMPANY "CREATIVE COOKING CONTEST"

HONEY CREAM DRESSING

1 can Cheddar cheese soup
1/2 cup milk
1/2 cup sour cream

1/2 cup honey
3 cups whipped topping

In bowl blend soup, milk, sour cream and honey until smooth; chill four hours or more. Fold in whipped topping. Serve on fruit salads. Makes about 5 1/2 cups.

Won the Grand Prize of $25,000 in the 1979 Campbell Soup Company Creative Cooking Contest.
CHARLIE POULOS, KNOXVILLE, TENNESSEE

CAMPBELL SOUP COMPANY YOU HAVE A WAY WITH CAMPBELL'S CONTEST

SPINACH SALAD WITH CREAMY MUSHROOM DRESSING

1 (10 oz.) package spinach, washed and torn
12 strips bacon, crisp fried and crumbled

4 hard-cooked eggs, peeled and sliced
1 medium onion, sliced in rings
Salt and pepper

Dressing:

1 can cream of mushroom soup
1/4 cup tarragon vinegar
1 1/2 tablespoons sugar
1/4 cup water
1/4 teaspoon celery seed

1/4 teaspoon margarine
1 teaspoon dry mustard
Salt and pepper
Dash of Worcestershire

Assemble spinach, crumbled bacon, sliced eggs and onion rings in layers in large salad bowl. Salt and pepper to taste. Beat together soup, vinegar, sugar, water, celery seed, margarine, mustard, salt and pepper to taste and Worcestershire; heat, stirring until smooth. Allow to cool and pour over salad, tossing gently to coat. Serves 4 or more.

Won the Grand Prize of $20,000 in the 1978 Campbell Soup Company You Have a Way With Campbell's Contest.
KAY HERALD, CINCINNATI, OHIO

BETTER HOMES AND GARDENS®
BUSY PEOPLE'S
CONTEST

TACO SALAD PIE

1 beaten egg
1/2 cup hot taco sauce
2 cups cheese-flavored croutons, crushed
1/4 teaspoon salt
1/2 pound lean ground beef
1/2 cup sliced green onions
3 beaten eggs

1 (15 1/2 oz.) can chili beans with chili gravy
1 cup shredded Cheddar cheese (4 oz.)
Shredded lettuce
Chopped tomatoes
Dairy sour cream
Sliced pitted ripe olives

In mixing bowl combine the 1 beaten egg and the taco sauce. Stir in the croutons and salt; let stand 5 minutes or till liquid is absorbed. Add beef and 1/4 cup of the onions; mix well. Press into bottom and up sides of a 9 inch nonmetal pie plate to form a shell. In a nonmetal bowl combine the three eggs, the undrained chili beans, cheese, and remaining onion. Microcook, covered, on High power of counter-top microwave oven for 3 minutes, stirring after each minute; pour mixture into meat crust. Cook, uncovered, 12 to 13 minutes or till filling is almost set, giving dish a quarter turn every 4 minutes. Let stand 10 minutes before cutting into wedges. Top each wedge with lettuce, tomatoes, a dollop of sour cream, and olives. Makes 6 servings.

Won $250 in the 1979 Better Homes and Gardens® Busy People's Recipe Contest.
JEAN W. SANDERSON, LEAWOOD, KANSAS

VENTURE-MOULINEX LaMACHINE FAVORITE RECIPE CONTEST

SAUCY SOLE SUPREME

2 pounds fillet of sole
1 tablespoon butter or
   margarine
1/2 teaspoon salt
8 ounces fresh mushrooms, sliced

1 (14 oz.) can artichoke hearts,
   quartered
Eggplant Sauce
Lemon slices
Parsley sprigs

Dot fish with butter. Sprinkle with salt. Place fish in 12x8x2 inch baking dish. Pour water into dish and cover with foil. To poach; bake in 400 degree oven 5 to 10 minutes. Drain off liquid. Sprinkle mushroom slices and 1/2 of artichoke heart pieces over fish. Pour Eggplant Sauce over all and top with remaining artichoke pieces. Bake covered for 20 minutes; uncover and bake an additional 5 minutes. Garnish with lemon slices and parsley. Serves 6.

Eggplant Sauce:

1 (16 oz.) can tomatoes with
   juice
1 (8 oz.) can tomato sauce
1 cup eggplant, peeled and coarsely
   chopped
1/2 cup chopped onions
1/2 cup finely chopped celery
1/4 cup dry white wine

2 tablespoons chopped parsley
1 tablespoon Worcestershire
   sauce
2 teaspoons sugar
1 teaspoon basil
1/2 teaspoon oregano

Combine all ingredients in a large saucepan. Bring to a boil, reduce heat and simmer 40 minutes or until thickened.

Won the Grand Prize of an 8-day trip for two to Paris, France and $1,000 cash in the Venture - MOULINEX ® La Machine Favorite Recipe Contest. JEAN W. SANDERSON, LEAWOOD, KANSAS

WOMAN'S DAY®
JAMES BEARD CREATIVE
COOKERY CONTEST

ITALIAN ONION DELIGHT

3/4 cup WISH-BONE® Italian
  Dressing
6 medium onions (6 cups
  sliced)

1/4 teaspoon oregano
1/3 cup grated Parmesan
  cheese

Slice onions and separate into rings. Heat 1/2 cup salad dressing and oregano in large fry pan. Add onions and saute until transparent. Pour remaining 1/4 cup salad dressing over onions and stir. Sprinkle cheese over top and serve at once. Makes 6 to 8 servings.

Won Second Prize of Ten Piece Revere Limited Edition Buffet Service in the 1977 Woman's Day® James Beard Creative Cookery Recipe Contest. JEAN W. SANDERSON, LEAWOOD, KANSAS

THE GREAT JELL-O® BRAND RECIPE SWAP

MOLDED SANGRIA

1 cup sectioned navel oranges,
  peeled
1/2 cup very thinly sliced tart
  apples, peeled and cored
1/4 cup brandy
1 tablespoon Cointreau
2 cups dry red wine

3 whole cloves
1 cinnamon stick
1 (6 oz.) package Jell-O® Brand
  Lemon Gelatin
Juice of 1 lime
1 (12 oz.) bottle club soda,
  chilled

Marinate orange sections and apple slices in brandy and Cointreau for 30 minutes at room temperature. Bring wine, cloves, and cinnamon to a boil. Strain to remove spices, pour wine over gelatin, and stir until dissolved. Add lime juice and chilled soda. Chill until slightly thickened. Stir in fruit and marinade. Spoon into sherbet glasses. Chill until firm. Makes 5 1/4 cups or 8 to 10 servings.

Won the Grand Prize of $25,000 in the 1972 Great Jell-O® Brand Gelatin Recipe Swap Contest. Recipe reproduced courtesy of General Foods Corporation, owner of the registered trademark JELL-O.
MRS. VIRGINIA T. SMITH, LOS ANGELES, CALIFORNIA

COUNTRY STAND FRESH MUSHROOM CONTEST

POPOVER MUSHROOM PIZZA BAKE

Base:

1 pound ground beef
1 pound COUNTRY STAND
Fresh Mushrooms, sliced
½ cup chopped green pepper
½ cup chopped onion

1 can (10½ oz.) pizza sauce
with cheese
1 teaspoon oregano, crushed
1 teaspoon garlic salt
1½ cups (6 oz.) shredded
Mozzarella cheese

Popover Top:

2 eggs
1 cup milk
1 tablespoon vegetable oil

1 cup all-purpose flour*
½ teaspoon salt
½ cup grated Parmesan cheese
½ cup thinly sliced ripe pitted
olives

Preheat oven to 400°. Prepare Base. In large skillet or Dutch oven cook and stir ground beef, mushrooms, green pepper and onion until meat is browned. Thoroughly drain off fat. Stir in pizza sauce, oregano and garlic salt. Simmer 10 minutes.

Meanwhile prepare Popover Top. In small bowl of electric mixer, blend together eggs, milk and oil. Add flour and salt. Beat at medium speed about 1½ minutes or until smooth. Do not overbeat.

Spoon hot beef mixture into shallow 2-quart baking dish. Sprinkle with Mozzarella cheese. Pour Top evenly over base. Sprinkle with Parmesan cheese and olives. Bake about 30 minutes or until puffy and golden brown. Garnish with tomato wedges if desired. Serve immediately. Makes 6-8 servings.

*Stir flour; then spoon into measuring cup.

Won Second Prize of Free Grocery Money for 1 Year ($50 a week) in the 1979 Country Stand Fresh Mushroom Recipe Contest sponsored by Ralston Purina Company.
MRS. RODNEY BATHKE, WELLS, MINNESOTA

SWEET 'N SOUR MUSHROOMS

Mushrooms:
1 egg, beaten
2 tablespoons all-purpose flour

½ teaspoon salt
1 pound COUNTRY STAND
　Fresh Mushrooms

Stir-Fry:
1 can (8 oz.) chunk pineapple in
　unsweetened pineapple juice
3 tablespoons cornstarch
¾ cup sugar
⅓ cup cider vinegar
¼ cup soy sauce
1 tablespoon catsup

2 tablespoons vegetable oil
2 small cloves garlic, minced
2 small onions, quartered and
　separated
2 carrots, peeled and thinly
　sliced
1 medium-size green pepper,
　cut into ½-inch pieces
Hot cooked rice

To Prepare Mushrooms: In small bowl beat together egg, flour and salt. Coat mushrooms very lightly. Fry in deep hot fat (360°) 2-3 minutes or until lightly browned. Drain on absorbent paper. Keep warm.

To Prepare Stir-Fry: Drain pineapple. Add enough water to juice to make ⅔ cup. Remove ¼ cup and combine with cornstarch. Set aside. To remaining juice add sugar, vinegar, soy sauce and catsup. Set aside.

Heat oil in large heavy skillet or wok. Stir-fry garlic, onion and carrots 2 minutes. Add sugar mixture. Bring to boiling. Gradually stir in cornstarch mixture. Continue to cook, stirring constantly, until thickened and bubbly. Stir in mushrooms, pineapple chunks and green pepper. Heat through (about 5 minutes), stirring occasionally. Serve over rice. Makes 4 servings.

Won the Grand Prize of Free Grocery Money for 3 Years ($50 a week) in the 1979 Country Stand Fresh Mushroom Recipe Contest Sponsored by Ralston Purina Company.
CATHLINE INGRAM, NORTHEAST HARBOR, MAINE

SAUCY MUSHROOMS
Especially good with steaks or hamburgers

2 tablespoons bottled oyster
　sauce
2 tablespoons dry sherry
2 teaspoons soy sauce
½ teaspoon sugar

4 tablespoons butter or
　margarine
1 pound small COUNTRY
　STAND Fresh Mushrooms
¼ cup finely chopped onion

Combine first 4 ingredients. Set aside. In large skillet heat butter over medium-high heat until sizzling. Add mushrooms and onion. Cook about 10 minutes or until liquid has evaporated and mushrooms and onion begin to turn golden brown around edges. Reduce heat to medium. Add oyster sauce mixture. Cook and stir 1-2 minutes or until mushrooms are glossy and sauce thickens. Makes about 2 cups.

Won Second Prize of Free Grocery Money for 1 Year ($50 a week) in the 1979 Country Stand Fresh Mushroom Recipe Contest sponsored by Ralston Purina Company.
JANE K. McGUIRT, WILMINGTON, NORTH CAROLINA

SUPER BRUNCH

½ pound **COUNTRY STAND Fresh Mushrooms, sliced**
2 tablespoons butter or margarine
2 tablespoons cornstarch
½ teaspoon salt
1⅓ cups milk
1 can (8 oz.) asparagus cuts, drained

4 eggs, poached
2 English muffins, split, toasted and buttered
½ cup mayonnaise
¼ cup dairy sour cream
⅛ teaspoon ground turmeric
Paprika

In large skillet saute mushrooms in butter 5-10 minutes or until liquid has evaporated. Stir in cornstarch and salt until completely mixed. Slowly stir in milk. Add asparagus. Heat until sauce just comes to a boil and is thickened. Stir occasionally.

Meanwhile, place a poached egg on each muffin half on a heatproof platter or in individual casseroles. Spoon ¼ mushroom sauce over each.

Blend mayonnaise, sour cream and turmeric. Spread over sauce. Sprinkle with paprika. Broil 5-7 minutes or until top is bubbly and lightly browned. Makes 4 servings.

Won First Prize of Free Grocery Money for 2 Years ($50 a week) in the 1979 Country Stand Fresh Mushroom Recipe Contest sponsored by Ralston Purina Company.
MABEL HAUGEN, BELOIT, WISCONSIN

KRAFT MARSHMALLOW CREME "SECRET INGREDIENT" CONTEST

CAPPUCCINO CANDY

2 cups sugar
½ cup PARKAY margarine
1 cup evaporated milk
1 (12 oz.) pkg. semi-sweet
 chocolate pieces
1 (7 oz.) jar KRAFT
 Marshmallow Creme
1 cup chopped nuts

1 tablespoon grated orange
 rind
1 tablespoon instant coffee
 granules
2 teaspoons orange flavoring
 or orange juice
2 teaspoons brandy flavoring

Combine sugar, margarine and milk in heavy 2½-quart saucepan. Bring to full rolling boil, stirring constantly. Continue boiling 10 minutes, stirring constantly to prevent scorching. Remove from heat; stir in chocolate pieces until melted. Add marshmallow creme, nuts, orange rind, instant coffee and flavorings; beat until well blended. Pour into greased 13 x 9-inch baking pan. Cool at room temperature; cut into squares. Makes 3 pounds.

Won First Prize of $1,000 in the 1980 Kraft Marshmallow Creme "Secret Ingredient" Recipe Contest — "Candies, Frostings and Other Treats" Category.
GLORIA WARD, YUMA, ARIZONA

APPLENUT CHESS PIE

1 (7 oz.) jar KRAFT
 Marshmallow Creme
2 teaspoons vanilla
2 teaspoons lemon juice
3 eggs, beaten
2 tablespoons PARKAY
 Margarine, melted
1 cup peeled, finely shredded
 apples

¾ cup packed brown sugar
¾ cup chopped walnuts
2 tablespoons flour
1 (9 inch) unbaked pie shell
Ginger Creme Topping

Combine marshmallow creme, vanilla and lemon juice, mixing with wire whisk until well blended. Add eggs and margarine; mix well. Stir in combined apples, sugar and nuts; pour into pastry shell. Bake at 425°, 10 minutes. Reduce heat to 350°; continue baking 45 minutes or until top is firm. Serve with:

Ginger Creme Topping:

1 cup dairy sour cream
½ teaspoon ground ginger

1 (7 oz.) jar KRAFT
Marshmallow Creme

Add combined sour cream and ginger to marshmallow creme, mixing with wire whisk until well blended. Makes 2 cups.

Apples can also be shredded or chopped in food processor.

Won the Grand Prize of $5,000 in the 1980 Kraft Marshmallow Creme "Secret Ingredient" Recipe Contest.
BETTY ROCKWELL, ENCINITAS, CALIFORNIA

LEMON CREME DIP

1 cup KRAFT Marshmallow
Creme
1 cup KRAFT Real Mayonnaise
or LIGHT 'N LIVELY Reduced
Calorie Mayonnaise

½ cup KRAFT Lemon & Spice
Dressing
Assorted fruit

Combine marshmallow creme and mayonnaise, mixing with wire whisk until well blended. Add dressing; mix well. Chill. Serve over fruit; garnish as desired. Makes 2 ½ cups.

Variation: Substitute ½ cup KRAFT Oil and Vinegar Dressing, 1 tablespoon lemon juice and ¼ teaspoon grated lemon rind for KRAFT Lemon & Spice Dressing.

Won First Prize of $1,000 in the 1980 Kraft Marshmallow Creme "Secret Ingredient" Recipe Contest — "Dips/Sauces/Beverages" Category.
MILDRED KLEIN, FOUNTAIN VALLEY, CALIFORNIA

RAZZLE DAZZLE RASPBERRY PIE

1 (7 oz.) jar KRAFT
  Marshmallow Creme
1 cup raspberry sherbet
1 (8 oz.) container raspberry
  yogurt

½ cup chopped toasted
  almonds
2 cups frozen whipped topping,
  thawed
1 baked 9-inch pastry shell

Combine marshmallow creme and softened sherbet, mixing with wire whisk until blended. Stir in yogurt and nuts. Fold in whipped topping. Pour into pastry shell; freeze until firm. Garnish as desired.

Won First Prize of $1,000 in the 1980 Kraft Marshmallow Creme "Secret Ingredient" Recipe Contest — "Frozen/Chilled Desserts" Category.
MARILEE WHEATON, NORTHRIDGE, CALIFORNIA

MOLLY'S APPLE CREME PIE

1 (20 oz.) can pie sliced apples
1 unbaked (9 inch) pastry shell
1 cup KRAFT Marshmallow
  Creme

1 tablespoon grated lemon rind
1 teaspoon lemon juice
1 cup raisins

Drain apples, reserving 1 tablespoon liquid. Arrange apples in pastry shell. Combine marshmallow creme, reserved liquid, lemon rind and juice; mixing with wire whisk until well blended. Add raisins; mix well. Spread marshmallow creme mixture over apples.

¼ cup flour
2 tablespoons packed brown
  sugar

¼ teaspoon cinnamon
2 tablespoons PARKAY
  margarine

Combine flour, brown sugar and cinnamon; cut in margarine until mixture resembles coarse crumbs. Sprinkle over marshmallow creme mixture. Bake at 375°, 40 minutes.

Variation: Substitute 3 cups fresh apple slices for 20 ounce can pie sliced apples and 1 tablespoon water for reserved liquid.

Won First Prize of $1,000 in the 1980 Kraft Marshmallow Creme "Secret Ingredient" Recipe Contest — Baked Desserts Category.
ROSE TUBIN, WEST PALM BEACH, FLORIDA

KRAFT MARSHMALLOW CREME "EASY SECRET INGREDIENT" CONTEST

PEANUT BUTTER AND JELLY CREME PIE

1 ½ cups chocolate wafer
  crumbs

¼ cup PARKAY margarine,
  melted

Combine crumbs and margarine; press onto bottom and sides of 9-inch pie plate. Chill.

1 (7 oz.) jar KRAFT
  Marshmallow Creme
¼ cup milk
¼ cup chunk style peanut
  butter

2 cups whipping cream,
  whipped
½ cup Kraft grape jelly
1 tablespoon chopped peanuts

Combine marshmallow creme and milk, mixing with electric mixer or wire whisk until well blended. Add peanut butter; mix well. Fold in whipped cream. Spread jelly on bottom of crust. Pour marshmallow creme mixture over jelly; sprinkle with peanuts. Freeze until firm.

Won First Prize of $1,000 in the 1981 Kraft Marshmallow Creme "Easy Secret Ingredient" Recipe Contest — "Easy Recipe for Kids" Category.
JAN HILL, SACRAMENTO, CALIFORNIA

PINA COLADA PARTY PIE

2 cups flaked coconut

¼ cup PARKAY margarine,
  melted

Combine coconut and margarine; press onto bottom and sides of 9-inch pie plate. Bake at 350°, 15 minutes. Cool.

1 (6 oz.) can frozen pineapple
  juice concentrate, thawed
2 tablespoons rum

1 (7 oz.) jar KRAFT
  Marshmallow Creme
1 cup whipping cream,
  whipped

Gradually add pineapple juice and rum to marshmallow creme, mixing with electric mixer or wire whisk until well blended. Fold in whipped cream; pour into crust. Freeze until firm. Garnish with pineapple or cherries, if desired.

Variation: Substitute 1 teaspoon rum flavoring for 2 tablespoons rum.

Won First Prize of $1,000 in the 1981 Kraft Marshmallow Creme "Easy Secret Ingredient" Recipe Contest — "Start with a Convenience Product" Category.
MRS. VINCENT DOWLING, TACOMA, WASHINGTON

FROST-ON-THE-PUMPKIN PIE

1 ¼ cups graham cracker
  crumbs
¼ cup sugar

¼ cup PARKAY margarine,
  melted

Combine crumbs, sugar and margarine; reserve 2 tablespoons. Press remaining crumb mixture onto bottom and sides of 9-inch pie plate. Bake at 375°, 8 minutes. Cool.

1 (8 oz.) container pineapple-
  orange flavored yogurt
1 (7 oz.) jar KRAFT
  Marshmallow Creme
1 cup canned pumpkin

¼ cup sifted confectioners'
  sugar
½ teaspoon pumpkin pie spice
1 (8 oz.) container frozen
  whipped topping, thawed

Combine remaining ingredients except whipped topping, mixing with electric mixer or wire whisk until well blended. Fold in 1 ½ cups whipped topping; pour into crust. Spread remaining topping over pie; sprinkle with reserved crumbs. Freeze until firm.

Won First Prize of $1,000 in the 1981 Kraft Marshmallow Creme "Easy Secret Ingredient" Recipe Contest — "Special Occasion Dishes" Category.
MRS. MADELLA BATHKE, WELLS, MINNESOTA

WALMALLOW CREME PIE

2 (7 oz.) jars KRAFT
  Marshmallow Creme
3 eggs, slightly beaten
½ cup PARKAY margarine

2 tablespoons lemon juice
1 ½ cups chopped walnuts
1 (9 inch) baked graham
  cracker crust
2 cups whipped topping

In 2-quart saucepan, combine marshmallow creme, eggs, margarine, juice and nuts. Cook over low heat, stirring constantly, until mixture darkens and thickens. Pour into crust; chill several hours or overnight. Spread with whipped topping before serving. Garnish with walnut halves, if desired.

Variation: Substitute 1 cup whipping cream, whipped for whipped topping.

Microwave: Microwave margarine in 2-quart bowl on High 1 minute or until melted. Add marshmallow creme; microwave 1 minute. Add eggs, juice and nuts; mix well. Microwave 4 minutes; mix well. Continue microwaving 2 to 5 minutes or until mixture darkens and thickens, mixing well every 2 minutes. Continue as directed.

Won First Prize of $1,000 in the 1981 Kraft Marshmallow Creme "Easy Secret Ingredient" Recipe Contest — "Make-Ahead Desserts" Category.
HARRIET MASON, WALNUT CREEK, CALIFORNIA

CREMEDOODLES

1 (7 oz.) jar KRAFT
  Marshmallow Creme
1 cup peanut butter
½ cup honey

2 (1.5 oz.) chocolate bars,
  crumbled
1 ½ cups raisins
1 cup chopped walnuts
2 cups shredded coconut

Combine marshmallow creme, peanut butter and honey, mixing with electric mixer or wire whisk until well blended. Add chocolate, raisins and nuts; mix well. Shape rounded teaspoonfuls of mixture into 1-inch balls; roll in coconut. Chill or freeze. Makes 6 dozen.

Won the Grand Prize of $5,000 in the 1981 Kraft Marshmallow Creme "Easy Secret Ingredient" Recipe Contest — "Easy Recipe for Kids" Category.
HILDA BORRI, MARK, ILLINOIS

PLANTERS OIL GREAT CUISINES OF THE WORLD CONTEST

TORTILLA SUNRISE

½ pound ground beef
¼ cup finely chopped onions
2 tablespoons minced fresh parsley
2 tablespoons minced fresh cilantro (optional)
2 tablespoons minced fresh mushrooms
½ teaspoon jalapeno salsa (or ⅛ teaspoon hot pepper sauce)

½ teaspoon salt
¼ teaspoon fresh ground black pepper
6 tablespoons Planters Peanut Oil
2 tablespoons grated Parmesan cheese
8 (8 inch) flour tortillas
5 small eggs
1 tablespoon milk
1 lemon or lime, quartered
Parsley sprigs

In a small bowl combine ground beef, onions, parsley, cilantro, mushrooms, salsa, salt and pepper. Blend well.

Heat 2 tablespoons Planters Peanut Oil in a large skillet over medium heat. Add meat mixture; break up as it cooks until no longer pink and mixture is a fine even texture. Drain well. Cool slightly. Stir in Parmesan cheese.

Spoon ¼ meat mixture in the center of one flour tortilla. Form a depression in the middle of meat. Carefully break and slip 1 egg into depression. Brush the edges of filled tortilla and another unfilled tortilla with a mixture of 1 egg beaten with 1 tablespoon milk, rubbing the outside edges of tortillas until they become very sticky. Invert unfilled tortilla over filled one and firmly press edges together, crimping with a fork to seal. Repeat with remaining tortillas and filling.

Heat ¼ cup Planters Peanut Oil in a large skillet over medium heat. Fry espinadas, one at a time, 7 to 8 minutes, turning once. Drain. Keep warm while cooking remaining espinadas. Garnish with lemon and parsley sprigs to serve. Makes 4 servings.

Won the Grand Prize of 18 Day Around The World Trip for 2 or $18,000 Cash, in the 1981 Planters® Oil, A Division of Standard Brands, Inc. Recipe Contest.   HARRY A. PETERSON, TEMPLE CITY, CALIFORNIA

WORLD'S CHAMPIONSHIP CHILI COOK-OFF CONTEST

RENO RED

3 pound round steak, coarsely ground

3 pound chuck steak, coarsely ground

1 cup Wesson oil or kidney suet

1 (3 oz.) bottle of Gebhart chili powder

6 tablespoons cumin

2 tablespoons MSG

6 small cloves garlic, minced

2 medium onions, chopped

6 dried chili pods, remove stems and seeds and boil 30 minutes in water (or 3 oz. bottle New Mexico chili pepper)

1 tablespoon oregano, brewed in ½ cup Budweiser beer (like tea)

2 tablespoons paprika

2 tablespoons cider vinegar

3 cups beef broth

1 (4 oz.) can diced Ortega green chiles

½ (14½ oz.) can Hunt's stewed tomatoes (or to taste)

1 teaspoon Tabasco (or add to taste)

2 tablespoons masa flour

Brown meat in Wesson oil or kidney suet, adding black pepper to taste. Drain meat and add chili powder, cumin, MSG, garlic and chopped onions. Cook 30–45 minutes using as little liquid as possible; add water only as necessary. Stir often.

Remove skins from boiled pods, mash pulp and add to meat mixture (or add 3 ounces New Mexico chili pepper), strained oregano and beer mixture, paprika, vinegar, 2 cups of beef broth, Ortega green chiles, Hunt's stewed tomatoes and Tabasco sauce. Simmer 30–45 minutes. Stir often.

Dissolve masa flour into remaining beef broth, pour into chili. Simmer 30 minutes, stirring often.

Won the Grand Prize of $20,000 in the 1979 International Chili Society® World's Championship Chili Cook-Off.
JOE AND SHIRLEY STEWART, MENLO PARK, CALIFORNIA

"BUTTERFIELD STAGELINE"

5 pounds beef brisket (cubed small)
1 pound ground fresh lean pork
2 large onions, chopped fine
5 cloves garlic, minced fine
½ can Ortega chilies (7 oz.)
2 cans Hunt's Tomato Sauce (8 oz.)
1 cube Wyler's Beef bouillon
1 (8 oz.) can Budweiser
½ ounce Montezuma Tequila

2½ cups water
13 tablespoons Gebhardt's chili powder
5 tablespoons ground cumin
¼ teaspoon dry mustard
¼ teaspoon MSG
1½ teaspoon brown sugar
Pinch of oregano
Salt and pepper to taste
4 tablespoons Wesson Oil

Cook in large covered pot (iron preferably) or Crock-pot.

1. In pot, simmer beer, tequila, tomato sauce, bouillon cube, water, garlic, Ortega chilies, and all dry ingredients.

2. Brown separately beef, pork and onions in oil. Add salt and pepper to taste.

3. Add to pot.

4. Cover and simmer for at least three (3) hours, stirring frequently.

Serves 8-10 (8 ounce) servings.

Won the Grand Prize of $20,000 in the 1981 International Chili Society® World's Championship Chili Cook-Off.
FRED DREXEL, VAN NUYS, CALIFORNIA

NEVADA ANNIE'S CHAMPION CHILI

3 medium onions
2 medium green peppers
2 large stalks celery
2 small cloves garlic
½ (or more) small, fresh jalapeno pepper, diced
8 pounds lean chuck, coarsely ground
1 (7 oz.) can diced green chilies
2 (14½ oz.) cans stewed tomatoes

1 (15 oz.) can tomato sauce
1 (6 oz.) can tomato paste
2 (3 oz.) bottles chili powder
2 tablespoons cumin
Tabasco sauce to taste
1 (12 oz.) can beer, divided in two portions
1 (12 oz.) bottle mineral water
2 or 3 bay leaves
Garlic salt to taste
Salt and pepper to taste

Dice and saute the first 5 ingredients. Add the meat and brown it. Add the remaining ingredients, including ½ can beer (drink the remainder, says Annie). Add water just to cover the top of the mixture. Cook about three hours on low heat, stirring often. Makes 24 or more servings.

Won the Grand Prize of $15,000 in the 1978 International Chili Society® World's Championship Chili Cook-Off.
LAVERNE "NEVADA ANNIE" HARRIS, LAS VEGAS, NEVADA

"CAPITOL PUNISHMENT"

1 tablespoon oregano
2 tablespoons paprika
2 tablespoons MSG
9 tablespoons chili powder (light)
4 tablespoons cumin
4 tablespoons beef bouillon (instant crushed)
2 cans Budweiser Beer
2 cups water
4 pounds extra lean chuck (chili ground)
2 pounds extra lean pork (chili ground)
1 pound extra lean chuck (cut in ¼ inch cubes)

2 large onions (finely chopped)
10 cloves garlic (finely chopped)
½ cup Wesson Oil or kidney suet
1 teaspoon mole (powdered)
1 tablespoon sugar
1 teaspoon coriander
1 teaspoon Louisiana RedHot! Sauce (Durkee)
1 (8 oz.) can Hunt's Tomato Sauce
1 tablespoon Masa Harina flour
Salt to taste

In a large pot add paprika, oregano, MSG, chili powder, cumin, beef bouillon, Budweiser Beer and two cups water. Let simmer. In a separate skillet brown 1½ pounds meat with 1 tablespoon Wesson Oil or kidney suet until meat is light brown. Drain and add to simmering spices. Continue until all meat has been added.

Saute finely chopped onions and garlic in 1 tablespoon Wesson Oil or kidney suet. Add to spices and meat mixture. Add water as needed. Simmer 2 hours. Add mole, sugar, coriander, Louisiana RedHot! Sauce and Hunt's Tomato Sauce. Simmer 45 minutes.

Dissolve Masa Harina flour in warm water (pasty) and add to chili. Add salt to taste. Simmer 30 minutes. (For hotter chili, add additional Louisiana RedHot! Sauce to taste.)

Won the Grand Prize of $20,000 in the 1980 International Chili Society® World's Championship Chili Cook-Off.
BILL PFEIFFER, SAN ANTONIO, TEXAS

"LIPTON SOUP MIX MICROWAVE MAGIC RECIPE CONTEST"

CARROT MEATLOAF

1 envelope Lipton Onion Soup
  Mix
2 pounds ground beef
½ pound ground pork
2 cups shredded carrots

1 cup dry bread crumbs
½ cup milk
3 eggs
Meatloaf Glaze*

In large bowl, combine all ingredients except Meatloaf Glaze. In 9-inch glass pie plate, shape into ring. Heat covered on High (Full Power) 15 minutes**, draining and turning pie plate twice. Let stand covered 5 minutes. Top with ½ Meatloaf Glaze; serve with remaining. Makes about 10 servings.

*Meatloaf Glaze:
Combine -
½ cup catsup

¼ cup brown sugar
2 teaspoons Dijon-style
  mustard

Heat at High (Full Power) 1 minute.

**Or, set temperature probe to 170°F.

Won First Prize of $1,000 in the 1981 Lipton Soup Mix Microwave Magic Recipe Contest.
JANE CALABRASE, SUN CITY WEST, ARIZONA

"HEUBLEIN INC. A.1. GROUND BEEF RECIPE CONTEST"

BEEFBROSIA A.1. - BOBS

1 pound lean ground chuck
3 tablespoons A.1. Steak
  Sauce
½ teaspoon salt
1 egg, beaten
½ cup finely chopped green
  pepper
¼ cup minced onion
1 cup corn flake crumbs

1 egg, beaten
1 tablespoon A.1. Steak Sauce
1 cup flaked coconut
1 can (20 ounce) pineapple
  chunks, drained (reserve
  ½ cup juice)
6 wooden meat skewers
½ cup Mandarin orange
  sections, drained
Fresh mint sprigs, if desired

Line 13 x 9 inch baking pan with foil. Set aside. Combine first 7 ingredients. Shape mixture into 6 (4 x 5 inch) patties. In shallow dish, combine 1 beaten egg and 1 tablespoon A.1. Spread coconut on wax paper. Thread 6 pineapple chunks on each meat skewer. Roll in beaten egg mixture. Roll in coconut. Wrap with meat patty. Mold meat to completely encase pineapple. Place on baking pan. Bake in preheated 350°F. oven 20 to 25 minutes or until lightly browned. Meanwhile, in small saucepan, combine reserved ½ cup pineapple juice, remaining beaten egg mixture, coconut, pineapple chunks and oranges. Heat slowly. Keep warm until serving time. Place meatrolls on warm platter. Remove skewers. Spoon sauce over and around meatrolls. Garnish with mint, if desired. Makes 6 servings.

Won First Prize of $10,000 in the 1980 A.1. Steak Sauce Ground Beef Recipe Contest.
MRS. DOROTHY G. KENT, NEW PORT RICHEY, FLORIDA

FRENCH'S SAUCE, GRAVY, OR SEASONING MIXES CONTEST

SHRIMPLY CHICKENCHANTING

1 pint dairy sour cream
1 envelope French's Gravy Mix
  for Chicken
¼ teaspoon salt
6 chicken breast halves
¾ cup corn flake crumbs

¼ cup butter or margarine
1 cup cooked or canned
  shrimp, coarsley chopped
¼ cup chopped ripe olives
2 tablespoons diced pimientos

Combine sour cream, gravy mix and salt; divide in half and refrigerate one half. Coat chicken with remaining sour cream mixture, then roll in crumbs. Melt butter in shallow baking pan; arrange chicken skin side down, in pan. Bake at 350° for 45 minutes. Turn; bake 20 minutes longer, or until tender and brown. Add shrimp, olives and pimientos to refrigerated sour cream. Heat slowly; do not boil. Serve sauce over chicken. Makes 6 servings.

Won the Grand Prize of a $15,000 New Kitchen in the 1981 French's Sauce, Gravy, or Seasoning Mixes Recipe Contest.
ELLA MARGARET McCALL, PORTLAND, OREGON

"WEIGHT WATCHERS MAGAZINE ANNUAL READER RECIPE CONTEST"

FLORENTINE ROLL

2 cups frozen chopped spinach,
  thawed and drained
2 eggs
⅔ cup part-skim Ricotta
  cheese
1 tablespoon dehydrated onion
  flakes
¼ teaspoon salt

¼ teaspoon imitation butter
  flavoring
½ cup tomato sauce
½ teaspoon lemon juice
¼ teaspoon chopped fresh
  parsley
⅛ teaspoon ground nutmeg

In a blender container, combine spinach and eggs; process until pureed. Spread mixture evenly over a 9 x 13 inch area of a 10½ x 15½ inch nonstick jelly roll pan. Be sure that surface is smooth and edges straight. Bake at 350°F. about 20-30 minutes or until mixture is set but not dry. In a bowl, blend next 4 ingredients. Spread cheese mixture evenly over hot baked spinach. Beginning at the narrow end, roll up to enclose filling. Place roll on a nonstick baking sheet and return to oven for 15 minutes. In a small saucepan, combine remaining ingredients; bring to a boil. Reduce heat and cook about 10 minutes or until sauce is slightly thickened. Serve ½ of the roll with ½ of the sauce. Makes 2 servings (MdE) Each equivalent to: 2 serv veg, 1 egg, ⅓ c. SC, ½ Bns. Per serving: 265 cal, 22 g. pro, 13 g fat, 18 g car, 858 mg sod. (Nutritional value for imitation butter flavoring is not available and is not reflected in this figure.)

Won Second Prize Regal® Ware Seal-O-Matic® Cookware Set in the 13th Annual Weight Watchers® Magazine Reader Recipe Contest.
RUTH ROHLFING, RACINE, WISCONSIN

POWERHOUSE PIZZA

4½ ounces precooked smoked beef sausage, sliced ⅛ inch slices
2 cups cooked enriched rice
2 eggs, beaten
1 ounce Colby cheese, grated
½ teaspoon salt
2 cups tomato sauce
1 tablespoon enriched all-purpose flour

1 teaspoon Worcestershire sauce (optional)
1 garlic clove, crushed
½ teaspoon each oregano leaves and onion salt
⅛ teaspoon pepper
1 cup each sliced mushrooms and tomato slices
½ cup thinly sliced onion
½ cup sliced green bell pepper
2 ounces Mozzarella cheese, grated

Broil sausage slices on a rack in a pan, 4 inches from source of heat, until lightly browned. Set aside on paper towels. In a bowl, combine rice, eggs, Colby cheese and salt; spread mixture evenly in a 12 inch pizza pan or 9 x 13 inch shallow baking dish. Bake at 450°F. about 7-8 minutes or until crust is slightly firm. In a saucepan, combine tomato sauce and flour, stirring until smooth. Add next 4 ingredients and simmer, stirring 5 minutes. Spread sauce mixture evenly over baked crust; top evenly with sausage slices and vegetables and sprinkle with cheese. Bake for 10 minutes longer or until pie is thoroughly hot and cheese is melted. Cool slightly before cutting. Makes 4 servings (MdE) Each equivalent to: 1⅛ oz. MG (cured), 1 Brds, ½ egg, ¾ oz. HC, 1 Bns, ¾ X, 1¼ ser veg, 2 T LV. Per serving: 371 cal. 18 g pro, 17 g fat, 38 g car, 1652 mg sod.

Won Third Prize of Stationary Bicycle Exerciser in the 13th Annual Weight Watchers® Magazine Reader Recipe Contest.
TAMIA KARPELES, MILLERSVILLE, MARYLAND

CREAM OF PEANUT SOUP

2 teaspoons reduced-calorie margarine
2 tablespoons finely chopped celery
2 tablespoons chopped onion
2 teaspoons enriched all-purpose flour
1 cup water

1 packet instant chicken broth and seasoning mix
3 tablespoons smooth peanut butter
¼ cup evaporated skimmed milk
Celery ribs with leaves to garnish (optional)

In a saucepan, melt margarine over low heat; add celery and onion and cook until tender but not brown. Add flour and stir until mixture is smooth; add water gradually, stirring constantly. Add broth mix and bring to a boil; blend in peanut butter. Simmer for 5 minutes; add milk and serve at once. Garnish with celery ribs and leaves if desired. Makes 1 serving. (MdE) Equivalent to: 1 fat, ¼ ser veg, 2 T LV, 3 X, 3 T PB (omit 2 fats), ½ milk. Per serving: 402 cal, 20 g pro, 28 g fat, 24 g car, 1313 mg sod.

Won Fifth Prize of a Maxim® 3 Convection Oven in the 13th Annual Weight Watchers® Magazine Reader Recipe Contest.
JOANNA I. RINEHART, CHESAPEAKE, VIRGINIA

CLAM CURRY

1 tablespoon + 1 teaspoon reduced-calorie margarine
½ cup chopped leek
¼ cup sliced mushrooms
1 tablespoon chopped scallion
1 ½ teaspoons MSG (optional)
1 teaspoon curry powder
¼ teaspoon pepper

2 tablespoons enriched all-purpose flour
¼ cup clam juice
8 ounces drained canned minced clams
1 cup plain unflavored yogurt
1 cup cooked enriched spinach noodles, hot

In a medium saucepan, heat margarine. Add leek, mushrooms and scallion and cook until soft. Stir in MSG if desired, curry powder, pepper and flour; combine well. Stir in clam juice. Cook, stirring, over medium heat until mixture thickens; remove from heat. Stir in clams and yogurt; cook over low heat just until heated through. Serve each portion of clam mixture over ½ cup noodles. Makes 2 servings. (MdE) Each equivalent to: 1 fat, ¼ c + 1 ½ t LV, ¼ serv veg, ⅛ Bns, 4 oz. fish, 1 milk, 1 Brd. S. Per serving: 383 cal, 28 g pro, 12 g fat, 40 g car, 408 mg sod.

Won the Grand Prize of a Tappan® Convectionaire Oven in the 13th Annual Weight Watchers® Magazine Reader Recipe Contest.
MARY KAY GARCIA, LEWISVILLE, TEXAS

CHOCOLATE CHIFFON

¼ cup unsweetened cocoa
1 envelope unflavored gelatin
¼ cup granulated sugar
⅛ teaspoon salt

1 ½ cups skim milk
3 eggs, separated
1 teaspoon vanilla extract
¼ teaspoon cream of tartar

In the top of a double boiler set over boiling water, combine cocoa, gelatin, sugar replacement and salt. Gradually add milk and egg yolks, stirring until gelatin is dissolved and mixture is slightly thickened. Stir in vanilla and cool until mixture thickens but is not set. Beat egg whites with cream of tartar until stiff but not dry. Fold cocoa mixture thoroughly into egg whites. Spoon mixture into a 4-cup ring mold that has been sprayed with a nonstick cooking spray. Chill until firm. Makes 6 servings. (MME) Supplement as required. Each equivalent to: 2 ⅓ X, ¼ milk, ½ egg. Per serving: 83 cal, 7 g pro, 4 g fat, 6 g car, 130 mg sod. Shown with optional garnish of 3 servings cherries (30 large) and 6 tablespoons whipped topping (14 calorie SF per serving).

Won First Prize of Amana® Touchmatic® Radarange in the 13th Annual Weight Watchers® Magazine Reader Recipe Contest.
DONNA GAINES, SADIEVILLE, KENTUCKY

GRANOLA

1 ½ ounces uncooked old-fashioned oats
1 tablespoon raisins
1 date, chopped
½ teaspoon wheat germ
½ teaspoon shredded coconut
½ teaspoon sesame or sunflower seeds
1 teaspoon firmly-packed light brown sugar
1 teaspoon vegetable oil
½ teaspoon honey
¼ teaspoon vanilla extract
¼ teaspoon almond extract

In a bowl, combine first 6 ingredients in a separate bowl, stir together remaining ingredients. Combine mixtures and spread evenly on a baking sheet. Bake at 350° F. about 5 minutes or until lightly toasted. Makes 2 servings. (MMES) Each equivalent to: 1 Brd, ½ fruit, 2 ½ X, ½ fat. Per serving: 155 cal, 4 g pro, 5 g fat, 26 g car, 3 mg. sod.

Won Fourth Prize of Oneida Ltd. Silversmiths® Sea Crest® 5-piece tea and coffee service in the 13th Annual Weight Watchers® Magazine Reader Recipe Contest.
BETTY SCHABERG, GREENWOOD, INDIANA

SARA LEE POUND CAKE CONTEST

EASY LINZER COOKIES

1 frozen Sara Lee Pound Cake
(10 ¾ oz.), thawed
1 ¼ cups unblanched almonds,
ground
½ teaspoon ground cinnamon

⅓ cup butter, melted
½ cup red raspberry preserves
Confectioners' sugar

Crumble cake into coarse crumbs in blender; stir in nuts and cinnamon. Blend in butter until mixture holds together. Shape level tablespoons of mixture into balls; place on ungreased baking sheet. Make indentation in center of each ball with thumb; smooth walls of cookies to form shell. Bake in preheated 350° F. oven for 20-25 minutes. Cool cookies completely on baking sheet. (Cookies harden as they cool.) Roll gently in confectioners' sugar. Fill centers with raspberry preserves. Makes about 2 dozen cookies.

Won the Grand Prize of a trip for two to Paris, France, $1,500 spending money, plus a 1 week cooking course for 1 person at the Ecole De Cuisine "La Varenne," in the 1982 Sara Lee Pound Cake Recipe Contest.
ANDREA SENKOWSKI, CAMBRIDGE, MASSACHUSETTS

INDEX OF RECIPES

National Pineapple Cooking Classic

The Christian Brothers Annual Sherry Contest

Red Star's 3rd Baking Recipe Exchange

Knox Unflavored Gelatine "Knox Blox Recipe Contest"

Wesson "Salad of the Year" Contest

Baskin-Robbins Ice Cream Show-Off Contest

BAKE-OFF® contest

National Beef Cook-Off

Seagram's V.O. One Dish Supper Recipe Contest

Seagram's V.O. International Dessert Recipe Contest

Seagram's V.O. International Hors D'Oeurve Recipe Contest

La Choy Swing American Contest Recipes

National Farm-Raised Catfish Cooking Contest

French's Recipe Hunt Contest

National Chicken Cooking Contest

Lawry's World's Greatest Hamburger Contest Recipes

Lawry's Seasoning / Sauce or Gravy Mixes Recipe Contest

General Electric Microwave Cooking Award Recipe Contest

Campbell Soup Company "Creative Cooking Contest"

World's Championship Chili Cook-Off Contest

"Lipton Soup Mix Microwave Magic Recipe Contest"

"Heublein Inc. A.1. Ground Beef Recipe Contest"

French's Sauce, Gravy, Or Seasoning Mixes Contest

"Weight Watchers Magazine Annual Reader Recipe Contest"

Sara Lee Pound Cake Contest